ON BEING
HUMAN(e)

ON BEING HUMAN(e)

Comenius's Pedagogical Humanization as an Anthropological Problem

JAN HÁBL

Foreword by Jerry Root

PICKWICK *Publications* · Eugene, Oregon

ON BEING HUMAN(E)
Comenius's Pedagogical Humanization as an Anthropological Problem

Pickwick Publications
An Imprint of Wipf and Stock Publishers
199 W. 8th Ave., Suite 3
Eugene, OR 97401

www.wipfandstock.com

PAPERBACK ISBN: 978-1-5326-0056-2
HARDCOVER ISBN: 978-1-5326-0058-6
EBOOK ISBN: 978-1-5326-0057-9

Cataloguing-in-Publication data:

Names: Hábl, Jan | Root, Jerry (foreword writer)

Title: On being human(e) : Comenius's pedagogical humanization as an anthropological problem / Jan Hábl, with a foreword by Jerry Root.

Description: Eugene, OR: Pickwick Publications, 2017 | Includes bibliographical references and index.

Identifiers: ISBN 978-1-5326-0056-2 (paperback) | ISBN 978-1-5326-0058-6 (hardcover) | ISBN 978-1-5326-0057-9 (ebook)

Subjects: LCSH: Comenius, Johann Amos, 1592–1670 | Philosophical anthropology | Education, Humanistic | Christian education

Classification: BV4511 H235 2017 (paperback) | BV4511 (ebook)

Manufactured in the U.S.A.   02/20/17

This book has been supported by the Internal Grant Agency of Jan E. Purkyne University in Usti nad Labem, Czech Republic, Comenius Institute in Prague and Giving Hands in Bonn.

Contents

Foreword

C. S. Lewis scholar Bruce Edwards, writing of Lewis's approach to literary criticism, observed, "For Lewis every critical posture is always an implicit ontology, teleology, and eschatology. For in his implicit view of literacy, the critic is always defining the relationship of mankind not only to texts, but also to ultimate matters: the ground of being, the locus of meaning, and the possibility of transcendence."[1] Jan Hábl, with a similar degree of precision, looks at the work of Jan Amos Comenius and reminds his readers that sound educational theory must also add a sophisticated grasp of anthropology. By sophisticated I mean avoiding the temptation to see what it is to be human through rose-colored glasses. Educational theory failing to recognize the tragic brokenness evidenced in human history and witnessed to and recorded in literature is not helpful to the educational enterprise. Equally unhelpful is a low view of what it is to be human; such a pessimistic view also lacks in sophistication; it may fail to recognize that the history of humankind is full of the heroic, as well as the tragic. Every age needs an infusion of hope, a willingness to envision for successive generations the possibility that some degree of good can be achieved by every individual and every human endeavor. If one would wrestle with the topic of education well, and in a profoundly nuanced way, it must be admitted that humans possess great dignity, and yet, are capable of great depravity. Any theory of education worth its salt must be rooted in such a complex approach to anthropology. Comenius operated with such a theory. And, Hábl's work has done a great service for his readers by bringing their attention back to Comenius's understanding of anthropology and what it means for education.

1. Edwards, *Rhetoric of Reading*, 110.

Fundamental questions arise, how might the ruins of humanity be restored, for certainly the effort is worth it? Furthermore, how might the good of man be cultivated and encouraged? This is the challenge of education. And, again, fundamental to that challenge is the educator's anthropology. The practice of education must be rooted in principle. It is the tendency of pragmatics, no longer tethered to principle, to become rooted in the self-referentialism of the educator, or the educator's party, or school of thought, the collective. Comenius was no enemy to a kind of collective, or society; but he longed to have his society, his educational community undergirded by a demonstrable objectivity. This is what Lewis, in his work on educational philosophy, called the *Tao*, or "the doctrine of objective value." It is objective value, he wrote, that "provides a common human law of action which can over-arch rulers and ruled alike. A dogmatic belief in objective value is necessary to the very idea of a rule which is not tyranny or an obedience which is not slavery."[2] Lewis believed there is an objective world that existed independent of his thoughts about it. Human capacity to perceive and reason indicates a capacity to think about that world, not to mention what it means to be a human living in that world. Educators engaged in the practice of connecting students to the realities of that world can have their misunderstanding of that world corrected whenever there is no reality to sustain their claims. And those whose assertions stand up to scrutiny can make a case for their claim by an appeal to objective reality. Certainly these claims can be attested to by reason, authority, and experience. These are necessary checks and balances that must be employed whenever the educator's anthropology is mindful of the human potential for dignity and depravity. Sometimes understanding can be accurate and sometimes inaccurate, falsified by human limitation and self-interest. Here again, we see the need for educational theory to be built upon a sophisticated anthropology. Hábl's study, rooted in Comenius's anthropology, will not allow his readers to forget.

Hábl keeps in the forefront of our minds that Comenius is still hailed as one of the greatest educators of all time. And, as Hábl point out, one feature that made Comenius's pedagogy so effective was this clarity about what it means to be human. Hábl reminds his readers that Comenius saw pedagogy as a means of transformation in those places where proper human development is needed. There is also awareness here that human kind is broken and in need of mending. Education has a role to play in the

2. Lewis, *Abolition of Man*, 16, 43.

mending process. Again, Lewis voices a similar belief when he observes, "For the wise men of old the cardinal problem had been how to conform the soul to reality, and the solution had been knowledge, self-discipline, and virtue."[3] In this very approach there is also implied recognition of the greatness of humankind. Efforts directed towards an objective approach to education are likely to have in mind an anthropology that believes that men and women possess dignity and energies directed towards their benefit are a worth the effort. Again, humans possess dignity and depravity. And theories of education that neglect this fact are destined to fail because they lack anthropological soundness.

Furthermore, Comenius's anthropology cannot be divorced from his faith. It was the integrating principle for all of his work. And, like all things Christian, thinking about any matter must not be inert. Christian thought, Christian theology, and Christian anthropology should always be in various stages of development. Humans are in a process of development. Reality is iconoclastic. An image once held, and helpful, must give way to a more robust understanding or it becomes an idol. Change is necessary. But the kind of change needed in any given situation requires a degree of wisdom and guidance. Is the change needed one of kind? Do we chop down the old tree and make it into a table? Or, is the change one of degree? The tree does not have to give up its interior rings just because it adds new ones; but if it does not add new rings it dies. The Bible was a source of inspiration for Comenius. He studied it in the days before schools of *Higher Criticism* existed. His views were rooted in a tradition, and they were fined tuned by Brethren applications. The Scriptures, as Comenius would have encountered them, exhibited what I would call theological trajectories of thought. In the book of Exodus the law was given at the beginning of Israel's forty years in the wilderness. At the end of those wilderness days the book of Deuteronomy is given and the law is nuanced further. What is an interpreter to make of this? Was the omniscient God in heaven coming up with new ideas? Did he leave some things out of the original rendering of the law and later sought to correct his error? Or, did God give the law, and with it time for the Israelites to wrestle with its applications; to think about it. This implies a high view of anthropology. Furthermore, when the daughters of Zelophehad object to the manner in which the property of Canaan was to be distributed, God affirmed their concerns and reinforced their new applications by encouraging critical thinking about the objective revelation

3. Ibid., 45.

just given. So it is, throughout biblical history, coordinates are revealed and a trajectory of thought is encouraged along the lines of those coordinates. The greatest coordinate being the Incarnate Christ. Here too, anthropology is in view. Furthermore, though the Scriptures were given in an agrarian age, they still have application in an industrial age, and in a technological age, and whatever ages come next. In such a tradition it is no wonder that Hábl points out Comenius's pedagogy, influenced by his faith and tethered to his anthropology, is a developing one. Furthermore, we should not be surprised, as Hábl points out, of its ongoing relevancy given its roots.

Lastly, it is good to remember that educational theory, influenced by faith and tethered to an understanding of what it means to be human, has a long history. Comenius is a unique voice, but he is supported by a choir of others who have been equally influenced in ways similar to him. Education in a fallen world will always be engaged in repairing the ruins. Examples are not hard to find. Dante Alighieri wrote in the *Inferno*: "Consider your origin; ye were not made to live as brutes, but to pursue virtue and knowledge."[4] Similarly, John Milton, in his essay *Of Education*, wrote, "The end then of learning is to repair the ruins of our first parents by regaining to know God aright, and out of that knowledge to love Him, to imitate Him, to be like Him as we may the nearest, by possessing our souls of true virtue, which being united to the heavenly grace of faith, makes up the highest perfection."[5] Furthermore, French Physicist and Philosopher, Blaisé Pascal wrote in the *Pensees*, "Man is obviously made to think. It is his whole dignity and his whole merit; and his whole duty is to think as he ought. Now the order of thought is to begin with self, and with its Author and with its end."[6] Philosopher and Mystic, Evelyn Underhill, also wrote explicitly

> Now the very object of education is to interpret life to the child: to bring some order into the confused mass of objects and experiences which besiege the awakening consciousness, and so put the growing human creature more fully in touch with the world in which it finds itself. The ultimate aim is gradually to set up a full, true relation between pupil and environment; and for Christians, the ultimate fact about that environment is, that it is the work of

4. Alighieri, *Inferno*, 39.

5. Milton, *Of Education*, 59.

6. Pascal, *Pensees* (Great Books), 200.

God, indwelt by God, and a means of serving, knowing and glo-
rifying God."[7]

And lastly, the English woman of letters, Dorothy Sayers, mystery writer,
and translator of Dante, wrote, "Christian Education is based on a coherent
philosophy interpreting all experience: That is, it educates a child to be:
a) a man, b) among men, c) in a universe which makes sense."[8] The thread
that holds these pedagogical opinions together is a shared and common
Christian faith, and a common view of humankind, such as we find in Comenius. Hábl has serves his readers well guiding us through the terrain of
Comenius's anthropology and its effects on his theories of education.

Professor Jerry Root, Ph.D.
Wheaton College, Wheaton, Illinois

7. Underhill, *Collected Papers*, 220–22.
8. Sayers, "Foreword," vii.

INTRODUCTION

Presentation of the Problem

Humanity and Humanization in Current Pedagogical Discourse

> Thus nothing about human affairs is working. The state of thought, piety, and politics among all people is out of order. Many people and in some cases whole nations neither know God nor think about His interests, nor have they experienced their humanity, living their brutal lives like the cattle of the field. And could it even be said that the very things which make us most human, are in confusion and decay?
>
> *Obecná porada* [General Consultation], Panegersia, 5.34[1]

T he school must be a "humanitas officinae," that is, a workshop of humanity, a relatively young Comenius wrote in his early Didactics. In his later work, reflecting his most mature thought, A General Consultation on the Restoration of Human Affairs [*Obecná porada o nápravě věcí lidských*], he spoke similarly when he clarified the meaning of his lifelong pedagogical and corrective efforts: they were "to help man become truly humane" (Pampaedia, 2.8). If one is to become what one should be, it's necessary that she be knowledgeable, and therefore, educated. The obvious question then arises: What, exactly, is a human being? And what ought one to be? Salt should be salty. A river should be clear. A knife should be sharp. But what

1. The *Obecná porada* is composed of seven books, one of which is the Panegersia. The numbers indicate chapter and paragraph.

ought people to be? In what does their nature, or essence, consist? What makes them human? And how should that be cultivated? In other words, in this book I will enquire into the ontological and moral character of human beings, in connection with so-called pedagogical humanization.[2]

Humanization was one of the key principles in the transformation of the educational systems in the second half of the twentieth century in Europe.[3] Its importance arose from the specific situation in which European society found itself in the post-war period, and specifically in the post-totalitarian period in the Eastern part of Europe. Humanity is a precious commodity; the more intensely we feel the lack of something, the more precious it becomes. It is true that during the last century, in the area of the techno-scientific revolution, Western civilization has recorded extraordinary advances which have brought unprecedented power and affluence. Humanity, however, has lagged behind, even so far as to be in crisis. The culture of excess and prosperity contrasts sharply with the reality of the poverty of millions of hungry, destitute, illiterate, and marginalized individuals and nations of the "third" world, which the "civilized" world does not dare to "civilize" anymore, recognizing it has lost the right because of the profusion and persistence of its own problems.[4] Its advanced technocracy has generated a series of dehumanizing "side-effects" such as the alienating individualization, indifference, and depersonalizing of human relationships. Instead of the hoped-for progress of humanity, sociologists point to the reality of a decrease in moral literacy, a dramatic decline in social capital (nobody trusts anyone), the global threat of self-destruction, conflicts of civilizations, various forms of extremism and the like.[5] Human beings are even considered to be an endangered species.[6] In the spirit of Erich Fromm: despite the techno-scientific saturation, humanity in our

2. I have dealt with pedagogical humanization not only in my *Lessons in Humanity from the Life and Work of Jan Amos Comenius*, but also in *Teaching and Learning Through Story*. To a large extent this text comes out of those two books, but what is new here is the addition of anthropological questions about the ontological and moral character of human beings.

3. See for example Helus, "Humanizace školy," 427–40; Skalková, *Humanizace vzdělávání*; Walterová, "Humanizace vzdělávání," 327–33; Harbo, "Humanizace vzdělání," 247–55.

4. Skalková, *Humanizace vzdělávání*, 46–47.

5. Helus, "Culture of Education," 671–85.

6. Sokol, *Filosofická antropologie*, 15–16.

world is "under-nourished." Naděžda Pelcová commented on the "precarious" anthropological situation thusly:

> The more we know about ourselves—our biological processes, metabolism, psychological activities, motivation for decision-making, history, the social groups we join—the more unable we are to answer the question of who we are.[7]

In response to this situation the concept of a so-called "new humanism" has emerged in pedagogical circles, say the educational experts. "The question of humanism has re-appeared with a new intensity in the last decade of the twentieth century," says, for example, Jarmila Skalková.[8] Pedagogical literature has abounded with various innovative plans and proposals whose "crystalizing themes of transformational change should be"—in the words of Štefan Švec—the very "idea of humanization."[9] Skalková even sees the demand for educational humanization as "a world movement that permeates every sphere of contemporary life."[10] Likewise Vladimíra Spilková says unequivocally: "The idea of humanization is one of the key principles of transformation in the contemporary educational system."[11] Features of authoritarian pedagogy, such as directive policies, uniformity, monotony and the like, which deform humanity, must be replaced by new alternative approaches, whose task is, in Skalková's words, "to put in place a new climate for teaching founded on spontaneity and the joy of teaching . . . , individual freedom for teaching and learning, space for creative work, imagination, the forming of conditions to promote the physical and psychological development of the individual."[12]

Similarly, Karel Rýdl explains humanization as "the process of improving and humanizing training and education in the sense of bringing it closer to the needs and expectations of the individual."[13] Moreover this "*pedocentrism* of the new generation," as Zdeněk Helus calls it, constitutes an "optimistic educational position" which believes in "the possibility of

---

7. Pelcová, *Vzorce lidství*, 9.

8. Skalková, *Humanizace vzdělávání*, 41.

9. Štefan Švec, "Humanistická didaktika," 24–48.

10. Skalková, *Humanizace vzdělávání*, 41.

11. Spilková, "Pedagogika," 25.

12. Skalková, *Humanizace vzdělávání*, 53.

13. Rýdl, "Didaktické perspektivy," 351.

improving and self-developing" the individual as "the highest good," as "the measure of all things" and the "complete person."[14]

However, in spite of the humanistic rhetoric and intentions, the coveted humanization has still not appeared. Admittedly it is true that contemporary pedagogy does relatively well in terms of the so-called "preparation of the individual for life."[15] It knows how to equip pupils with the given amount of useful information and the pragmatic skills or competencies needed for successful self-assertion (usually in the marketplace), but it fails in the formation and cultivation of that human dimension of personality that would guarantee a humane—in current terminology—pro-social use of all of the school acquired equipping, and it fails in spite of a significant (and more or less alternative) didactic arsenal. Pavel Floss notes, for example, that despite the humanistic language of official documents, current education continues to remain "essentially functionalistic," that is, it produces "efficient workers and experts" in various fields, but fails to cultivate "the whole person."[16] Skalková likewise says that the current process of "educating and training and also managing internal school activities does not leave any room for cultivating individual abilities and talents, for ethics, aesthetics and emotional development, for the development of interpersonal relationships, or for the self-fulfillment of the individual."[17] Ever since Rousseau it has been proclaimed that the ultimate goal of modern education is "kalokaghatia," that is, a harmonically and versatilely developed human being who will, together with other such human beings, comprise a harmonic society. The failure to achieve this goal does not have to be argued, because the problematic state of contemporary western society can be observed by the "naked eye."[18]

14. Spilková, *Proměny primárního*, 33–34.

15. The relativity and controversial nature of this statement is evident for example in the urgent appeal of some leading Czech personalities, warning of the rapid decline of education in the Czech Republic. The appeal is freely accessible on the internet: see for example <http://ktv.mff.cuni.cz/IFO-RUM-4389.html>. Aleš Prázný also notes that neither have these objectives been accomplished "with appropriate efficiency," however, continuing in the spirit of "humanistic ideology" it is still hoped that this is just a temporary stopgap that will be removed as soon as some kind of "technically improved implementation of the goal" is found. See Prázný, "Komenský," 236–40.

16. See for example the formulation of educational goals that are part of the current Education Act 261/2004 Sb., valid from Jan. 1, 2005. For further discussion see Floss, *Poselství*, 26.

17. Skalková, *Humanizace vzdělávání*, 52.

18. Compare Pelcová, "O krizi," 139–60.

The critical question then is, why? Why, in spite of the great amount of theoretical and practical efforts, has this humanization not occurred? Does the problem lie in inadequate pedagogical methodology? In a lack of financial resources? Or perhaps in human resources—that is, in inadequate motivation, scholarship, or competence of teachers? Or is the problem structural, pedagogical, political, economic, or something else?

GOALS AND METHODOLOGY

In this work I do not want to question the importance of seeking adequate answers to the above questions, because the problem is clearly complex. However, I believe that one of the key reasons for the failure of humanizing efforts is primarily philosophical: specifically, anthropological. As the title of this book suggests, in the search for answers for authentic humanization I will turn to the works of Jan Amos Comenius, and for good reason. Comenius's pedagogical system—whose significance and value there is no need to demonstrate—contains a specific anthropological dimension which has disappeared in modern pedagogical discourse, yet which, I believe, is indispensable for the pedagogical formation of authentic humanity. It is as follows: Comenius believed that humans are ontologically, that is, in their very being, "good," noble, valuable, endowed with innate dignity. Morally, however, we are twisted, "fallen" into evil. This is the source of the fundamental ambivalence of human nature. In Comenius's words, humans are by nature "the noblest of all creatures," however in their actions they are often "like an animal," as if they weren't even human. Or said another way, our *humanity* is fine, our *humaneness*, however, is depraved, as is evident by all the inhumane things a person is capable of doing. From now on I will refer to this concept of Comenius as *anthropological realism*.[19] This specific "configuration" of the ontological and moral aspect of human nature may seem trivial, but we will see that for the question of pedagogical humanization it is crucial.

---

19. It's necessary to add a minor terminological caution here: Comenius is often associated with the term *optimism*. However, what is meant is *pedagogical*, not anthropological optimism. Pedagogical optimism expresses the conviction that man is essentially educable, i.e., pedagogical efforts can shape the nature of man. The pedagogical pessimist, on the other hand, does not believe it is possible for education to achieve substantial change. In this context, it can be said that Comenius was a pedagogical optimist. However, this optimism was largely based on his anthropological realism.

The educational importance of this concept of anthropology is well demonstrated if we consider the "competitive" alternatives: What would humanization look like if it was based on the assumption that a person has no ontological value? Or has neither ontological nor moral value (anthropological pessimism)? Or the opposite, what would it look like if it was based on the assumption that people are wholly good—both ontologically and morally (anthropological romanticism)? In the history of anthropological discourse these alternatives have appeared regularly, and in various mutations still circulate—see Hobbes, Locke, Rousseau and others.[20] I intend to demonstrate that the uniqueness of Comenius's project for the pedagogical "remedy of human affairs" is situated, among other things, in his specific anthropology containing the ontological and moral differentiation of human nature. It is the primary objective of this work. I also want to present the argument that this very concept of anthropology is one of the most inspiring initiatives for solving the problem of pedagogical humanization.[21]

I will, however, approach Comenius's work critically, because Comenius's anthropology presents a specific exegetical problem. To the question of how Comenius understood human beings, or what his anthropology was, it is not possible to give a simple answer because we find more than one anthropology in his work. We will see that the development of Comenius's philosophy was markedly dynamic. His conceptions were changed by both external and internal situations—sometimes partially, in details, sometimes radically. Thus a secondary aim of this work is to analyze the particular anthropological accents or stages, bringing them into the broader ideological context of Comenius's philosophic development, and showing their implications for the question of pedagogical humanization.[22]

In terms of methodology this will be an analytic-synthetic interdisciplinary study, drawing on research primarily from the fields of education, Comeniology, and philosophy of education; in the chapter devoted to the interpretation of Comenius's most famous allegory, the *Labyrinth of the World and the Paradise of the Heart*, I will also draw from literary

20. Compare Kreeft, *Ethics*, 55.

21. There is no doubt that Comenius's work has inspired many other initiatives. This is attested to by, among other things, the wealth of perspectives in Comeniological research—didactic, psychological, linguistic, philosophic, theological, etc. In light of the theme of this work, I will limit myself to the anthropological assumptions of pedagogical humanization.

22. Compare Pešková, "Jan Amos Komenský," 21–28; Patočka, *Komeniologické studie 1, 2, 3*; Pelcová, "Komeniův výchovný sen," 229–41.

hermeneutics, especially narratology. Selected texts will undergo descriptive analysis for subsequent connections with the theme of educational humanization, and a key analytical tool will be this anthropological point of view. In other words—to Comenius's pedagogical system I will pose the question, on what kind of anthropological pre-understanding is it based, and what does it mean for the phenomenon of educational humanization?

I have based my research on three main sources. 1) In the area of pedagogy, primarily on the work of Zdeněk Helus and Vladimíra Spilková, especially on those pieces which deal with the issue of humanization.[23] 2) In the area of Comeniology and philosophy I refer to the *Comeniological Studies* (Komeniologické studie) of Jan Patočka and the lifelong works of Dagmar Čapková and Radim Palouš. 3) The field of anthropology is wide, but of the many authors whose work is linked with the philosophy of education I refer mainly to Peter Kreeft, Jaroslava Pešková, and Naděžda Pelcová.

From the start I want to emphasize that the purpose of this text is not a sentimental evoking of the name "Jan Amos Comenius," or a nostalgic mourning over the faded glory of the "good old times." It is not possible to replace the school of today with the school of Comenius's time, nor is it even desirable. My intention is to serve contemporary pedagogy (that is, the theoreticians and practitioners of education) with a critical and constructive complement of those sources that have proven to be vital, functional and have withstood the test of time.

---

23. I am also taking into account the text of Jarmila Skalková, whose humanizing imperative is highly visible in post-revolutionary literature. See for example her previously-mentioned *Humanizace vzdělávání a výchovy jako soudobý pedagogický problém.*

CHAPTER 1

Theatrum

Teaching and Learning through Wonder

Not without reason is the world called, in the Greek language, *cosmos*, that is, beautiful; and in Latin, *mundus*, meaning pure. Everything in it is beautiful, pure, delightful and charming, and the visible beauty is painted by the invisible God. If one does not see beauty in the world, one sees little. . . . Oh, what must be the wondrous and abundantly loveable beauty of our God, from whom all diverse beauty flows! Whatever is noble in a created thing didn't arise out of itself, but from the well of that which is beyond.

Theatrum universitatis rerum

THEATRUM UNIVERSITATIS RERUM

Comenius's thoughts exhibited a certain dynamism over the course of his life. Regarding his understanding of human nature, there is a clearly visible evolution. The classification and interpretation of Comenius's thoughts, I would submit, are closely linked to the so-called "major" discoveries of the 1930s. Certain Comeniologists were able to track down some extremely important manuscripts of his, which had been assumed to have been lost. Before these discoveries, the classification of the development of Comenius's thinking and work into periods was usually determined by external and accidental factors, such as where he was living, historic events, and so on. These discoveries enabled contemporary Comeniologists to classify his work according to internal factors, that is, factors that Comenius himself considered to be important and that significantly shifted his thinking.

The discoveries mentioned above are basically three—the first was Souček's "Leningrad Discoveries," which he found in 1931 after a long search. The findings consist of six extremely important manuscripts, which include, among other works, *Prima Philosophia, Geometrie, Cosmographiae compendium.* The second discovery was made by G. H. Turnbull in 1933. In Hartlib's papers he found a relatively large number of various manuscripts. Some of them were originals of previously known works of Comenius, but he also found a series of completely new documents and letters. The greatest findings came with the third discovery. After a long period of focused research in the area of Slavic Studies, D. Čiževskyj discovered a large manuscript of 2,000 pages in the archives of the Francky orphanage in Halle in 1934 (on Christmas Eve). They turned out to be four parts (of seven) of Comenius's pivotal work: *De rerum humanarum emendatione consultatio catholica* (General Consultation Concerning the Restoration of Human Affairs).[1]

In addition to those major discoveries there were also smaller ones, in the areas of correspondence, preaching, and so on. The impact of all of those discoveries on Comeniological research was huge. The new information provided a deeper understanding of the historical, political, philosophical, and literary background of Comenius's work. Patočka emphasized the importance of the findings when he said, "It's true that certain of the philosophic ideas on which Comenius's pedagogical works were based have long been known. However it was never suspected that the Czech thinker's ideas had grown into such a large system whose originality, despite certain similarities with his contemporaries, is beyond doubt."[2]

In light of these discoveries it is possible to distinguish four or five main stages in Comenious's thought: 1) encyclopedic or preparatory; 2) comforting—with an emphasis on resignation; 3) narrative allegory; 4) educational pansophy; and 5) emendation or reformation, which somewhat

---

1. Comenius published the book in Latin, and it was translated into Czech much later. In this text I will quote from the Czech version, *Obecná porada*. For further particulars see Patočka, *Komeniologické studie 2*, 7–63.

2. Ibid, 21.

overlaps the preceding period.[3] Each of these stages is characterized by a specific understanding of the human being; of course, the endpoints of the stages are only relative. Sometimes there was a comparatively abrupt shift from one to the next, other times the change was slower and more gradual. Individual chapters in this book correspond to the stages listed above, thus in each chapter I first outline the biographical context of that stage in the development of Comenius's thinking, and then analyze the key works of that period.

BIOGRAPHICAL CONTEXT: THE REFORMATION, BRETHREN TRADITION, AND STUDY

It is not my intention to repeat already well-known facts about Comenius's life, but rather to follow the roots of his concept of humanity. I will focus primarily on those moments in his life that are relevant to this work, that is, which formed his understanding of the human being.

Jan Amos Comenius was born on March 28, 1592, most likely at Uherský Brod in Moravia. There were five children in the family of Martin and Anna Komenský (the Czech version of the latinized Comenius), four girls and a boy (the boy being the youngest). He spent his early childhood in Nivnice (a little village close to Uherský Brod), where his family owned a mill.[4] They were quite affluent burghers who enjoyed considerable respect not only in the area surrounding Uherský Brod, but also in the Unitas Fratrum (literally, "Unity of Brethren," known outside of Bohemia as the "Moravian Brethren"), the church to which they belonged.

The Unitas Fratrum was a specific branch of the Czech reformation movement founded in 1457. It was inspired by the visions of radical piety and religious simplicity of Petr Chelčický (around 1380–1460). It arose in the period of the Hussite wars, when the radical Hussite movement was declining and the moderate Utraquist church was looking for a conciliatory path with the Roman Catholic church. The Unitas wanted to restore the radical tendencies of the original Hussite movement. However, it should be underlined that by being conscious followers of Petr Chelčický, the pacifistic rejection of force in matters of faith and conscience was always an integral part of their radicalism. Josef Smolík rightly reminds us that

3. Compare Floss, *Od divadla*, or Patočka, *Komeniologické studie 1*, 175.

4. Adjoining the village of Nivnice is the village of Komňa, where his father's family came from and probably also where the family name came from.

the Unitas never accepted the principle of "cuius regio, euis religio,"[5] whose implementation always carried with it elements of violence.[6] It was their radicalism and separatism that caused much persecution of the Unitas from the beginning of their existence. The characteristic non-compromising desire for spiritual purity included, in their early periods, rejection of magisterial power, oath-taking, and participation in war. They also avoided worldly education and vocations such as commerce, which they considered a hindrance to proper spirituality.

The emphasis on practical piety did not, however, prevent the Unitas from developing and cultivating their theology, which reflected both its inner life as well as its relationship to Catholicism and Utraquism at home, and Protestantism outside the borders of Bohemia and Moravia. Out of this interaction gradually emerged some characteristic theological accents of the Unitas, which Comenius inherited.

One of the key theological concepts the Unitas held—besides the traditional Christian doctrines—was a precise differentiation of things essential to salvation from those which are merely ministrative or incidental.[7] The concept was elaborated by the second principal leader, Lukáš Pražský (1458–1528). Terminologically, the categories of *substantialia, ministeralia, et accidentialia* can be traced back to medieval scholasticism. What was unique in the Unitas's theology, however, according to Jarold K. Zeman, was the utilization of these categories within a soteriological perspective.[8] The Unitas consistently classified all matters of faith and practice under this trichotomy.[9] According to their theology, the things essential to salvation were: 1) "on God's side"—the grace of God the Father, the merit of Jesus Christ, and the gifts of the Holy Spirit; 2) "on the human side"—faith, love, and hope. The things ministrative to salvation included the Holy Scripture, sacraments, discipline, and the church as such. Liturgy and church government were considered incidental.[10] The implied hierarchy of values assigned to the respective concerns in Christian life had, according to the Unitas, an important bearing upon the unity of all of Christendom, and

5. Whose realm, his religion.

6. Smolík, *Teologické a ekumenické motivy*.

7. Amedeo Molnár called it a "formal principle of Brethren theology." See Říčan, *Dějiny*, 424.

8. The term *soteriological* means "pertaining to salvation."

9. Compare Zeman, "Restitution and dissent," 7–27.

10. For further details see Molnár, *Bratr Lukáš*.

unity was of course, for the Unitas, one of the key doctrines.[11] As we will see later, it continued to be key for Comenius's irenic efforts as well.

Josef B. Souček observed that the theologians of the Czech Reformation had to deal with no other so pressing a question as that of "in what does the true unity of the church consist, and in what does it not?"[12] As indicated, the reasons for interrupting the external bond with the established church were neither arbitrary nor incidental;[13] it was the soteriological concern expressed in the well-known phrase "the need of salvation" (*nouze spasení*) which moved the Unitas to the separation. But in no case was it exclusivist. Article 8 of the Unitas Fratrum Confession best illustrates their ecumenical vision. It clearly states that each denominational part (e.g., Roman Catholic, Lutheran, Ultraquist, etc.) is to be viewed as "united." Each is a mere branch of the one Universal Church for which is reserved the term "Ecclesia." For the local church the Unitas used the word "sbor" (congregation).[14] Thus, the Unitas did not claim themselves to be the one universal catholic church, but one of many expressions of the catholic church; and, at the same time, this theological framework granted to every denominational body its legitimacy. This attitude disclosed quite a degree of theological "modesty," in Souček's judgment.[15] Jarold K. Zeman further inferred that the consistent use of the terminology *unity, church, congregation* (Unitas, Ecclesia, Congregatio) served as "a reminder of the dialectical tension between the ecumenical and separatist motifs in [the Unitas's] ecclesiology.[16]

Another theological motif which needs to be mentioned because of its implications for Comenius's specific notion of human engagement within

11. Molnár was commenting on this when he said, "the Brethren were convinced that a lack of discrimination among these categories had created the greatest confusion in the history of Christian thinking . . . ." See Říčan, *Dějiny*, 424.

12. Souček, "Hlavní motivy," 106.

13. It should also be mentioned that the separation took place with a certain amount of hesitation, for it appeared that some traditional doctrines had deep roots in the Brethren ecclesiological thinking. Thus, when in 1467 the Brethren chose (by lot) their own ministers, independent of the apostolic succession in the Roman Catholic church, they sought confirmation of this act by a Waldensian elder. They appear to have accepted the legend about Peter Valdes, who was a contemporary of Pope Sylvester, as a mediator of an uncorrupted line of a kind of "counter-succession." For more details see Molnár, *Valdenští*.

14. Or "Gemainde" in German-speaking Brethren circles. See *Bratrské vyznání*, 144.

15. Souček, "Hlavní motivy," 107.

16. See Zeman, "Restitution and dissent," 24.

the world, is justification by faith. This doctrine deals with the method of salvation. How can a person become righteous before God? Can one earn salvation by good works? Can it be bought as an indulgence? The answers were developed gradually, helped especially by the work of Lukáš Pražský. By the end of the fifteenth century, he made it clear that there is only one righteousness that is of any value: "the righteousness merited through Christ the Lord."[17] The Unitas listened with great interest and understanding to Luther's radical soteriology. They did not, however, embrace his views without any reservations. According to the Brethren theologians, there is not as sharp a discord between law and grace as Luther claimed, for grace presupposes law and confirms it. That is why his polemical statements concerning the Epistle of James were foreign to the Unitas. They fully employed the Reformation concept of remission of sins by the imputation of Christ's righteousness through faith alone, as is clear from the second redaction of the Brethren Confession of 1564.[18] But at the same time, they retained their old emphasis that justification and sanctification belong inseparably together.[19] This characteristic emphasis, which was part of their original doctrinal heritage according to Souček,[20] was expressed by the term "living faith." They derived this concept from James's polemic against "dead faith."[21] Thus in the Brethren view, good deeds are necessary "manifestations of living faith."[22] We shall see that this emphasis on human deeds and activity became one of the key aspects of Comenius's anthropology concerning the emendation projects.

The last theological theme to mention, because of its relevance to Comenius's anthropology, is the eschatological expectation of the Unitas. Their eschatology was closely connected to their actual existence, as Molnár observed when quoting the editor of the writings of the Unitas's archivist Jaroslav Bidlo:

> I came to the conviction that one of the main reasons the Brethren established their own church order was their firm conviction that the end of the world was nigh, and therefore they were called to form a circle of morality in the midst of the overall decline, and

17. Citation from Strupl, *Confessional Theology*, 279–93.
18. See Article 6 of the Brethren Confession, 137–40.
19. See Article 7 of the Brethren Confession, 141–44.
20. Souček, "Hlavní motivy," 112.
21. See James 2:26.
22. See Article 7 of the *Brethren Confession*, 142.

thus preserve the rightly renewed church until the approaching end of the world.[23]

Molnár further observed that to identify such an expectation with chiliasm would be too hasty, for the conviction of the Brethren, that a sanctified way of life was appropriate for the coming judgment, had nothing to do with impatient millennialist calculations of the date of the final events. The Unitas very carefully monitored the signs of eschatological pressure in their own situation. As a result, they felt a calling to radical holiness, although they knew that "such things have always been present."[24] The true church knows that "for the whole time of her existence she is in an eschatological situation." Thus, she should not be restlessly concerned with worldly and fleeting things. In other words, the radical desire for purity was not a "programmatic escape from the world," as Molnár put it. Rather, it was an "attempt to serve the world so that it recognizes its state before God and His judgment."[25] Nevertheless, the anticipation of the apocalyptic conclusion of the times was not as dark and depressive in the Brethren understanding as one might expect. This is especially true when considering the difficult context in which the Unitas Fratrum theology originated. Perhaps it was the dark circumstances which caused the Brethren to focus their attention on the "joyful hope and coming fulfillment of the delightful will of God."[26]

These theological accents emerged gradually and underwent significant development as the Unitas interacted with various churches and theological views during the first 200 years of her existence.[27] As hinted above, the Brethren did not hesitate to correct their past errors. At the same time, they had the courage to make definite pronouncements which were to determine their future theological course. Thus, we can distinguish, with Milos Strupl, six more or less clearly delimited periods of the Brethren theological development, with varying doctrinal emphases, within the overall history of the Unitas Fratrum. They were not of the same length, nor were they marked by an equally intense theological productivity.[28] Molnár

23. Molnár, "Eschatologická naděje," 63.

24. Ibid., 64.

25. Ibid.

26. Compare ibid.

27. For further details on the Brethren interaction with Calvinism, Lutheranism and other theological influences, see for example Molnár, "Martin Luther," 109–28; Říčan et al., *Bratrský sborník*; Říčan, *Od úsvitu reformace*.

28. Milos Strupl distinguishes these periods as follows: first 1468–95; second

commented on this characteristic of the Unitas Fratrum with the following words:

> The Unitas never proclaimed the exchangeability of its dogmatic expression. The Unitas was convinced that the continuity of its theology was given primarily by its attachment to the essential tenets of the Christian faith, as they are attested to in the midst of Christ's confessors by the Holy Scripture. Although the ecclesiological and theological exposition of the essential principles among the Brethren was based on the Apostles' Creed and the dogmatic tradition of Western Christendom, it did not lay claim to being a changeless rule.[29]

It is important to keep in mind that the quest for theological identity had been pursued against the backdrop of almost constant religious persecution. The Brethren were well aware of the threats connected to their doctrinal convictions; in spite of that, they dared not only to hold them but also to publish them, live them out, and suffer for them. From this it follows that they cannot be suspected of enacting any doctrinal changes for opportunistic or pragmatic reasons, whether ecclesiological, political, social, or economic. In other words, the relentless push for constant reformulation of their confessional statements was motivated by nothing less than an inner need for genuine consistency or, in František M. Dobiáš's words, "a conscious and obedient yielding to the newly recognized and newly formulated truth."[30]

In summary, the theological heritage into which Comenius fell was as follows: an emphasis on saving faith and knowledge of one's dependence on God, pacifism, a desire for religious unity, fundamental openness to the truth, a desire for spiritual purity, active moral consistency, and hopeful eschatological expectations. I consider that, in addition to the traditional

---

1495–1531; third 1531–46; fourth 1546–74; fifth 1574–1628; sixth 1628–62. Each period is usually tied to one or more particular leading theologians such as brother Řehoř, Jan Klenovský (first period), Lukáš Pražský (second period), Jan Roh, Jan Augusta (third period), Matěj Červenka, Jan Augusta (fourth period), Jiří Strejc (fifth period), J. A. Komenský (sixth period). The theological productivity of the Brethren was different in each period, but in total they produced almost 40 official confessional documents (including apologies) within fewer than twenty years. For details see Strupl, *Confessional Theology*, 279–93.

29. Říčan, *Dějiny*, 409.

30. Dobiáš, *Víra a vyznání*, 21.

Christian doctrines, this heritage was the most important factor forming Comenius's anthropology and his work.[31]

As a result of the above-mentioned developments, the Unitas church in which Comenius found himself at the end of the sixteenth century was quite a different church from the one of the previous period. It was different both theologically and practically. Although the accents on spiritual purity remained strong, as the Brethren theology deepened it found a more conciliatory relationship to the "world." According to Brethren historians, "they critically affirmed the social responsibility of the believer."[32] The original primitivism was practically gone; there was no problem with receiving as members rich or educated people, even aristocracy, providing they showed signs of purity in their lives.[33]

At the age of twelve, Jan Amos lost in a very short time his father, mother, and two sisters, probably from the plague. His guardians (the family of Jan's aunt) sent Comenius to work at hard manual labor, thus depriving him of a quality primary education. Comenius had previously attended school in Strážnice, where he first met Mikuláš Drabík (who markedly influenced him, as we shall see). But the Strážnice school didn't fulfill his intellectual needs. In his autobiographical notes Comenius gave us the insight that his unhappy experience compelled him to think about the positive aspects of orphanhood. In his judgment they consist in the fact that an orphan is more intensely aware of how precious some things are, especially a quality education.[34] Not until age sixteen was he sent, by his church, to the Grammar School of Přerov.[35] His natural talents and aptitudes were soon discovered by the rector and by Bishop Jan Lánecký, who accepted the orphan into his household as a son and gave him the name Amos, mean-

31. Compare Neval, *Die Mach Gottes*, 523.

32. See the article on *Historie Unitas Fratrum* published on the home page of the Jednota Bratrská at <http://www.jednotabratrska.cz> [accessed 2012–07–14].

33. It is estimated that during this period the Unitas had about 150 congregations in Bohemia and Moravia and represented about 2–3 percent of the overall population. The members of the Unitas consisted mainly of craftsmen, peasants, and intellectuals of the middle civic class. See Králík, *Otázky*, or Říčan, *Dějiny*.

34. See Molnár and Rejchrtová, *J. A. Komenský*, 32, 34.

35. The field of Brethren activity was quite large before the fatal year of 1620. There were more than 50 Brethren Schools at the beginning of the seventeenth century. J. Vomáčka describes the Brethren schools as "incomparable to the conventual and cloistral schools for their virtuousness, folksiness, openness to the world, bright approach to life and thoughtful use of the mother tongue" (Vomáčka, *Proměny školního vzdělávání*, 31). For further details see Molnár, *Českobratrská výchova*.

ing Loving.[36] Through the Bishop, Comenius was brought to the favorable notice of the leading nobleman protector of the Unitas, Karel of Žerotín, who made further university studies possible for the boy.[37]

At age nineteen Comenius was sent with other young men to the Reformed University of Herborn in Nassau where he studied philosophy and Protestant theology.[38] Here the foundations of his specific philosophical and theological scholarship were laid. In a remarkably short time (two years),[39] Comenius managed to acquire a proper university education, attending the courses of outstanding teachers such as Alsted, Guberleth, and Piscator. Through them (especially through Alsted), Comenius received not only classical learning in philosophy and theology; he also became familiar with the latest events in the scientific and academic world.

Among the other significant formative influences on Comenius's thinking were Johann H. Alsted's encyclopedism, Wolfgang Ratke's famous educational reforms, the helio/geocentric disputations, and Johann Piscator-Fischer's chiliastic expectations and last but not least, the irenistic[40] thoughts of some scholars who came across Comenius's path. These were thinkers such as Johanes H. Althusius and David Pareus, whom Comenius met at the university in Heidelberg. After a short holiday in Amsterdam Comenius spent an additional year of study at the university. Among other things he saw how terrible are the consequences of religious oppression, and how difficult it was to bring together the divided Protestants in Germany. Jan Patočka summarized that period in Comenius's studies as follows:

> There is no doubt that during those three and half years spent abroad [Comenius] made an extraordinary effort to assimilate as

36. Kvačala alerts us to the different interpretations of the name Amos. It might be a translation of the Czech "Jan," that is, "Loved by the Lord," who was John the Evangelist. Bishop Lánecký apparently wanted Comenius to know that his skills and gifts were an expression of God's love, and that he should therefore use them properly. See Kvačala, *Jan Amos Komenský*, 14.

37. It was also during the Přerov period that Comenius first encountered the teachings of the Polish Socinians, which, as he himself later recalled, caused the first great shock to his inherited faith. See Molnár and Rejchrtová, *J. A. Komenský*, 35–37.

38. Patočka points out that the Unitas wouldn't send their youth to Prague University because at that time they considered the environment there to be too liberal. See Patočka, *Komeniologické studie 3*, 396–97.

39. Sadler explains this as a result of Comenius's "intense sense of purpose and the work of excellent teachers." See Sadler, *J. A. Comenius*, 15.

40. The term comes from the Latin *irené*, which means "peace." For details see the Glossary of Special Terms.

much knowledge as he could. He missed no opportunity to learn. He visited Amsterdam, he witnessed a public autopsy, he observed life in the United provinces which were economically and socially the most developed in Europe, he went to Marburg to meet famous scholars such as R. Goclenius.[41]

When Comenius returned home to Moravia, he enthusiastically began to implement the plans he had conceived during his studies. He wanted to raise the general level of Czech literacy and culture, because, at the time, it lagged behind the rest of Europe. In addition to other works,[42] he embarked on two major projects: an encyclopedic Latin-Czech glossary called *Thesaurus linguae Bohemicae*, a phraseological, grammatical, and stylistic dictionary. He worked on this project for more than 40 years, until 1656, when it was lost in the fire at Leszno. Unfortunately, the second project, *Theatrum universitatis rerum*, suffered the same fate. It was planned to be a gigantic encyclopedia of twenty-eight volumes that should have provided the readers with an overview of the general knowledge of all things. As Comenius prepared the materials for his works, he read influential thinkers such as Nicolaus Cusanus, Jakob Böhme, and others,[43] who stimulated him to new creativity.

In 1614 Comenius became the headmaster of the school in Přerov where he himself had studied only six years earlier. Two years later he was ordained as a minister of the Unitas Fratrum, and his first appointment was to the church in Fulnek, in northern Moravia. At the same time he was also the rector of the local Brethren school. Before moving to Fulnek Comenius married Magdalena Vizovská, a girl from a respected and influential family. During the following relatively peaceful period the Comenius family, which had moved to the new place, was very well received by the church

41. Patočka, *Komeniologické studie 3*, 368.

42. Eg. Grammaticae facilioris praecepta (Principles of a Simpler Approach to Grammar), De antiquitatibus Moraviae (On Antiquities of Moravia), De origine et gestis familiae Zierotin (On the Origin and History of the Zerotin Family), Retuňk proti antikristu (Against the Antichrist) and others. In this period Comenius also acquired a remarkably good map of Moravia. See the Appendices.

43. Comenius knew most authors from primary sources. As for Cusanus, it is a question whether he knew him only from Ulrich Pinder's anthology *Speculum inttellectuale* or whether he read some of Cusanus directly. However, Patočka has clearly demonstrated that Cusanus's influence on Comenius was particularly significant, for his concept of a harmony or unity in which contradictions fuse—together with other philosophical assumptions—became one of the foundational aspects of Comenius' pansophy. See Patočka, *Komeniologické studie 1*, 138–39 or Králík, *Otázky*.

of Czech and German speaking believers. Within a year their first child was born, a son named Jan. Joy in his personal life and relative prosperity did not, however, diminish in the least Comenius's sharp awareness of the social and political problems of his day, as reflected in his *Listové do nebe* (Letters to Heaven). In these letters he expressed a great interest in the poor and in encouraging the rich towards emendative action.[44]

During that time Comenius also became acquainted with the work of the prominent German Lutheran thinker Johann V. Andreae, who strongly inspired Comenius with his magnificently conceived reformation projects. Andreae was a very able critic of his contemporary social problems such as the immorality of clergy, means of upbringing and education, the political organization of states, etc. His literary style vividly and colorfully reflected the forms he adopted such as drama, dialogue and allegory. His thought was originally related to Rosicrucianism: the authorship of three tracts regarded as manifestos of Rosicrucianism (*Fama Fraternitatis, The Confessio Fraternitatis, Chymishe Hochzeit*) is ascribed to him. Later, however, he distanced himself from the Rosicrucian Brotherhood for its mystical and esoteric tendencies and elaborated his own emendative projects such as *Christianopolis* (an ideal utopian Christian city) and *Societas Christiana*, an international society of Christian scholars, which Andreae himself founded in 1619. Comenius's interest in Andreae's thought was so great that he initiated and kept up a correspondence relationship with him. Later, when Andreae lost some of his manuscripts due to the too often devastating conflagrations caused by Thirty Years War, and announced his search for any surviving copies of his earlier, hitherto unpublished dialogue called *Theophilus*, Comenius offered to him his own personal copy, and thus that work could have been published in 1649.[45]

The period of relative quiet, full of intensive pastoral and teaching work, soon ended for Comenius—but that is another chapter. We find this stage of his life, when Comenius began to create, socially and existentially saturated, equipped with traditional Brethren theology and Reformation philosophy, and filled with a meaningful life mission. Not surprisingly, for him the cosmos was primarily a beautiful and exciting wonder.

---

44. For further details on this subject see Novák, "Úvod k listové," 3–5; Patočka, *Komeniologické studie 3*, 431–32 ; Lášek, *Komenský kazatel*, 56.

45. For details see Kopecký, *J. V. Andreae*; Polišenský, *Jan Amos Komenský*.

"THOSE WHO SEE THE BEAUTY": EDUCATION THROUGH WONDER

The first stage of Comenius's anthropological thinking was closely connected to the resources from which he drew during his youth and student years. As we saw earlier, from the time of his studies Comenius carried the evolving concept of a grandly conceived encyclopedic work[46] whose task was to teach people wisdom; that is, the ability to see in creation the greatness, beauty and power of God's providence.[47] The *Theater of the Universe of Things* should later be complemented by the *Theater of Scripture*, so that the reader can learn the entire contents of what is known to humankind, both in the natural world and the supernatural,[48] as both worlds harmoniously point beyond themselves to the other as their source and goal. Or in the words of Comenius's himself:

> Not without reason is the world called, in the Greek language, *cosmos*, that is, beautiful; and in Latin, *mundus*, meaning pure. Everything in it is beautiful, pure, delightful and charming, and the visible beauty is painted by the invisible God. If one does not see beauty in the world, one sees little. . . . Oh, what must be the wondrous and abundantly loveable beauty of our God, from whom all diverse beauty flows! Whatever is noble in a created thing didn't arise out of itself, but from the well of that which is beyond.[49]

Because the created world is so remarkable and worthy of our attention, Comenious speaks of it as a theater, as the wonderful theater of God's work. It's enough just to look and wonder, the reality itself will teach people about God's plan and wise governance through its grandeur, fullness and beauty. One must step as an actor/participant onto the stage of the theater of the world and participate in this drama written by the author/Creator; each has their own role which they must play wisely and well. Patočka, referring to Stanislav Souček,[50] called Comenius's view of the human being an "extensive anthropology," explaining that human wisdom, accord-

46. His *Thesaurus linguae Bohemicae*, *Theatrum univesitatis rerum* and *Amphitheatrum universitatis rerum*.

47. It's necessary to add that in the aftermath of the Lešno fire, only small fragments were saved.

48. Comenius revealed this in the surviving preface to *Theatrum*. See Komenský, *Theatrum*, 111–12.

49. Ibid., 146.

50. Souček, "Dva české prasménky," 271.

ing to Comenius at this stage, was simply one's understanding of "his [sic] complete dependence in his [sic] cosmic position and creative, moral, and historical conduct."[51]

Nevertheless it would be a mistake to conclude that the grandeur of creation led Comenius to an anthropological romanticism or idealism. This is evident from a surviving fragment from the second volume of *Theatrum*, where Comenius dealt with the "corruption, deviation and confusion of man [sic] and everything in his [sic] soul and body."[52] With regard to this Radim Palouš observed that, "this in itself is not an unusual perspective, but is the necessary precursor for Comenius's later turn from passive observations to an active calling to repair what was broken."[53]

In terms of the main thesis of this work, it is necessary to not overlook the fact that even in this early stage of his thinking, Comenius had already recognized that a person has both an ontological and moral dimension. Human beings, as part of the "beautiful" creation, are ontologically valuable, but also morally "corrupt," "led astray," and "confused." It is true that at this time Comenius was focused more on the ontological beauty of humankind—there is moral decay here, but so far he wasn't emphasizing it too much. For now he still hadn't contrived a corrective plan, he was only leading his listeners/readers to contemplation and wonder.

51. Patočka, *Komeniologické studie 1*, 178.

52. Komenský, *Rozložení Theatrum*, 119.

53. Palouš, *Komenského Boží svět*, 9.

CHAPTER 2

The Depths of Safety

Teaching and Learning through Resignation

Come to the light, you morose, depraved, corrupt world, so that
we can see how beautiful you really are. Listen, World! You are the
big den of Satan. . . . A mixture, I say, of strange confusions and
misperceptions, you are such a confusion that it is impossible to
distinguish the beginning, middle or end of anything. . . . There is
no law, or justice, or counsel, no reason, no love, no compassion,
no shame, no fear, or morality, or respectfulness or piety. . . . Why
should I bother with you, you miserable, painful, blind, running to
damnation World? But I am Your servant, Jesus Christ.

Výhost světu (Banishment of the World)

BIOGRAPHICAL CONTEXT:
WHITE MOUNTAIN AND THE THIRTY-YEARS WAR

The Czech insurrection against Emperor Ferdinand II, which marked
the beginning of the Thirty Years War in 1618, was the beginning
of Comenius's life afflictions.[1] The consequences of the fatal defeat of the

---

1. Comenius naturally sided with the anti-Habsburg camp, the so called 'corpus
evangelicorum,' which was formed at the beginning of the Thirty Years War by an alliance of Sweden, Norway, Denmark, Netherlands, England, and the northwestern German princes. His open participation in this alliance caused the persecution that followed.

Bohemians at White Mountain in 1620 reached Fulnek one year later, and ended this period of a peaceful life with a focus on his literary and preaching work. In 1621 the "Spaniards" (Habsburg guards) arrived, and because Comenius had participated in the coronation of the Protestant king, Fridrich Falcký (Frederick of Palatine), he and other non-Catholic clergy were expelled from the country by the decree of October 28, 1621, which essentially was an arrest warrant. For the safety of himself and his family Comenius decided to hide. He left his family in Prerov, which at the time was under the protection of Žerotín, and hid himself in various places in Northern Moravia, probably in the area of the Žerotín Estate. For several years the region was sacked by soldiers, who in addition to looting and killing, usually also brought the plague and other diseases. While in one of his hiding places Comenius guessed that the heart of his wife must be full of "sorrow and grief," so he wrote a brief treatise for her and his other loved ones. It was called *Přemyšlování o dokonalosti křesťanské* (Thoughts on Christian Perfection), and in it he made clear that the full perfection of a person tested by adversity consists in complete submission to God, which is a conclusion not unlike that of the Paradise section of the later *Labyrinth*. The booklet accompanied a personal letter dated February 18, 1622, which begins with the famous salutation: "My dear wife Magdalena, my jewel, dearest to me after God . . . ." In the letter we learn that she was expecting their second child—he hopes that she will "happily survive" the coming birth. However, his wife never read either the letter or the booklet. She and the two children, including the one Comenius had never seen, died in the plague. The family tragedy was further compounded. The library that Comenius had been carefully building since his student days was publicly burned by the Jesuits in Fulnek Square, the church building of the Unitas was demolished, and the community dispersed. Comenius thus lost literally everything he had. In his own country he was an outlaw, all of his social and personal security collapsed. It is not surprising therefore, that in 1623 he put the following words into the mouth of *Truchlivý* (Mournful):[2]

> Evil on every side, a cruel, bloody sword is destroying my beloved homeland, conquering chateaus, castles, and cities; towns, villages, beautiful homes, and churches plundered and burning, property looted, livestock captured and slain, the wretched poor afflicted, suffering, in places captured and murdered. . . . And what is most

2. An allegorical work in which the title character argues with Faith and Reason about the meaning of life.

painful is that the truth of God is being suppressed, the pure divine
service has been stopped, ministers banished or put in prison. . . .
There is no one under heaven who would take in the innocent or
help the suffering. All hope, even that which we had in God until
now, is falling away: we call to Him, and He doesn't listen nor does
He want to help; we are abandoned right and left, there is nothing
left but to die. Oh, may death come and obliterate![3]

In the following period, Comenius had to continue to hide with other
ministers in various places in Bohemia. As a consolation for the others and
probably himself as well, he wrote books which Patočka describes as those
"which have no precedent in Czech literature."[4] Probably the most famous
ones are *Labyrint světa a ráj srdce* (The Labyrinth of the World and the
Paradise of the Heart) and *Centrum Securitatis* (The Center of Safety), in
which the old literary themes are remolded into a new and original form.[5]
The experience of great affliction wedded with the rich imaginative spirit of
Comenius gave birth to an unusual allegory that struggled to understand
human wandering in the world, as we will see later.

The years before the exile to Poland were busy for Comenius. Without
a doubt these years were filled with anxious expectations. As a pastor, he
had to keep faith and hope alive in his troubled co-believers. Some hopes
were raised by prophecies of K. Kotter and K. Poniatowská, who predicted
an early fall of the anti-reformation oppressors and ultimate deliverance of
the nation. Comenius was at first distrustful and even "suspicious," according to his own words, but after overcoming the initial hesitations of a theological nature,[6] he gladly received and even passionately defended them.[7]

3. Citation from Molnár and Rejchrtová, *J. A. Komenský*, 61–62.

4. Patočka, *Komeniologické studie 3*, 400.

5. In *Centrum Securitatis* Comenius combined two pictures from Cusanus's *Ludus Globi*, according to Jan Patočka. Patočka dealt with this issue several times in his writings. See, for example, Patočka, *Komeniologické studie 3*, 262–73. Novák also reminds us of the influence of the German theosoph J. Böehme; see Novák, "Úvod k Centrum Securitatis" 383.

6. In 1629 Comenius wrote a polemical tract of sixty-three paragraphs called *De veris et falsis Prophetis* (On True and False Prophets), in which he theologically dealt in detail with all disputed questions such as: Who is a prophet? The subject and form of prophecy. Why and when God sends prophets? How to distinguish true and false prophets? The relation between revelation in the Scripture and new revelations. And of course, the issue of the possibility of continuity of revelation.

7. For details of Comenius' own account concerning the problems of the prophecies, see Molnár and Rejchrtová, *J. A. Komenský o sobě*, 62–74.

The "revelations" caused much controversy among both Comenius's contemporaries and later among the interpreters of Comenius.[8] There is no dispute about the problematic nature of the prophecies—some were very specific, some multivalent, even ambivalent, some were fulfilled (supernatural origin or an accident?), and many were never fulfilled.[9] How does Comenius's faith in such doubtful visions fit into his overall thought? Modern interpreters, approaching Comenius through the rationalist prism, tended to condemn Comenius's faith in revelations as an irrational side of his personality or even as a mental deviation, which spoiled an otherwise quite positive picture of the great thinker. Josef Volf, for example, considered the prophecies to be "sick figments of over-excited minds."[10] Similarly, František J. Zoubek viewed Comenius's faith in prophecy as "the only thing which clouds the memory of Comenius."[11] Perhaps one of the most critical judgments comes from Jaromír Červenka, who saw in Comenius two irreconcilable, almost schizophrenic, levels of personality: the rational and the irrational.[12] The dual-personality interpretation was also held by T. G. Masaryk, who distinguished the "rational" and the "mystical" side of Comenius's personality. It should be noted that Masaryk, however, did not view the mystical side negatively.[13]

More recent Comeniologists have striven to understand Comenius within his religious, cultural, and political context, a far more fruitful approach. Thus, his faith in revelations is viewed as one of the factors which helped Comenius to face the severe crisis of faith and life in 1620 and activated him to enter the public arena of social and political matters. As with every great thinker, Comenius "struggled to overcome the mental framework and thought structures of his time," Josef Válka commented. Válka

8. The issue became the subject of a number of Brethren synods which wanted to resolve both the problem of authenticity and of the possibility of continuity of revelations. Also the wider public, both educated and uneducated, was interested, even excited, in such things. It seems that there were as many critics as defenders of the revelations. Some of the greatest critics were Samuel des Martes (Samuel Maresius), Nicholas Arnold, Matyáš Prokopius and Nicholas Megander, who considered the continuation of prophecies impossible, absurd and needless. The supporters of Comenius were Christopher Pelargius, Jan Cyrill, Abraham Menzel and others.

9. For a detailed analysis see the unpublished Master's thesis of Pavel Heřmánek, *Jan Amos Komenský*.

10. Volf, "Horologium Hussianum," 305–12.

11. Zoubek, "O proroctvích," 3–16.

12. Červenka, *Pokračování*, 427–28.

13. For details see Masaryk, *Lecture*.

explained that Comenius, finding the prophetic phenomenon widely accepted and consistent with his theology, "transformed them into an instrument of resistance against the Habsburg-papal politics."[14] Moreover, Válka
rightly observed that Comenius "relies primarily on a general meaning of
the revelations, not on the particular wording." As such, he placed them
into the European political conflict, which he understood "as the final battle between the powers of evil and powers in the service of freedom, which
make restoration possible."[15] Other recent interpreters have paid attention
to the psychological aspects of the whole issue. In what state of mind were
those prophets? Were they suffering from some disease? Were they victims
of their own imagination or projections? In the case of Drabík and Poniatowska, Comenius himself may have put these projections into their minds,
because he was in contact with them and informed them about the political
situation in Europe.[16] The fact remains, however, that the content and form
of their visions seemed to both express and respond well to the emotions of
oppressed political and religious exiles, who strove for righteousness, truth,
and godliness. It was therefore not surprising that Comenius, along with
many of his fellow believers, gladly "succumbed" to the prophetic visions.[17]

In 1626 Comenius was sent to The Haag to deliver Kotter's revelations
into the hands of the exiled King Frederick of The Palatinate, for the prophecies assigned him a leading role in the political overturn. At the same time,
the leaders of the church, anticipating the worst, sent Comenius to negoti-
ate a potential settlement (to which they might flee) for the Czech Brethren
in Protestant Lezsno.

One of the light moments in the otherwise uneasy life of an outcast
and widower was Comenius's new marriage in 1624 to the daughter of
his older colleague and friend Jan Cyril, Dorota Cyrilová, with whom he
later had four children. Another biographically important event happened
when, on one occasion, Comenius received an invitation to visit the library
of Silberštejn castle in Vlčice, which was close to Comenius's hiding place at
that time,[18] and whose count Adam Zilvar was sympathetic to the Brethren.

---

14. Válka, "Problém výkladu revelací," 118.

15. Ibid., 117.

16. Compare Heřmánek, *Jan Amos Komenský*.

17. Compare, for example, Schaller, "Několik poznámek," 172–76.

18. The hiding place was at the estate of Jiří Sádovský of Sloupno at Bílá Třemešná,
near Dvůr Králové in Eastern Bohemia.

There he came across a copy of Elias Bodin's *Didactics*, which later turned out to be an important source of inspiration.

THE JOY OF RESIGNATION:
EDUCATION THROUGH RELIANCE

The horrors of the Thirty Years War, which personally affected Comenius, called his attention again to the problematic aspects of the world and away from its beauty and harmony.[19] The writings of this period are usually called the "Consolation Works": *Truchlivý, O sirobě* (On Orphanhood), *Hlubina bezpečnosti* (The Depths of Safety), the *Labyrinth*,[20] *Výhost světu*, etc. It wasn't that the world no longer awoke amazement in Comenius, but that it no longer appeared to him only as a theater of God's goodness; now it also was like an intricate labyrinth, a dangerous place to live. The seemingly reliable assurance of normal life had fallen apart, truth had been lost, people were doing harm to each other, and reality had been somehow skewed—as though seen through "glasses of delusion" (a picture from the *Labyrinth*). And this had led to all kinds of human afflictions: drudgery, wandering, and despair.[21] It was necessary to seek a place of refuge, an impregnable fortress, a fixed point, a *centrum securitatis*. At this stage Comenius was not yet talking about fixing what was wrong, or contriving a project for rebuilding the "labyrinth." He wasn't looking for a remedy, but rather rest, on a personal existential level. He was trying to formulate, for himself as well as others, a consolation which would empower each one to meaningfully deal with the "futility and misery" of the world.[22] How did he find the way out?

"Return to the home of your heart and shut the door behind you," he advised the pilgrim at the end of the *Labyrinth*, in God's voice. The

19. It is viewed similarly by Jaroslav Pánek, and Antonín Kostlán. Compare Pánek, *Labyrinth of Czech Lands*, 15; Kostlán, "K 'negaci světa,'" 149–55.

20.. Comenius's *Labyrinth* was unique for its narrative form as well as for its pedagogy, therefore I will give it special attention in the following chapters.

21. Comenius used all these words and more in the subtitle of his *Labyrinth*, which actually sums up the whole point of the work: "An illustrious [or, A bright] painting ofhow, in the world and all its things, everything is but a chaos and confusion, whirling and toiling, illusion and deception, misery and difficulty and despair; but for those whose home is their own heart, cloistered with the only Lord God they find true and full comfort and joy.

22 "Futility and misery" are Comenius's words from the introduction to the *Labyrinth*. See Comenius, *Labyrint*, 190.

tired pilgrim obeyed and entered. Outside the door remained a fainting, wandering, delusion and "frightful darkness and gloom of which neither the bottom nor the end could be fathomed by the human mind." Inside he was the guest of Christ Himself, who greeted the pilgrim with the words "I have watched you, my son, while you were straying, but I did not wish to see you stray any longer, and have brought you to me by leading you into yourself. For here have I chosen a palace for my dwelling; and if you dwell with me, you will find here all that you sought in vain in the world—peace, happiness, glory, and an abundance of all good things. I promise you, my son, that here you shall not be disappointed as you have been in the world." The pilgrim's answer was unequivocal: "Hearing this speech . . . joyfully and trustfully he stretched out his hands and said, 'Here I am, my Lord Jesus, take me to Thyself,' I cried. 'Thine I desire to be and to remain for ever.'"[23]

With poetic language comparable to that of the *Labyrinth* Comenius handled a similar theme in *Hlubina*—only with different imagery.[24] Here—influenced by Nicolaus Cusanus—the world was compared to a large wheel that rotates harmoniously, if it is properly related to its center. All of the spokes have only one center, which is God. A person is safest in that center, because there all motion and anxiety ceases. Conversely, the farther one goes away from the center, the faster and more dangerously the wheel turns. And there is precisely the problem for humankind: they want to be their own center, independent of their Creator. This, however, causes all kinds of confusion and disconnectedness and their world is as if it went out of balance. The remedy isn't some kind of repair of a badly functioning wheel/world, but simply a return to the center, to the place designated for human beings, where people find safety and fulfillment. This return to God He himself made possible when He made Himself visible to human beings through Christ the Savior. The way back was revealed. The one who wants to find his center of safety must rely fully on Christ. The key concept in this turning is *resignare*.

The word "resignation" might at first seem negative or despairing, but a careful reading of *Hlubina* reveals that for Comenius this concept contained no negativity whatsoever. The Latin word *resignare* that Comenius

23. Comenius, *Labyrint*, 296–98.

24. Both Centrum securitatis and the Labyrinth were inspired by literary models of the day. *The Labyrinth* was inspired by three major works of J. V. Andreae: *Peregrini in partia errors*, *Rei publicae*, *Christianae descriptio*, and *Civis Christianus sive Peregrini quondam errantis restitutiones*. Centrum Securitatis was inspired by N. Kusánus's *De ludo globi*.

used is contrasted to the term *samosvojnost,* which is a not easily translatable Czech archaism meaning *having one's ultimate goal and end in oneself,* and it has a very negative connotation. "Samosvojný" describes one who relies solely on himself or herself, who lives only for himself or herself, or as Comenius put it, one who "founds his fortune on the mere insecure world," and who "wants to belong to himself, be his own counsellor, his own guide, his own guardian, his own lord, his own little god."[25] In this searching for meaning and safety in places where it is not, that is, anywhere outside the true center, Comenius saw the beginning of all evil and all human "disconnectedness." The term *resignation,* then, expresses the exact opposite of *samosvojnost.* Comenius did not give a brief or simple definition, but in several chapters of *Hlubina* (primarily 9, 10, and 11) he explained, illustrated, gave biblical references,[26] and even made up his own parables, with which he tried to better capture the importance and bliss of the longed-for state of *resignare.* The term *resignatio* [resignation] is often used interchangeably with phrases such as *entrust oneself, give oneself, rely on,* or *dive into the depth of God's mercy.* Such a desirable attitude is warranted for several reasons: 1) the limited nature of human knowledge, 2) the human tendency to carelessness, 3) the human inability to have control over either oneself or circumstances, 4) human unsteadiness and uncertainty, which are all things whose opposites might be found in God.[27] If a person resigns, that is, returns to her true center, if she hands herself over to God, there follow "many exceedingly pleasurable benefits," which Comenius enumerates in the tenth chapter, and which he evidently experienced himself. The resigned have 1) peace with God; 2) spiritual security in spite of physical dangers; 3) perpetual good-heartedness; 4) a safe distance from worldly confusions; and they 5) do not fear any harm; 6) bear suffering

---

25. Komenský, *Hlubina bezpečnosti,* 36.

26. For example (I am using here the 1611 English Authorized Version; Comenius would, of course, use the Czech Bible Kralická from 1613): John 5:30 "I seek not mine own will, but the will of the Father which hath sent me."; Luke 22:42 "not my will, but thine, be done."; Ps 37:4 "Delight thyself also in the lord; and he shall give thee the desires of thine heart."; Isa 30:15 "For thus saith the Lord god, the Holy One of Israel; In returning and rest shall ye be saved; in quietness and in confidence shall be your strength."; Phil 1:20 "According to my earnest expectation and my hope, that in nothing I shall be ashamed, but that with all boldness, as always, so now also Christ shall be magnified in my body, whether it be by life, or by death."

27. Komenský, *Hlubina bezpečnosti,* 72–82.

with praising of God; 7) are amazed by God's benevolence; 8) do not fall harmfully; 9) die joyfully.[28]

Although the expression *hopeful resignation* may sound like a contradiction to a modern reader, from the above citations it is clear that Comenius did not understand resignation as something negative, hopeless, or undesireable, but exactly the opposite. A person can see the futility of his efforts, stop his searching and groping around in places where there is nothing, and with hope turn to that place which gives his life meaning, peace and safety in the midst of every hardship. In this context it is necessary to recall Comenius's (the Brethren's) eschatological expectations, which are evident from many of Comenius's writings, not only from this period. In *Truchlivý*, for example, he expressed the idea that present afflictions are signs of the soon coming of Christ and with Him the final victory of good and justice.[29] Therefore for Comenius resignation was never completely negative, and thus hopeless, but something completely concrete and specific, namely "resignation to worldliness as manifested in the givens of the time," as Palouš put it.[30] It means resignation to the addiction to anything earthly, fragile, or temporary. As in the *Labyrinth*, so also in *Truchlivý* and *Hlubina*, Comenius wrote a lot about misery in the world, but still offered a way out: "not intending to persist in deception, but to expose to himself and others deception as deception and delusion . . . the pilgrim in his current despondency could not elevate the world, but he could however come out of it, to go from the outside world into the heart."[31] One could return to the center, rely on God and find safety, and look forward to the future with hope.

Understanding Comenius's experiences during the early 1620s, which found its expression in the theme of resignation, is the key to understanding the later development of his thinking.[32] When in the second half of

28. Ibid., 82–90.

29. See for example the end of the first part of *Truchlivý*, where Comenius had Truchlivý say "cheer up over the promises of God." Komenský, *Truchlivý I*.

30. Palouš, *Komenského Boží svět*, 10.

31. Ibid.

32. Jan Blahoslav Čapek observes that because of the subjective expressions of pain and sorrows, Comenius has been often incorrectly identified as a baroque writer, but a careful reader, continues Čapek, notices that Comenius's subjectivism is far from "the typical baroque desolation, aimlessness and despair," but rather it expresses "a collective pain or life trials caused by the external events of persecution and personal loss." Čapek further states that "in Komenský we can neither find any traces of baroque sensuality or

the twenties Comenius's thoughts shifted increasingly towards thoughts of pansophism and emendation, it was not a shift away from his concept of *resignare*. Comenius had never turned away from a full submission to and reliance on God, on the contrary, all his efforts arose from this assumption, whether they were projects of didactics or pansophy.[33] His attitude of commitment and hopeful expectation was not inconsistent with the potential for emendation which he discovered later; on the contrary, Comenius's "resignation" to God functioned as the foundation of emendation. Comenius's resignation wasn't substituted or overthrown by emendation, but rather complemented and enhanced by it.[34] In other words, the anthropology of innate reliance (*resignare*) laid the foundation for an anthropology of action (*emendare*), which is both understandable and internally consistent, because positive hope usually leads to positive actions. Hopelessness doesn't lead to anything.[35]

Regarding the anthropological duality (ontological—moral) which is the central theme of this book, it's obvious which of the components came to the forefront of Comenius's attention at this time in his life. He still saw humanity as ontologically noble, but morally it was "exceedingly" inadequate, unstable, weak, suffering from an over-reliance on oneself and disconnectedness. The miserable poverty of humanity was for Comenius at that time so great, that it even called for "banishment from the world." If Comenius saw any hope for the world, it had to stand somehow outside the

---

desire of sensual depiction of the transcendent, as was common in , e.g., Terezia of Avila or in Rubens." See Čapek, *Několik pohledů*, 18.

33. In the *Great Didactic*, in the second chapter for example, Comenius presents the final goal of human being: "to be so connected with God, the peak of all perfection of glory and bliss, as to enjoy with Him the highest perfection of glory and blessedness forever," which is a very similar anthropology to that of *The Depths*, *The Mournful*, and the *Labyrinth*. The mentality of 'resignation' was both implicitly and explicitly expressed in Comenius' writings throughout his life. In his late *Unum Necessarium* (The One Thing Necessary) from 1669, he said, for example: "[Christ] commanded us not to worry too much about the earthly things, but to rely on God's fatherly care;" elsewhere Comenius quoted the apostle Paul to make his point: "I have learned, in whatsoever state I am, therewith to be content" (Chapter 4); and elsewhere he added: ". . . to be born again, be changed into a new creature in the likeness to God . . . is possible only through the complete and meekest committing of oneself to the will of God" (Chapter 6). See also his later writings such as *Clamores Eliae* or *Angelus pacis*.

34. Compare Patočka, *Komeniologické studie 2*, 226.

35. For the idea of internal hope in hopeless situations, compare Neval, *Die Mach Gottes*, 523.

world in a grasping onto that which transcends both the world and human beings.

CHAPTER 3

Labyrinth

Teaching and Learning through Story

May the mercy of God be praised that He opened my eyes also, so that I was able to perceive the manifold vanities of this pretentious world, as well as the frauds everywhere, hidden under the appearance of outward splendor. I have learned to seek peace and security of mind elsewhere. Desiring to portray this more vividly both to myself and to others, I have devised this peregrination or wandering through the world. . . . It is no fable, even though it may have the appearance of one: it describes real life, as you will perceive when you have gained insight into it, particularly such among you as are somewhat acquainted with my life and circumstances. For I have described, for the greatest part, the vicissitudes of the few years of my own life; for the rest, the incidents were observed in other lives, or I have been told of them.

Labyrinth of the World and the Paradise of the Heart (To the Reader)

SPECIAL CHARACTERISTICS OF THE LABYRINTH

Comenius wrote something over two hundred writings, yet only the *Labyrinth* approached the narrative genre—albeit with qualifications, as we shall see later. Even so, the *Labyrinth* has become by far the most famous of Comenius's literary achievement and that is why I want to give

special attention to it in this chapter. The *Labyrinth* is a unique work, testified to on the one hand by the number of editions, and on the other hand
by the unprecedented number of references to it—by scholars, laity, and
artists. I will present the scholarly ones later in the text, but here are some
extracts from various Czech and Slovak authors expressing sentiments
from the period of the National Revival:

> What is present suffering after all? Refining only strengthens.
> What happiness is there in the world? Dreams are only a scintillation.
> What is the world? Only a labyrinth; and heaven is the goal
> Until we cease our worldly wandering.[1]

◆

> And so you strut through the great labyrinth of the world
> In the footsteps of nature, avoiding vain dreams,
> And with you through paradise a team of apprentices
> enter by the gate of language into the castle of all arts . . . .[2]

◆

> Nothing have we taken with us
> Everything is lost—
> We have but our Bible—
> And the Labyrinth of the world.[3]

◆

> Oh let us escape from the whirl of life, from the "labyrinth" of the land!
> Let us also enter as you did—to the paradise of our hearts![4]

From the ranks of experts in a wide range of fields resound only su-
perlatives: "One of the best books in all of Czech literature" (Jungmann),[5]
"Discerning view of the world, massive and fascinating flight of imagination . . . deep and honest emotion.[6] Similarly, in Antonín Škarka's judgment, the *Labyrinth* surpasses every other work of our older literature."[7] Jan

1. Excerpt of a poem from a play written for the jubilee celebrating 300 years since
Comenius' birth (1892) called *J. A. Komenský*, by Jan Peliška. Taken from Souček, "Dva
české prameny."

2. Excerpt from the poem *Památce J. A. Komenského* by A. Hejduka. Taken from
Souček, "Dva české prameny."

3. Verse from a poem by Jan Kollár. First published in 1832, now in Prague in the
Museum of Czech Periodocals.

4. From the poem by P. O. Hviezdoslava, called *Ján Amos Komenský*. Taken from
Souček, "Dva české prameny."

5. Quotation from Jungmann taken from Bílý, "Úvod."

6. Ibid, 9.

7. Škarka, "Doslov," 9.

Patočka even says that the *Labyrinth* is a work which has no "precedent in Czech literature."[8]

It is evident, then, that in the *Labyrinth* Comenius succeeded in, on the one hand, doing justice to a theme which spoke (and still speaks) to the Czech soul, and, on the other hand, choosing a very effective form. I believe it is precisely in this that its magic lies. In contrast to others of Comenius's works the *Labyrinth* is a story, and a didactic one at that (although it's not solely didactic), which is very important for the theme of this work. The notion of "didactic" isn't used here in the modern sense of the word, that is, as a theory that pertains to the systematic aspects of teaching, but in the wider sense, in the same way Comenius used the word in his later *Didactics*. It rather indicates a philosophic approach to education, or to the educative purpose, which was carried throughout the work.

Comenius laid his didactic cards on the table in the introductory chapter, called "To the Reader," where he revealed the work would be nothing less than a search for the "highest good" (*summum bonum*) in human life. In this he revealed the breadth of his educational aim. He intended to lead the reader into the area of practical philosophy, that is, ethics—which Josef Jungmann pointed out in his *History of Czech Literature* when he ranked the *Labyrinth* among the "moral writings."[9] But it would also be a lesson in apologetics, for the author would defend the "true" good and the "real" truth against all depravity.[10] Comenius admitted that it's not an easy task, but it isn't impossible. He believed that in the same way Solomon himself looked for "rest for his own mind" but couldn't find it anywhere until his eyes were opened to "perceive the manifold vanities of this pretentious world, as well as the frauds everywhere, hidden under the appearance of outward splendor. . . . [He had] learned to seek peace and security of mind elsewhere."[11]

Comenius further informed the reader that when he was thinking about how to "portray this more vividly both to myself and to others," the idea of *story* occurred to him, (which is the way some contemporary

8. Patočka, *Komeniologické studie 3*, 400.

9. Bílý, "Úvod," 18; Nový, "Dialektika," 95.

10. In Comenius' *Labyrinth* however, it is not yet possible to speak of rationalistic apologetics typical of the period of modernity. With regard to the narrative method he uses, his defense is rather closer to the concept of *non-reductive apologia* as discussed in the study by Ivana Dolejšová (*Accounts of Hope*).

11. http://www.labyrinth.cz/en/to-the-reader. All English quotations from the *Labyrinth* will come from this 2005 internet translation by James Naughton.

translators interpreted the word "treatise" in the original text).[12] Then in the dedication to Charles the Elder from Žerotín, Comenius said it was a "drama." So in which genre can we classify the *Labyrinth*? Antonín Škarka responded that the label "drama" is okay here because of its "lively story lines, quickly changing scenes and acts and abundance of monologues and dialogues . . . ." According to Škarka, Comenius here crossed over the border of traditional educational treatises and created a work of "fiction," which was unprecedented at that time.[13] To conclude the genre definition, it seems that Comenius's "treatise" is dramatic, allegorical, didactic, and narrative all at the same time.

The author revealed the contents of his work in the subtitle, using his well-known dualist style—first we see the "vagueness and confusion, whirling and grinding, illusion and deceit, poverty and want . . ." of the world, and then the "true and full intellect, satisfaction and joy" to which it's possible to attain in your own heart.

This goal could theoretically have been reached using the traditional treatise form, as was the custom in Comenius's time, which was to describe the problem, analyze it and respond with the appropriate argument. Comenius himself also employed that method in many of his other works from that time and later—for example, *Hlubina bezpečnosti, Pres boží* (*God's Press*), and his thorough analysis of "human affairs" in the introductory chapters of the *Velká* and *Česká didaktika* (Great Didactic and Czech Didactic) and "public affairs" in *Obecná porada* (General Consultation, Panegersia, 5: 28). In the *Labyrinth*, however, he chose a different form. Instead of a theoretical essay he displayed narrative scenery, created a plot, let allegorical figures do the talking and raised questions like: "Have you ever heard of the Cretan Labyrinth?" Didactically, psychologically, and aesthetically the effect is powerful.

In other words, the uniqueness of the *Labyrinth* lies in the nature of its pedagogical discourse. If in other works Comenius was dealing with humanity, or humanization, in the *Labyrinth* he illustrated it. The *Labyrinth* is a specific example of pedagogical humanization, it is the application of Comenius's theory of education (albeit still early). Good teachers and educators know intuitively about the power of story and have always used it liberally. Pedagogically speaking, they have communicated their curriculum in a narrative form. Remember, for example, the stories of Moses, Homer,

---

12. Ibid.

13. Škarka, *Slovesné umění*, 35–36.

Plato and Jesus, whose "teachings" still have a significant cultural influence today. Joseph Hillis Miller noted that we don't know of "any human society . . . , that hasn't had its stories and narrative customs, its myths, . . . tribal legends and stories about its heroes."[14] This raises the key question, what is so magical about the narrative form? Where is its formative strength? What gives the story (in our case, allegorical) such didactic functionality? How, concretely, does Comenius carry out his humanization in the *Labyrinth*?

In this chapter I will attempt to answer the above questions. It won't be an exhaustive discourse on narrative as a literary phenomenon, but rather an interdisciplinary case study in which I will read a literary text (Comenius's *Labyrinth*) with pedagogical glasses. That is, I will try to interject literary insights into a pedigogical discussion about the effectiveness of story as a tool for pedagogical humanization.

EDUCATION THROUGH NARRATIVE ALLEGORY

The existence of a wide range of pedagogical disciples and subdisciplines proves that pedagogy is well aware of the multiple layers of human personality. It knows that a person is a rational being, but is also emotional, moral, aesthetic, relational (socially), physical, spiritual, and so on. Our emphasis in describing humanity depends on which direction we look at the human being from. Biologists may notice certain components of humanity, psychologists others, maybe sociologists others, and professional cultural anthropologists notice still others. Good pedagogy as a humanistic and synthetic discipline tries to take into account the results of research from other sciences inasmuch as it strives, as far as possible, after what brings the most complete development of humanity, or nurturing of a person. The individual layers of human personality respond to specific teaching strategies which are aimed at developing that particular layer or component. Cognitive skills are usually learned by methods other than those used to learn, say, social or moral skills. From the perspective of psychological effectiveness the story, or its telling, tends to be ranked in teaching manuals among the motivating strategies.[15] This is very relevant to the theme of this work. That stories can activate, motivate, draw in, engage, etc., is well known. The question is, "How?" How does a story captivate its readers? By

14. Miller, "Narativ," 30.

15. See for example Hanesová, ⊠Aktivizujúce metódy⊠; Skalková, *Humanizace vzdělávání*; Kalhous et al, *Školní didaktika*.

what means does it touch or affect the various layers of human personality? In the following eight subchapters I present partial answers based on my analysis of Comenius's *Labyrinth*, while at the same time I keep an eye on my central theme—how Comenius spoke of the ontological and moral nature of human beings.

BIRTH OF THE MODEL READER

A story requires a lot from its reader or listener. First, it invites the person to enter into a complex interpretative game which always requires interaction. Consider, for example, what the author (or story) asks of a reader when he (it) begins with the words:

> I was thus musing, we suddenly found ourselves (I know not how) upon an exceedingly high tower, so that I seemed to touch the clouds. Looking down from this tower, I saw a city beautiful in appearance, shining, and prodigiously wide-spread, but not so great that I could not discern its limits and boundaries all around. The city formed a circle, and was surrounded with walls and ramparts, but instead of moats there yawned a gloomy abyss, to all appearances boundless and bottomless. Light shone only above the city, while beyond the walls it was pitch dark (chapter 5).

Upon entering this world the reader must first enter into an agreement with the author, that she will accept the rules of the game. In this way emerges an intimate, rather mysterious and often latent tie between the so-called model author and model reader. First the reader hears the voice of the storyteller (not Comenius, the empirical author, but the model author), gradually presenting a set of instructions and messages—which are obeyed if she has decided to become that model reader. The reader is invited into a specific initiative, to make "a guess about the intention of the text."[16] In terms of intellectual engagement it's the foundational step of the reader. The reader is literally "born together with the text, which is the driving force behind interpretive strategies."[17] Still elsewhere Umberto Eco has noted that many texts (and I think this text by Comenius is among them) aspire to create two model readers—the first on the level of understanding what

16. Eco, *Meze interpretace*, 68.
17. Eco, *Šest procházek*, 26.

the text says, and the second on the critical level of appreciating the way the text says it.[18]

In the case of *The Labyrinth*, the reader first has to accept that it's an imaginary world. She knows that such a city does not actually exist, nor was that narrator ever in a high tower "seeming to touch the clouds," but accepting the author's imaginings, she also pretends to believe them. Only then can the reader receive what the author has prepared—not only aesthetically but also morally and otherwise. Therefore the reader is not surprised to meet Searchall Ubiquitous (one of the main characters) or the "bridle of curiosity," or to walk to Fortune Castle. However, the rules of the fictional world are neither arbitrary nor random.[19] If Comenius's traveler met Little Red Riding Hood or Beowulf in the labyrinth it would be both disturbing and improper, as if Red Riding Hood met Robin Hood on the path. At best the reader would be merely confused, at worst he would be outraged by the author's violation of the agreement, which illustrates the practical power of stories.

A story requires still more work from the reader, work which engages him whether he wants it to or not. C. S. Lewis (with reference to Samuel Alexander) noticed a certain epistemological law: the perceiving or discerning "I" can never enjoy the given state of mind and at the same time observe it from a contemplative distance.[20] However possible it is to go from one mode of knowing to another, it is not possible to experience both at the same time. To *experience*, for example, some emotion or thing of beauty is quite another thing than to *reflect* on it. The process of reading a story—whether on the model or empirical level—is the kind of epistemic action through which a reader *experiences*, that is, his mind is fixed, linked, or absorbed by the imagined reality. He experiences something that is impossible to experience through purely rational discourse.[21]

The reader must also complete those details that have been left incomplete, which every narrative necessarily contains. Umberto Eco notes in this regard, that "every narration is inevitably and inescapably brief" because, if it has to build a world full of events and characters, it cannot

18. Ibid., 64.

19. On the subject of the narrative "framework" of fictional worlds see Doležel, *Narativní způsoby*.

20. Lewis acknowledged this reference to Alexander in his autobiography *Surprised by Joy* (published in Czech by the Česká křesťanská akademie in 1994 as *Zaskočen radostí*). For more on this topic see Hošek, *C. S. Lewis, mýtus*.

21. Compare Hošek, *C. S. Lewis, mýtus*.

explain everything. "A story only suggests," continues Eco, "and then asks the reader to fill in the blanks." In other words, a text is "a lazy instrument that requires the reader to do part of its work."[22] When, for example, Comenius says in chapter 8, "My companions then led me to a street where, they said, married people lived," he doesn't have to clarify that the street was paved with stones or that the way from the square (in the previous chapter) to this street takes half an hour. If the text calls forth the need to complete some detail or link, it's the reader's work to do it. Roman Ingarden comments on this: "Because of the limited number of words and sentences allowed in the structure of a work, it isn't possible to express clearly and exhaustively the infinite number of characteristics and situations presented by individual subjects."[23] The reader has to imagine, predict, evaluate, infer, relate, believe, compare, classify, project, and so on. That is, "to think narratively," as Jiří Trávníček says.[24] This creates the necessary emotional and aesthetic aspect of the reading that brings into the mix the hopes, fears, and excitement which flow out of the reader's identification with the characters or the story itself. From the perspective of didactic usefulness, it's a mental exercise that's worth its weight in gold because it engages the reader in a very comprehensive way. With reference to Chris Crawford, Trávníček notes: "Thinking narratively we move around in a situation, while thinking only logically we have to rely on concepts, that is, abstract themes. Therein lies the . . . appeal and virtue of narrative thinking." In terms of the ontogenesis of the human psyche it's sort of like the peak or highest state of human thought, which includes three lower forms, as Trávníček continues: "Storytelling is not only a special area within language (spoken thought), it is also the time-causal sequence of situations in which the individual actors are engaged (social thought), and is identified by its place (spatial thought)."[25] From this comes the magic of story.

MYTHOS, OR PLOT

Aristotle noted in his *Poetics* that one of the most important aspects of a good story is the plot. In his terminology "mythos," which is translated variously—outline, structure of events, plot, *děj* (Czech), *syžet* (Russian)—together

22. Eco, *Šest procházek*, 9.
23. Ingarden, *O poznání*, 46.
24. Trávníček, *Vyprávěj mi něco*, 18.
25. Ibid.

with *fabule*, create the core of every story.[26] The beginning, development and climax are normal parts of every story. In other words, in order to be a "well-told" story it must contain: 1. an initial situation— Joseph K. awakes in his bed, Neo is awakened by his computer, a man is created by God, a pilgrim finds himself in a labyrinth; 2. some fundamental change (complication, twist, conflict)—Joseph K. is absurdly accused, Neo swallows the pill of truth, the created one revolts against his Creator, the pilgrim gets glasses of deception; 3. its resolution—Joseph K. insists on a fair trial, Neo wakes up in "true" reality, the created one is saved, the pilgrim finds the paradise of the heart. Everything else, such as linguistic devices, time-frames, locations, characters, etc., are, according to Aristotle, secondary and supplementary. What is crucial is the quality of *mythos*.

Comenius's plot outline is, in this regard, straightforward. As an early Renaissance text, the *Labyrinth* doesn't have complex plot strategies, but follows a well-established framework: beginning, middle, end—entry, plot, climax. The reader is simply put into the situation:

> Having reached the age when human intelligence begins to distin-
> guish between good and evil, . . . it seemed to me highly desirable
> to consider well which of these groups of folk I should join and
> which profession I should choose for my life work. . . . Thereupon
> I sauntered out by myself and began to consider where and how I
> should begin (chapters 1, 2).

Then comes the central plot, brought about by the fact, which the reader understands, that the allegorical guides of the hero/pilgrim are trying for the whole journey to deceive (and control) him, but "luckily" (his own word) he gets a secret chance to escape their snares. The "glasses of illusion" that they forced him to wear did not fit him properly, so when the pilgrim "raised my head [and looked] under them" (leaned back his head and looked out of the corner of his eye), he was able to see things "in their proper, natural aspect," that is, such as they truly are. The plot is then more or less rhythmically lengthened as the pilgrim goes through the town and has a look at his "labyrinth-world" in each of its spheres, until the denouement when he finds the way out, or rather, he is found and taken out, of the

---

26. Wolf Schmid clarifies the terminology with his reference to B. Tomaševský: "Fabule is what really happened, plot is how the reader came to know it" (Schmid, *Narativní transformace*, 13).

labyrinth. The resolution has its own rhythm and length because it is more or less a mirror image of all that went before.[27]

Clearly this is not a very sophisticated storyline or suspenseful plot. Comenius didn't use all the opportunities the epic genre offers, or at least those which we know today are offered by this genre. The individual episodes are somewhat repetitive and follow a predictable framework. The pilgrim comes to one of the streets in the labyrinth, sees it the way his guides want, through the glasses of deception, and then again with his own eyes as it really is, and in the end leaves in disappointment to look further. It goes on like this throughout the first part, until he finds paradise. And then the paradise part of the narration "degenerated" into almost one long monologue, only occasionally punctuated by appearances of a Savior, and thereby considerably reducing the epic nature and drama of the story, making it instead more like a descriptive-explanatory treatise.

Nevertheless *The Labyrinth* still has basic plot contours. The reader can participate in the structure of the narrative. From the psychological perspective it isn't important whether the climax will be a surprise to the reader, but that she will participate in the storyline. Jiří Trávníček noted that this is one of the elementary ways in which a person (first in childhood) acquires stories. Before curiosity, the perception of causality, time, and other phenomenon of narratives can enter the game. "Participation in the structure" is crucial for the reader (as well as the listener), as every parent who tells their child fairytales from their earliest childhood knows. Although they have heard the story many times, they want to hear it again and again, without any changes and exactly as it was before. But even adults tend to enjoy this. They return to their favorite book or film that they have already read or seen many times. The pleasure from joining in the storyline and final resolution is worth it. The Magnificent Seven finally disperse, Sherlock convicts the murderer, Harry overcomes Voldemort, the pilgrim finds the paradise of the heart. They are all variations of the same structure. It seems that Vladimir Propp, a classic writer of Russian formalism, had it right. In his particularly influential work *The Morphology of Fairytales* he demonstrated that the structure of the outline of this type of narrative is transferable from one story to another, even though the individual scenes in the stories might be different. Propp showed that Russian fairytales are

---

27. The traditional division of the work into two opposing parts is questioned by Lubomír Doležel, (Doležel, "Kompozice"). Instead of two parts in the *Labyrinth* Doležel sees three, and he determines the type of narrator by the criteria for division. I will return to this problem in the section on narrative perspective.

all variations of the same structural form.[28] Thus, the reader's motivation isn't necessarily knowledge, the point isn't to know how it will turn out—the reader already knows that—but to a far greater degree she yearns to be part of the story, to participate in it and to "be there." So it becomes a kind of ritual, an almost sacred moment, when the reader (or listener), the storyteller, and the text "harmonize according to established rules."[29]

It is precisely this "storyness" that raises Comenius's *Labyrinth* above the other literature of his time, which were all treatises, and brings about something "natural and universal,"[30] in the words of Miller, which is typical of all stories—the plot draws in the reader. In educational terminology: it motivates. And therein lies the magic of story.

ALLEGORY

That the book will contain allegory, Comenius announced up front in the dedication, where he wrote that the first part "depicts the follies and inanity of the world" and the second part "partly as through a veil, partly openly" describes the true and lasting happiness of those who find their way out of the labyrinth. With this the author gives the reader insight into how the text should be read. Again this is not trickery. The text isn't trying to trip up the reader. She simply has to decode the allegorical level of the text in order to find its real and intended level. The interpretation of allegorical language—as well as any other kind of language—is of course notoriously controversial. However there is something Umberto Eco calls "the rights of the text," which is based on its relationship to its author, the referent (that to which the meaning refers), the circumstances of its origin, and so forth. In other words, the meaning of a text can be understood variously, but not arbitrarily.[31]

For his project Comenius used a series of allegorical and related linguistic devices—from denotative abstract allegory through connotative allegory, to only partially allegorical parody, characterization, and irony, with various kinds of personifications and metaphors. Many of them are freely mingled together (compare Kolár and Petráčková, "Komentář"; Mirvaldová,

28. Propp, *Morfologie.* For a deeper discussion on this theme see for example the historical overview of Zofie Mitoseková (Mitoseková, *Teorie literatury*).

29. Trávníček, *Vyprávěj mi něco,* 13–14.

30. Miller, "Narativ," 30.

31. Compare Eco, *Meze interpretace,* 7.

"Alegoričnost"). A few examples for illustration: we often encounter objects, characters or storylines whose aesthetic imagery is explicitly (denotatively) verbalized—for example a bridle made from "the headstall of Curiosity" and the "steel of Tenacity," "glasses of deception" made from the "glass of Assumption" and frames "of Habit." In another chapter the pilgrim meets with the character Fate, who sorts people by means of labels with words like "Rule!," "Hoe!," "Write!," "Dig!," "Judge!," etc. And similarly with "talking names," or denotatively expressed characters—whether positive or negative: Kindness, Obsequiousness, Pleasure, Mammon, Justice, Wisdom, and so on. The characters Delusion and Searchall Ubiquitous have special roles, as we shall see. Hypocrisy is exemplified by a denotatively allegorical storyline when the pilgrim is taken to the "marketplace of the world" where, when people meet each other, they simply change their masks as needed.

Comenius also widely used connotative allegory. In this extensive quotation from chapter 8 is a description of the activities of engaged couples:

> And behold! There stood a gate which, according to the guide, was called Engagement. Before it was spread a spacious square full of both sexes who were walking about and peering into each other's ears, nose, teeth, tongue, hands, feet, and other limbs. They likewise measured how tall, broad, stout or slender each was. . . . Especially were they curious (as I have seen most frequently) about each other's purses, money-bags, and pocketbooks, measuring and weighing how long and wide, full, tight, or thin they were. . . . At times one drove away his rival, only to be himself chased away in turn; another, routing a group of rivals, himself thereupon ran away also. Some lost no time in examining, but seized the nearest he could grasp. Thereupon, the couple led each other hand in hand through the gate.

Sometimes the denotative and connotative allegories are mixed. See this description of his submersion into his own heart after the pilgrim is summoned by a mysterious voice, and his subsequent representation of allegorical human nature (chapter 37.):

> Collecting my thoughts as well as I could, and shutting my eyes, ears, mouth, and nostrils, and all other outward passages. I entered into the inner recesses of my heart, and lo! it was dark. But after peering into it, and looking about a little, I perceived after a while a very faint light streaming in through some cracks, by which I was able to distinguish above in the vault of this, my chamber, a large, round glass window. But it was so dirty and so thickly smeared

with filth that no light could penetrate it. Looking about me by this dim light, I discerned various pictures on the walls which, as it appeared to me, possessed once upon a time considerable beauty; but now the colors were faded and some limbs of the figures were severed or broken off. I approached closer and noticed their names: Prudence, Humility, Justice, Purity, Temperance, and so forth. In the middle of the room were scattered some damaged and broken ladders; also broken pulleys and pieces of ropes. Besides, I saw large wings with plucked feathers.

The way the author communicates the didactic content of his "curriculum" is worth noting. In the turning point of the whole narrative, when the pilgrim finds his way out of the labyrinth, the reader should learn something fundamental about human nature. The pilgrim's connotative submersion into the depth of his heart isn't an escape from the evil world but insight, the discovery that even his own heart is not in order, not completely clean or perfect. Admittedly there are some valuable—denotatively named—artifacts like Humility, Justice, Temperance, etc., but all are broken in some way and dirty. Likewise ladders, pulleys, and wings, with whose help it would have been easy to climb upward, are "plucked and scattered." In other words, the reader is led with the help of allegory to reflect on her human nature, to recognize both "talents" and "sins," her ontological dignity and moral depravity. Human beings long for the true, the beautiful and the good, but at the same time they are capable of evil. Thus, one's nature is neither wholly alright nor wholly lost. There is a problem, but there is also a way out. In the following five sections of this chapter we will see how Comenius expressed his educational anthropology without using allegory in the *Didactics* (both *Great* and *Czech*) and in other emendational works; a human is the "most magnificent" and at the same time the "most detestable" being in all creation. If one isn't to "fall into non-humanness" one must be educated, led away from everything inhuman and taught how properly to live. People need the "forging place of humanity." But more on that later.

The very composition of the work also has its allegorical nature which is evident both in the basic contrast between the two main parts and in the almost encyclopedic layout. Comenius calls his fictional world a labyrinth, but in reality this world is very orderly and clear. The city is a closed circular formation rising out of the darkness. A beam of light illuminating the area of the city from above evokes the idea of a theater stage, which is an image Comenius often resorted to in his later works. Individual scenes—streets, gates, squares and so on—are placed on the stage, and as we saw with Pilgrim's experience in the tower of the city, it's possible to examine them comfortably with the naked eye. Aleš Haman notes that this panoramic visibility is reminiscent of the "encyclopedic" pictures of the Dutch painters.[32] The confusion or "maze-likeness" of the city then does not lie in its form, but in the befuddled state of its inhabitants. Chaos is brought about by the deceit, hypocrisy, and absurdity of human behavior. It's this that the author wants to unmask, disclose. And so with almost encyclopedic clarity he subjects the entire hierarchy of the society of his day to allegory. Thus he gives us the opportunity to analyze, along with the pilgrim, the state of married couples, tradesmen, knights, philosophers, ministers, the nobility and soldiers, which is to say almost all "human affairs." This universality— the Kožmíns have reminded us—foreshadows all of Comenius's later understanding of the world, and his corrective efforts.[33] The only social class the author does not analyze is the peasantry. I will discuss the reasons later.

Of particular note is the allegory in which Comenius's didactic spirit awakens. In chapter 8 the pilgrim can't stop himself from saying something when he sees the helplessness of parents and their spoiled children. First he notices "with what pain, tears and risk of life" children are brought into the world, then how hard the "twofold" task is as the little ones grow up—the parents have to both curb their excessive enthusiasm and at the same time spur them on to do the things they should. But the children often don't accept either the bridle or the spur and raise such a fuss that the parents are driven to utter "weariness" and "tears." Many parents are too lax with their children and when the children tear themselves away it causes the parents shame and sometimes even death. The pilgrim begins to admonish both parents and children: the parents against overly sentimental love and excessive indulgence, the children for their rowdiness and disrespect, but with little success. The beginning teacher meets displeasure from both children and parents—they gave him "dark looks and caustic remarks" and some even "threatened [him] with death." Remember that this was written in 1623 by an author who had had only a few years of teaching experience in Přerov and Fulnek. From the perspective of today's reader, the author's inclusion of this allegory could have a surprising side effect. Many educators might be encouraged and comforted that even the "Teacher of Nations"

32.. Haman, "Estetický rozměr světa," 8.
33.. Kožmín and Kožmínová, Zvětšeniny, 47.

couldn't avoid the typical phenomenon of every teacher: frustration with the students (even though he was still young).

Particularly helpful to the theme of this great work is chapter 10, where Comenius allegorized the educational system, or "state of education" of his time. In essence it is a specific kind of meta-didactic discourse, which is an instructive text on education as such. First the pilgrim is lured by his guides' vision of the "easier, more peaceful and for the mind a more useful life" of an intellectual. Apparently he will no longer need to be bothered with "unprofitable manual toil," but can instead devote himself wholly to "splendid causes," which will in the end make him "like God" with an abundance of knowledge. The pilgrim can't resist. "Why do you tarry?" he urges his guides, eager to be among the learned.

When they arrive at the "street of the learned" the pilgrim observes the entrance examinations of the young people registering for study. The following passage is famous:

> The first of these [examinations], required of all, aimed at ascertaining what kind of purse, posterior, head, brain (which they judged by the nasal mucus), and skin each of the candidates brought. If the head were of steel, the brain of quicksilver, the posterior of lead, the skin of iron, and the purse of gold, they praised him and willingly conducted him farther.

Those who pass the test are taken by "guards," also called "reformers." Their work is to prepare the students for study by "re-forming" their "hands, tongue, eyes, ears, brain, and all other external and internal organs," in order to be "of a different order from those of the ignorant masses." Of course, it can't happen without "toil and pain," and the pilgrim sees how the poor souls were beaten with "fists, pointers, canes and sticks on their cheeks, head, back, and seat until they shed blood, and were full of bruises and scars, weals, and callouses." Many candidates are discouraged, tear themselves out of their reformer's hands and simply run away. But our pilgrim, who still longs for that profession, suffers all of it "with hardships and bitterness" in order to continue further. He subsequently arrives at a crossroads where he has to choose between "philosophy, medicine, law, and theology," that is, between the four schools in the universities of Comenius's day. They continue further to some square where there is gathered a "crowd of students, masters, doctors, priests, both youths and greybeards." But many of them—to the pilgrim's surprise—"had eyes but no tongue; others had a tongue but no eyes; some had only ears but no tongue or eyes; and so forth." Each was missing something.

There follows a tour of the library, where the pilgrim observes how the students stuff themselves with the "best and wittiest" pieces, "slowly chewing and digesting" them. Some of them really benefit from this, but he sees that for others, "whatever they crammed in passed out at both ends undigested." Some of them in the end "became dizzy or lost their minds," still others "grew pallid, pined away and died." Some students learned from this and instead of allegorically consuming the books only stored them "in their rooms, . . . they placed the books on or took them off the shelves, pleased with looking at them; they continued putting up and taking down the books, approaching or retreating, pointing out to each other or to strangers the excellent appearance of them."

"What are these folk playing?" wonders the pilgrim and receives the answer from Delusion that if a person wants to be counted "among the learned" it isn't necessary to actually read the books, it's enough to have a nice library. To this the pilgrim reacts with the words (my paraphrase): As if a blacksmith was a blacksmith only because he had a hammer and pincers. But he only "thought to myself" and said nothing to his guides, conspiratorially telling us, the readers, and by this creating "just between us" a special bond because we know something "they" don't. Thus, a charming narrative tension is established here, with the author slyly winking at the reader. We are drawn in.

Then comes an especially current description of something we might call today *publication dilution*. Comenius speaks of "disorder in the writing of books," and borrows an illustration from the apothecary, where medicine was prepared for general use. This is what he sees: There were "one or two . . . who collected fragrant roots and plants, cut them up, shook, cooked and distilled them, preparing delightful gins, potions, syrups and other medicines which are useful to the life of man." And opposite them were hundreds of those who "only picked out things from the pots of others and transferred them into their own." Still others, "who seized the pots of others to fill up their own, diluting the contents as much as they could, using even dishwater; and others condensing the mixture by adding all sorts of hodge-podge, even dust and sweepings." It greatly angers the pilgrim, but he is assured that "it is also an art." That doesn't appease him though, and he continues—this time aloud—fussing at the quackery, although that only earns him hatred. So in the end he resigns himself, but he can't help remarking again that he is bearing these misdeeds only with great displeasure. But there wasn't anyone "to set matters right."[34]

Then follows a description of the "quarrels, strife, scuffles and tumult" in "the Market-place of the Learned," which again upsets the pilgrim because his guide promised him that here he would find the "most peaceful profession." He has a glimmer of hope when some people appear who are calling for peace and the settling of every dispute. There even appears the possibility to organize some kind of conference in which the reconciling can take place. It is an obvious reference to the irenic trends Comenius had met in his own studies. He is met with the same outstanding personalities. The pilgrim catches sight of "Aristotle with Plato, Cicero with Sallustius, Scot with Aquinus, Bartoly with Bald, Erasmus with the men of the Sorbonne, Rama and Campanella with the peripatetics, Copernicus with Ptolomy, Theophrastus with Galen." A number of pairs, each known for their controversies, are presented in dialogue. When they can't agree they are asked to make the briefest outline of their argument. But when these are presented there are so many they couldn't all be read in "six thousand years" (that is, all of history, according to the dating used in Comenius's time). Consequently everyone scattered to their quarrels and our pilgrim was "grieved to tears." This strict rejection of the ancient philosophical tradition isn't aimed at philosophy as such, which Comenius not only knew very well but used liberally in his later works. According to Eduard Petrů ("Filozofie") he was criticizing the philosophical methods that are based only on a rational interpretation of the world and ignore other sources of knowledge—especially sensory and spiritual (Scripture). Philosophy that doesn't make use of every available source of knowledge must necessarily become reductionist, its view of the world incomplete and therefore deserving of criticism.

The conciseness, pertinence and talent for observation demonstrated by Comenius is outstanding. And he clearly has the ability to anticipate the reader's allegorical literacy—some allegories he leaves without clarifying comments, but where he expects the picture won't be understood, he provides an explanation (of course, using allegorical code). Thus, for example, he lets the guide explain that "the head that is not of steel would crack: without the brain of quicksilver the pupil could not make a mirror of it;

---

34. Self-critically I'm afraid this text also suffers from a certain publicational "dilution" as it analyzes what has already been analyzed many times. On the other hand, some things are worth repeating.

LABYRINTH

without the skin of sheet-iron he would not survive the formative process;
not possessing the seat of lead, he would hatch nothing but miscarry everything; and without the purse of gold, where would he obtain the necessary
leisure or teachers, both living and dead?"

Why the head would split or why the mind should become a mirror,
etc., the author doesn't explain. He expects the reader's experience as well as
the story's context will make the picture understandable. Both wittily and
engagingly, Comenius creates the opportunity to work out a solid critique
of the allegorized phenomenon, and in doing so reveals much of his early
ethics as well as his philosophy of education. I set forth his allegorical ideas
concerning education one by one (following his pattern) in the form of
question and dictum:

1. What is the proper motive for seeking an education? Education is not
   and must not be a purely pragmatic means of obtaining an easier life.

2. Is it possible to find a didactic approach that wouldn't be onesidedly
   loaded with cognitive components (so as not to crack the head)? How
   can specific material be truly understood and not merely mirrored?
   What approach could be taken that is without the abomination of violence? With what approach can the student remain actively engaged
   (not needing a "seat of lead")?

3. What are the necessary preconditions for a student being able to
   study? Money should never be one of them (the "purse of gold").

4. How to prevent fragmentary knowledge ("they had eyes and no
   tongue"); how to provide a solid, holistic education? Work out everything, from every side, in its entirety (omnes, omnia, omneno), says
   Comenius later.

5. In what way should the study materials (books) be handled, so as to
   allow the student to get the most from them? What about the student
   who doesn't read (who "studies without studying")?

6. How to tackle didactically the huge wealth of knowledge in a way that
   the student doesn't faint or become overwhelmed?

7. What makes a scholar a scholar? Outward appearances? A good library? Titles?

8. What is the true meaning and reason for writing a book or publishing
   a work? Why is there so much watering down, recycling and even

43

stealing from what has already been written many times? Shouldn't one write with an almost sacred respect for truth?

9. Shouldn't the mission of the university be to find unity in diversity (uni-versitas)? Isn't that type of humility which preserves the dignity even of those who have a different opinion part of academic excellence? Isn't virtue one aspect of scholarship? Or the ability to overcome personal interests, vanity, pride or other character defects so as to not hinder the meaningful and peaceful dialogue with another?

Given that this was written in the pre-didactic, pre-pansophic period of Comenius's work, the pertinence of his insights is fascinating. Long before the emergence of education as a separate discipline he was able to understand, name (and later also treat systematically) the key issues of the subject which are still relevant.

However, it is necessary to make a few critical comments about Comenius's strategy. The phenomenon of allegory as a literary-stylistic form works only as long as the author is able to create a consistent network of relationships between the external text and the internal (allegorical) meaning. Some of Comenius's illustrations have a problem with this. For example, in chapter 4 the reader is informed about the taming of the pilgrim by the previously mentioned Searchall Ubiquitous and Delusion, with the result that the pilgrim can't search the world freely but is forcefully dragged by his guides, who are the personification of the tendencies of his own mind. Later the reader finds that the author doesn't stick to this imagery because very often the pilgrim acts and speaks as if he had no bridle—"let's go" he orders when he feels like it, and his guides pick up and go. However other times it seems that the reins are really in the hand of Ubiquitous, as they should be according to the first rules given in the allegory—see for example the end of chapter 18, where Ubiquitous says: "'Let's go, we'll look further'; and taking me by the hand, he led." And even here, shouldn't it be "by the bridle," not "by the hand"?

Later in the central allegory there is a similar problem with the glasses of deception. As has been said, in chapter 4 the reader is conspiratorially informed that the glasses of deception were set crookedly on the pilgrim's nose, and therefore if he inclined his head he could see true reality out of the corner of his eye. But in the rest of the story it's as if the author forgot this imagery; he lets the pilgrim explore every deception and abuse in the world as if he wasn't wearing the glasses at all—with one exception:

in one tense situation in chapter 19 the pilgrim says that he straightened the glasses in order to "look more closely." What sense does that make? He adjusted the glasses so he could see better? If yes, then he should have seen the alluringly deceptive version of reality, but our pilgrim sees reality as it truly is, he sees "the depraved state of the nobility."

If I read correctly, that was the only reference to the glasses until chapter 36, which is the end of the first part of the *Labyrinth*. This brings up a certain complication. First it seems that the pilgrim, bound by Searchall's bridle, can in no way manipulate the glasses, and if he wants to see the world as it is he has to "incline his head." Until chapter 19, then, it seems that the pilgrim is walking the whole time with his head tilted back. According to the logic of the image it must be that way, because wherever he goes he immediately sees how things are, and at times it moves him to tears, other times he is horrified or disgusted. However in the incriminating chapter 19, this logic is broken. If the pilgrim can freely manipulate the glasses, why does the author force him in the previous chapters to tilt his head and squint out of the corner of his eye? And the picture is further complicated at the end of the first part, when the pilgrim is left to look at "the lot of the dead" (chapter 36). Here the pilgrim gives an eyewitness account of a dramatic scene:

> . . . I saw a sorry spectacle, for every one gave up his spirit in terror, lamentations, fear and trembling, not knowing what would become of him afterwards nor where he would find himself after leaving the world. I likewise feared it, but nevertheless desiring to understand it a little better, I walked between the rows of biers until I reached the end of the world and of light; there the friends of the deceased closed their eyes and blindly hurled their dead into the abyss.

The problematic part is still to come. Even though others close their eyes when faced with such horror, our main hero does a surprising thing (from the perspective of allegorical consistency):

> Casting off the glasses of delusion and rubbing my eyes, I leaned out as far as I could. There I saw nothing but frightful darkness and gloom of which neither the bottom nor the end could be fathomed by the human mind, and in which nothing but worms, frogs, serpents, scorpions, pus and stench were found; besides, a smell of brimstone and pitch, overpowering the body and the soul, issued thence, in a word, horror unspeakable!

The question is how the pilgrim's epistemology changed after he threw away the glasses (and rubbed his eyes). The problem—for the cohesiveness of Comenius's allegory—is that throwing the glasses away didn't change anything. But the glasses should cause him to see the exact opposite of reality, because they made "the distant things seem near and the near seem distant; the small things large and the large small; ugly things beautiful and the beautiful ugly; black things white and the white black, etc." (chapter 4). Nor does the situation get better in the case of the alternative "spiritual" glasses that the pilgrim gets in the "paradise of the heart" (in chapter 41). In summary: when he is wearing the glasses— whether delusional or not—he sees just as well as without them. It is possible to narrow the interpretive eye and overlook these irregularities, that is, to not deal with the details, but with the general intentions of individual allegories. For example, J. Patočka did this when, in the drama of the *Labyrinth* he saw the act of opening the human spirit as enabling a meaningful relationship with the surrounding world. The pilgrim's shedding of the glasses of deception is interpreted as the determination of a person "to look into the eyes of human finitude as it is concentrated in death," which opens the way to a fundamental change in the human spirit.[35]

Jan Blahoslav Čapek noted another level of problem—sometimes in his allegories Comenius fell into a mere charactural naming, other times he simply transfered the spiritual acts or characteristics to the physical acts (the schoolboys gorging themselves on books) or the identification of an allegory with a real picture ("Seneca, sitting among tons of gold, was extolling poverty"), and still elsewhere Comenius's allegories fell into "pseudo-visual ideograms," as in statements like "Plato chased ideas in the air." Čapek wrote that this "disunity and inconsistency" was caused by working in too much of a rush, given the circumstances of 1623.[36] The indulgence with which Čapek approached Comenius's inconsistencies is charitable, but the question remains whether it was haste that caused the inconsistencies. Comenius returned more than once in his life to the *Labyrinth* and made corrections. If he was aware of any defects in the beauty of his allegorical method he had ample opportunity to remove them.

---

35. Patočka, *Komeniologické studie 2*, 48. In a similar spirit other Comeniologists, who refer in some way to Patočka's interpretation, also hold the same view. Compare Schaller, "Komenský a otevřená duše"; Nastoupilová, *Pojetí odpovědnosti*; Krámský, "Komenského svět."

36. Čapek, *Několik pohledů*, 81.

It's necessary to emphasize that from the perspective of the overall purpose/design of the work these are only insignificant side issues. Many critics give a thoroughly positive evaluation of Comenius's allegory in *The Labyrinth*. Although he failed to find a "perfectly balanced allegorical method,"[37] his allegories did not sink into "schematization and abstraction," as did those of many of Comenius's contemporaries. On the contrary his allegories tended to be valued for "not being cold and monotonous," inasmuch as they reflected the author's own memories and experiences, and "they search out real life by means of an allegorical garment," said Čapek with reference to E. Denis a J. Jakubec.[38] Other allegorical works of Comenius's time[39] are more or less forgotten "not only because they were written in Latin, but also for their abstractly allegorical character," noted J. Patočka, and continued: "Comenius's *Labyrinth* lives and will live by the heart's blood that the author gave to it."[40]

Remember that the author's intention was primarily didactic, as he suggested in his introductory chapter "To the Reader." He wrote in his own words therefore, so that his knowledge and discoveries would be on the one hand portrayed more clearly to himself, and on the other hand they would be opened to others. Comenius's *Labyrinth* addressed his own pain while simultaneously teaching others how to deal with the difficulties that the post-White Mountain situation brought. Čapek reminded us, in this regard, of the socio-consoling function of the *Labyrinth*—it shows the underside of the power, wealth, and fame of those who rule the world—in order to comfort his fellow countrymen and loved ones who had lost everything.[41] It also addressed the moral questions: How can one succeed as a human being in the face of evil, violence, injustice, deception, etc.? How can one distinguish good from evil, the essential from the inessential, the true from the false?

For a treatise on this kind of question, the allegorical method is perfectly suitable. Allegory—a tool for hiding—paradoxically exposes reality. The process of uncovering what is veiled (by the allegory) produces

37. Ibid., 79.

38. Ibid.

39. Patočka was here referring primarily to Andreae's *Peregrini in patria errores* a *Civis Christianopolitanus*, but also to Campanella's *Sluneční stát* and Vodňanský's *Theatrum mundi minoris* among others.

40. Patočka, *Komeniologické studie 2*, 98.

41. Čapek, *Několik pohledů*, 78.

a specific distance between the fictitious and real dimensions of the text, which offers the reader a tremendous heuristic potential: through its coding the allegory forces the reader to pay attention to reality. This is very valuable didactically, because reality isn't trivial. In addition, the stimulation on the semantic level of self-irony, parody, personification, and caricature awakens the reader's imagination, enabling him to look at things in a new, often truer, light. As an example consider the allegory mentioned above, whose goal is to expose the ills of education. Comenius might have appealed to pedagogy to lead the students towards active engagement, he might have written a treatise or a whole book in which he criticized the fact that children in school tend to be too passive. But instead he simply says that one requirement for study is a "seat of lead." No further explanation is necessary. The reader's imagination completes the work. It is "an instrument of sense" or the "sense organ of meaning,"[42] and thus enables the reader not only to understand reality in a new way, but to actually enter into that reality. With the help of his imagination the reader penetrates the fictional world, experiencing its "fragrance," submitting to its rules, feeling the feelings of the characters, adopting their perspectives, identifying with or qualifying, experimenting with being this new "me" and so on. This visit to a fictional world—in our case an allegorical one —changes one's perception of the real world; the reader is "enchanted."[43] It is a kind of self-transcendence, for it "widens, enriches and transforms not only the reader's vision of reality, but also his very being."[44] The reader might even, as a result of this literary experience with the imaginary world "convert" to a different, deeper understanding of both the world and himself. He can laugh at himself or his own situation, or cry; he can see through it, get angry, be insulted or embarrassed, perhaps even discover something new about himself. In every case he is engaged—cognitively, emotionally, aesthetically, even, in the case of Comenius's allegories, morally, because the ultimate goal is to uncover the *summum bonum* of human life.[45] In this is the magic of narrative allegory.

42. Lewis, "Bluspels and Flalansferers," 265.

43. Tolkien, "O pohádkách," 161.

44. Hošek, *C. S. Lewis, mýtus*, 91.

45. Kožmín and Kožmínová, *Zvětšeniny*, 44.

HUMOR AND SATIRE

Humor and laughter was heard often and extensively in Comenius's stories, so I want to devote a whole sub-chapter to it. For the most part it is inseparable from the allegory, as I mentioned above, but again, for the author the point or function is more important than the form. Thus, Comenius said in the Introduction that it doesn't matter "how wittily" he painted his "wandering through the world;" the crucial thing was that God would use it to benefit him and his fellow-men (see "To the Reader"). In reality, though, he paid a lot of attention to wit and humor. It could almost be said that for Comenius, humor was a serious thing. In the *Labyrinth* satirical criticism was not an end in itself, but the main tool for revealing the "perversities" of the world. In addition to consolation, this also fulfilled a socio-ideological function. The things that needed to be changed in society were exposed through parody. Almost every chapter in (the first part of) the *Labyrinth* contains this element. We heard laughter which was sometimes compassionate, sometimes playful, almost situational, sometimes bitter: but always ironic or spoofing. All phenomena the author dealt with were subjected to this irony—including himself.

We can sense a certain bitterness, although mixed with sweetness— according to the author's own words (see chapter 8)—in all the ironies by which the author comes to terms with his personal pain, especially the loss of his loved ones. One of many examples: in this chapter portraying the state of marriage, the pilgrim is persuaded by his guides that he should try it too. He is initially reluctant, because he is not sure whether the "shackles" of marriage are worth the pleasure that these bonds offer. But in the end he allows himself to be persuaded and gives himself up to be "tied" to three other people (Comenius's wife and two children, whom he lost in Fulnek during the plague). Here they are nameless. Immediately afterwards they are struck by "a gale with lightening, thunder and a frightful hailstorm," forcing everyone to flee to find shelter, when suddenly a "chevron of death" kills "his three" and he remains "woefully lonely" and in "a horrible daze." To that his two guides pragmatically advise him that he can be glad because at least it will be easier to run. Given that we know from chapter 4 that Delusion and Searchall are positioned as revealers of the storyteller's thoughts, this is almost black humor. "Is he trying to quell the pain of his recent loss with these words?" wondered Čapek. I believe instead this is an allegorical shortcut, in which the realistic story predominates. Comenius simply describes what happened to him, how he felt, and how stupid and inappropriate it may sometimes be to advise a sufferer to find something good in something so horrible.

We can see specific self-irony when Comenius delves into the various professions of which he himself is a member—teacher, philosopher, Christian, clergyman. He himself is an intellectual, laughing at the "learned ones" who have the previously mentioned heads of steel, minds of quicksilver, lead bottoms, etc. He laughs at the method of "drilling into the head" and "pouring something in," making fun of the meaningless feuds and disputations about things like "snow, is it white or black; and about fire, is it hot or cold." He himself is a philosopher and he laughs at the "philosophers." The offer to visit the philosophers he enthusiastically welcomed: "God grant that I shall at last learn something certain." After all, philosophers are surely those who "know the truth of everything, without whose knowledge neither heaven manifests itself nor does the abyss hide anything; they guide human life nobly to virtue, enlighten communities and countries, and have God for their friend; for their wisdom penetrates His secrets." But in the end he discovers they are "like peasants in a tavern," each one howling louder than the next, and "each to a different tune." He himself is a Christian and laughs at the Christians whose "sermons are extremely eloquent and full of piety," pleasing themselves, but immediately after "got drunk and vomited, quarrelled and fought, defrauded and stole from one another by might and main, exuberantly shouted and skipped, jumped and whistled, indulged in adultery and fornication" more than others. Himself a minister, with a special sharpness he makes fun of the priests and bishops:

> Why do they not keep those in the lower ranks in order?" Desiring to discover the reason, I followed one of these men into his room, and then a second, a third, a fourth, and so on. I saw that they were so overburdened with their work that they could not spare time for supervision. Their occupation, not to mention all the work which they had in common with their clergy, consisted of keeping account of the revenues and the ecclesiastical treasures (as they called it). "I suppose that it is by mistake that they are not called fathers of profits, rather than of prophets."

But we feel a compassionate satire in the chapters picturing the life of the lower class, as for example the profession of craftsman:

> I saw that all these human occupations were but toil and drudgery, and each had some disadvantages and dangers of its own. I saw that those who were working with fire were scorched and

blackened like Moors: the clatter of hammers was ever jangling in their ears and had rendered them half deaf; the glare of the fire had blinded their eyes; and their skin was perpetually singed.

Similar laughter, but never mocking, we can also feel in his descriptions of the common (usually difficult) experiences of life that touch everyone. Consider disease. In a scene from chapter 14 many readers, both contemporary and current, can see themselves. The conciliatory tone is worth noting—doctors are doing their best; some more, some less, sometimes neglecting something, but even when they are practicing their profession as honestly as they can ("trying their best") it is hard work and the patients still "die in their hands." See this in context:

> Then I saw a number of wounded, both externally and internally, with putrid and rotting limbs, brought or conducted to the physicians; they approached them, examined the putrifications, smelling the stench emitted from them, and scrutinized the evacuations proceeding from both above and below, until the sight was disgusting; this they called diagnosis. Then they cooked, steamed, roasted, broiled, cauterized, cooled, burned, hacked, sawed, stabbed, sewed again, bound, anointed, hardened, softened, wrapped, or moistened, and I know not what more they did in order to effect the cure. In the meantime, their patients had been expiring under their hands, not a few of them lamenting the doctors' ignorance or carelessness as the causes of their death. In a word, I saw that although the art of these fine salve-mongers brought them a certain gain, it also involved them, on the other hand (if they wished to do justice to their calling), in a great deal of very strenuous and partly even disgusting labor.

On the other hand, Comenius doesn't spare the sharp flashes of irony whenever he is exposing what he considers to be sensitive social questions. See for example the description of the "happy wealthy" in chapter 24. Or the "exalted of the world" in chapter 26:

> Others had coffers full of lumps of earth and stones which they constantly rearranged, shutting and opening the lids, and neither wishing nor seeking to go anywhere for fear of losing their treasures. Some did not trust even the coffers and bound and tied so many of those things upon their persons that they could neither walk nor stand, but were obliged to lie, panting and groaning. Observing this, I remarked: "But, in the name of all the saints, are these people to be considered happy?

The author is similarly relentless when criticizing public administration, where it should be expected that the people would hold responsible those in the positions of judges, procurators, clergy and nobility. If they are to be in leadership they must first govern themselves, as Comenius repeats many times in various of his later didactic and pansophic works. Instead, in chapter 19 we see:

> I tarried and observed very diligently the procedure in the senatorial court, and learned that the names of the judges were as follows: Atheist, Lovestrife, Hearsayjudge, Partisan, Personrespecter, Lovegold, Bribetaker, Tyro, Knowlittle, Dontcare, Hasty, and Anyhow; the President and the Supreme Justice, or Primate, was My Lord Icommandit.

The encyclopedic outline of *The Labyrinth* allowed Comenius to satirize every social class, and thereby criticize them. It isn't necessary to go through them all here. With regard to humor as a didactic-literary tool it is worth noting two more things. In his satire Comenius completely ignored the broad social class of the peasant. It seems that this also had a didactic purpose. Jan Blahoslav Čapek noticed it and speculated on various possibilities. It doesn't appear that Comenius simply forgot such a (numerically) significant group. Nor is Čapek satisfied with the explanation that the peasants were missing because the *The Labyrinth* is depicted as a city. He asked the question whether it had to do with Comenius's conservative outlook from the Unitas tradition. The early Unitas Fratrum forbade many jobs, such as the holding official power, joining in armed combat, taking an oath or being involved in commerce. Agricultural work, however, was approved. At the time of Comenius the Unitas had undergone many changes in its two hundred years of existence. Comenius himself was a relatively unorthodox thinker, but the question is whether his silence about peasants expressed his quiet identification with some aspects of the original Unitas orthodoxy. Surely it was possible to find even among the peasants a subject for criticism or amusement. But it's also possible that in Comenius's system of values there were subjects about which he didn't joke.

This is connected to my second and final note on the question of humor. All the "fun" ended when the pilgrim left the labyrinth. It's made clear on the one hand by a change in genre, but I think there is also a semantic aspect. The minute the author began to deal with sacred matters, he stopped joking. Thus we can't read any of the paradise of the heart as a source of humorous hyperbole; it has to be read with the understanding that it will never be possible to fully attain such perfection of human character and society as are described in the Paradise of the Heart. It seems that Comenius wasn't against such a reading, because in the introductory chapter he advised the reader that what concerned the portrayal "of the happy life of hearts devoted to God . . . was sketched as the ideal" (that is, as an example). Comenius knew that such "perfected spirits" would never be met, but he wanted everyone who read about the paradise of the heart to desire that perfection.

There's no doubt that a man living on the border between the Middle Ages and the Modern Age for the most part desired different things and laughed at different things than people today do. Comenius's laughter was specific and often historically contingent. In every age and culture each individual must struggle again and again to answer the question: To what extent do I participate in my culture so as to be its critic but never its enemy? Even though Comenius spoke about "banishment" from the world at the beginning of the post-White Mountain period, it seems that in *The Labyrinth* he found his answer. His critical "laughter" is neither destructive nor an end in itself. It didn't run away from the world, and it was not merely a mockery of the world or a particular literary genre—as was the case with other authors of the time.[46] His purpose was to expose all types of falsehood with the goal of change. In every parody, hyperbole, and caricature Comenius denounces the contemporary value systems and human activities that create them (wealth, fame, power, etc.), exposing them as "paint" that "disguises the true nature of life."[47] In this he both prepared and identified the way to change. Paul Lehmann, who devoted his research to parody and satire in Medieval literature, alerted us about this function. These tools serve, according to Lehmann, to call into question the value system of a given society and thereby prepare the way for deep ideological and social change.[48] It seems that this phenomenon is both timeless and universal. Just as the time of Comenius needed change, so also change is needed in our time. And therefore Comenius is still relevant today. Much of human depravity and baseness tends to be comical (if not tragic). In *The Labyrinth* Comenius presented us with a story that not only allows us to laugh at

46. In his study *Parodie u Erasma Rotterdamského a Jana Amose Komenského*, Eduard Petrů noted that Comenius used "direct" or "life" parodies, in contrast to Erasmus, who rather resorted to "literary" or "genre" parodies; that is, he used parody within a certain genre to "make a caricature of contemporary idology" (Petrů, "Parodie.")

47. Compare ibid.

48. Lehmann's observations are taken from Petrů, "Parodie."

our own humanity, but also reveals the need for restoration of those things which are, although funny, wrong.

One more ontological note as a conclusion: slugs, camels, and mosquitos don't laugh at themselves; to them, there is nothing ridiculous about their nature or characteristics. But people do laugh at themselves. Their own humanity often brings laughter, often tears, often both at once. Why? Because of the characteristic human contraditions between the ontological and moral dimensions of human nature. One knows that one *should* be a certain kind of being and duly behave that way. And when one doesn't, it can be funny, or tragic, or tragicomical.[49] See Comenius's judges and prosecutors—by their very nature they should be fair and objective, however they behave otherwise and thus earn names like *Gold-lover, Gift-taker, Negligent* or *Careless*. Comenius specifically uses this humor to teach the reader. That is, to give readers insight into their own humanity, how they are (ontology), and how they should be (ethics), while allowing them to laugh at themselves. That also contributes to what I call the magic of the Labyrinth.

LANGUAGE AND OTHER LITERARY DEVICES

"The search for appropriate language to express what I want to picture is part of authentic storytelling," said Ingo Baldermann, and he continued "a narration gains authority primarily from this effort expended in the search for appropriate speech: speech that is able to open me and my audience to our own perception of new experiences."[50] Comenius's feeling for, and his work with, language is universally renowned. *The Labyrinth* is a showcase of literary devices shaped to complement the whole aesthetic effect of the story. I will try to outline some of these devices here.

We have already noted the contrast in language between the first and second parts. When we are in the labyrinth part of the book we come across

---

49. It's worth noting that when a person is especially immoral he is sometimes called by animal names or epithets like "bitch," "hyena," "snake," "beast" and the like. Jaroslav Seifert thought that was not entirely fair to the animal kingdom, writing somewhere that it is "only people who are evil to one another." If a person behaves in a totally inhuman way, which is not a hypothetical situation, then that person is usually called a "monster." Comenuis said "non-person." C. S. Lewis, in the third book of his cosmic trilogy *That Hideous Strength* used "unman."

50. Baldermann, *Úvod*, 94.

many Moravianisms,[51] popular sayings, proverbs, colloquialisms and ex-
pressive language, but then we find the Paradise to be full of noble biblical
sayings, quotes, and lofty rhetorical sentences.[52]

Another aspect of Comenius's verbal artistry is his work with composition. It has already been mentioned in connection with his allegorical
techniques. Now I want to emphasize the stylistic and aesthetic level of the
text. Comenius's finesse was evident not only in his choice of words, but also
in the way he made use of linguistic resources with regard to the narrative
as a whole. On the one hand the pilgrim's journey was rendered linearly—a
continuous addition of one scene after another on the same theme—and
on the other hand most of the chapters were built as an obvious gradation of individual actions and their effects, a characteristic which added to
the drama of the story. An example is the account of how, at the castle of
Fortune, the contenders for a dubious honor boasted about their crimes:

> one, that he had shed so much human blood as he could; another,
> that he had invented a new blasphemy wherewith to revile God;
> another, that he had sentenced God to death; another, that he
> had pulled the sun from the sky and had plunged it into an abyss;
> another that he had organized a new band of incendiaries and
> murderers for purging . . . , etc.

The following description of the secret paradise of joy from chapter 49
serves as a semantic counterpart:

> For how otherwise than happy and joyous can a man be who is
> conscious of, and perceives within himself, such light of God, such
> noble inner harmony caused by the Holy Spirit, such freedom
> from the world and its slavery, such sure and abundant care of
> God himself, such protection against enemies and accidents, and
> finally such constant peace, as has already been demonstrated?

A stylistic variation of this gradual accumulation of facts is the use of word
strings, occasionally completed with ordinal numbers:

> And all about us we observed various halls, workshops, forges,
> benches, stores, and booths full of quaint-looking implements.
> Men plied these tools in a curious manner, with clattering,

51. Comenius was from Moravia, which is the eastern part of the Czech Republic.

52. For a more detailed study on this theme see Kučera, "Lidová rčení," or Michálek,
"Tradiční rysy."

striking, squeaking, squealing, whistling, piping, blowing, blast-
ing, jingling, and rattling (chapter 9.)

One howled, another roared, or crowed, barked, whistled,
chirped, or twittered, accompanying their performance with
grotesque gestures. . . . Then several gourmands from behind the
tables caught sight of me and one began to drink to my health:
another winked at me, inviting me to sit down with him; a third
began to question me as to who I was and what was my business
there, while a fourth demanded rudely why I did not wish them a
"God bless you!" (chapter 25.)

An especially strong gradation of the central motif of futility is recorded in
chapter 28. Here "the pilgrim begins to despair."

Oh, woe is me! Shall I ever find satisfaction in this miserable
world? . . . But which of these do I possess? None. What have
I learned? Nothing. Where am I? I myself know not. . . . I saw,
observed, and learned that neither I nor anyone else is anything,
knows anything, or possesses anything, but that we all but imagine ourselves to know something. We grasp at a shadow while the
truth escapes us. Woe is us!"

The first part ends with an increasing, almost existential intensity.
After that the pilgrim is forced to affirm Solomon's "vanity of vanities" of
everything under the sun, and he longs to leave this world: "'I choose rather
to die a thousand times,' I answered, 'than to remain here where such things
occur and to look upon wrong, fraud, lie, guile, cruelty.'" He wants to be
consistent to the end, so he goes to see "the lot of the dead." The "unspeak-
able horror" he sees as he stares the futility of death in the face culminates
here with a unique literary intensity:

Is this the conclusion of so many of your splendid deeds? Is this
the goal of your learning and the manifold wisdom with which
you are so puffed up? Is this the desired peace and rest after your
innumerable labors and struggles? Is this the immortality which
you forever promise yourselves? Oh, that I had never been born!
That I had never passed through the gate of life, if after all the
futilities of the world I am to become a prey to this darkness and
horror! Oh, God, God, my God! If Thou exist, O God, have pity
upon me, a wretched man!

Equipped with statistical methodology, Josef Hrabák[53] noted that the gradation in the *Labyrinth* was organized not only semantically but also stylistically; that is, "the exigencies of the central motif are emphasized by the repetition of words continually expressing these images." Moreover, Comenius managed to do this "artfully," that is skillfully bringing together and combining words with the same sounds, thus forming new semantic ties. See for example the prevalence of the sounds "s" and "r" in the words associated with the picture of death: *ostrá kosa, hrozná postava, strojili šípy, kterého trefiti měla, chroptícího* [sharp sickle, terrible figure, set the arrow, hit the target, wheeze]. According to Hrabák the point wasn't the puns but the "sound metaphors," which contributed to the "semantic effect" of the text.

A compositional break in the work—that key turning point when the pilgrim at last finds paradise—comes just in time. The pilgrim's suffering could hardly be endured any longer. The author lets it continue to the very edge, but from an aesthetic and emotional perspective this is perfectly fine. As Aristotle noted, a long adventure has to include both catastrophe and catharsis.[54] The reader, in identifying with the main hero, experiences with him the tensions which gradually strengthen to the point of becoming unbearable. So when in chapter 37 the reader finally hears, along with the pilgrim, the mysterious call to return that leads him away from his wandering, it is a unique moment that becomes a catharsis for the reader too. This narratively important event was set up by a long series of escalating pain, adversity, and ruin at whose end the reader experiences a sense of relief that could not have been so great if the suffering hadn't lasted so long. If the waiting had been shorter, his emotional trepidation wouldn't have been so strong or the psychological effect so powerful. And strong emotions are very helpful for didactic purposes, because they help to integrate the information connected with those emotions into the cognitive structure of the reader's mind.[55]

The chapters in the paradise part of the work exhibit the same polar construction as those in the first part. Not only is it "attractive (in a literary way) because of the heightening of opposing types," as the Kožmíns commented,[56] but also because it deals with the fundamental controversy

53. Hrabák, "K stylistické výstavbě," 284.

54. Aristotle, *Rétorika, poetika*, 355.

55. Eco, *Šest procházek*, 89.

56. Kožmín and Kožmínová, *Zvětšeniny*, 50.

between a human life having a purpose or being in ruins, which reflects "the whole philosophic conception of the author" as expressed by the character Delusion: "you yourself are to blame, because you are asking questions about great and extraordinary things which nobody has asked before." However, as long as the pilgrim is still a human being he cannot help himself, he cannot be satisfied with delusion and destruction. The desire for truth and meaning in life is an existential part of his humanity. His desire is fulfilled, an exit from the labyrinth exists, hope endures. Comenius's practical philosophy is thus once again put into words.

The contrasting parallels in both parts are consistently maintained, even when the storyline is considerably weakened in the ways mentioned above. This creates a "structural integrity," in the words of Lubomír Doležel, based on the principal of "symmetry and parallelism."[57] In the first part of the *Labyrinth* the fictional world is deliberately painted in aesthetically negative colors. It is portrayed by a chaotic monstrosity accentuating the absurdity and disorder of everything, which engenders a sense of revulsion. In other words, it is perfectly "de-aestheticized."[58] In the end even nature, which should serve as the opposite pole to the pilgrim's troubled spirit, doesn't help. In Comenius's "world," as in "civilized" towns, it is never found. The only exception is the episode in which the pilgrim arrives at the sea. But even here the function ascribed to the sea is negative; it is an uncontrollable and dangerous element that impinges on human destiny in a thoroughly adverse way. In defense of Comenius's relationship to the sea it's necessary to say that this episode was added to the text only in the third edition in 1663, after Comenius had endured a dramatic voyage from Gdansk (Poland) to England in which he nearly died. It's possible that if he hadn't experienced that storm, that seafaring episode wouldn't have been in *The Labyrinth* and his attitude towards the sea would have been quite different. Comenius picked up a more positive approach to nature in the next phase of development of his thinking. He discovered its potential along with the "happy restorers of philosophy," Tommaso Campanella and Francis Bacon.[59] But it appears that, from the aesthetic perspective, Comenius

---

57.. Doležel, "Kompozice," 53.

58. Haman, "Estetický rozměr světa," 9.

59. We learn about the influence of Campanella and Bacon in a letter from Rafael Leszcynský in 1630. I discuss this topic more elsewhere; see Hábl, *Lessons in Humanity*.

stayed near the "medieval mentality" which was characterized by a "distaste for the sensual world," said Aleš Haman.[60]

The "world" in the paradise part of *The Labyrinth* is a contrast in its aesthetically positive nature. Here it is necessary to first undergo a "severe test" to become detached from worldly things and purify one's heart. But then aesthetically every image mediates a sense of freedom, safety, and harmony. In contrast to the noise and pomp of the world, the paradise of the heart is quiet. In place of darkness, light; in place of disarray, order; in place of strife, peace; in place of worry, joy; in place of want, bounty; in place of slavery, freedom; in place of fearful happenings, safety. In place of the reins of over-inquisitiveness the pilgrim receives the reins of obedience to Christ in the biblical allusion to the "yoke that is light." In place of the glasses of delusion he gets glasses whose frame is the Word of God and whose lenses are the Holy Spirit. With this equipment he is again sent into the world, this time to see "things which you would not have perceived at the time without the aid of these gifts" (chapter 41). The pilgrim again goes to the various roads of the world to see what real, true humanity looks like. In marriage he doesn't see "steel handcuffs," but "a joyful union of bodies and hearts." The authorities, governing with true Christian ethics, treat their subjects as loving parents treat their children. Scholars are friendly and welcoming, and they look for ways they can be helpful to their neighbor and contribute to the common good. There is also a picture of the ideal pastor in the Unitas Fratrum church:

> Men of fervent spirit but disciplined body, lovers of heavenly things but careless of earthly, diligent over their flock but forgetful of themselves, drunk with the Spirit but not with wine, of few words but of abundant actions, each striving to be the first in work but the last in boasting: in a word, intending the spiritual upbuilding of all in their every act, word, and thought.

It's clear that for Comenius the paradise of the heart was not an escape from the difficulties and complexities of the world, but rather a transcendence of its depressed version. Comenius was looking for and formulating a "concept that could project true reality back onto the world."[61] As the grotesquely deformed world was criticized, so the sought-after paradise was often idealized in the loftiest ethical maxims that the author (as a

---

60. On the subject of "negation of the world" see Kostlán, "K 'negaci světa.'"

61. Kožmín and Kožmínová, *Zvětšeniny*, 54.

theologian and philosopher of the Unitas Fratrum) had at his disposal—so that every reader would "desire this same degree of perfection for himself."

All of the layers of literarily dynamic text mentioned above—verbal, semantic, stylistic, compositional, etc.—are effective as a whole. Their distinguishing functions are complementary and intertwined, so that in their entirety they form the particular character or readability of the work. In addition to the quality of the content, the story has its formal beauty, gradation, contrast, tension, and so on.

THE NARRATIVE PERSPECTIVE

Most of the *Labyrinth* is told in the first person, which is a distinctive feature of the close union between the author and the narrator.[62] Statements like "I saw" and "I watched" are constantly repeated in an almost journalistic manner. Most of the situations described are not static, but as if they are just happening now. Again and again the pilgrim is absorbed in the events and dialogue, always having some task to perform, always having his actions and thinking confronted. Antonín Škarka notes that if it's possible to speak of the particular form of this novel, then it can only be with the adjective "subjective." With the narrator's preoccupation with his own heart and constant attention to himself the *Labyrinth* approaches, according to Škarka, "the form of a psychological and philosophic novel, though not yet highly developed."[63]

This narrative perspective creates the space for specific literary elements. The pilgrim's subjectivized view of the world is deliberately naïve, as if he is seeing the world for the first time. In every new situation he is allowed to wonder almost as a child would, why things are as they are. Why are the trades so rife with "drudgery and moaning?" Where does the nobility that rules us come from? Why do wagoners have to carry their various burdens and costs? Through these naïve questions the author autor first invites an examination of the fundamental problems of the present world, and then develops an unconventional vision of reality in order to describe things as yet unseen and unknown.[64] In the forefront are the descriptions of the phenomena which the author believes deserve critical examination.

62. Doležel, "Kompozice," 39.
63. Škarka, *Slovesné umění*, 39.
64. Kožmín and Kožmínová, *Zvětšeniny*, 43.

According to Jaroslav Kolár and Věra Petráčková,[65] Comenius thus created an effective and powerful tool for interpreting his critical view of the world and also "outlining his own ideas about how to correct it."[66]

The narrative perspective, to a large extent, determines the structure of the work.[67] The first thirty chapters preserve a distance between the observer and the things observed. In the following five chapters, where the pilgrim endures the catastrophic climax of his labyrinth experiences, that distance recedes into the background and the storyteller becomes the main figure in the narrative. And from chapter 36, in the paradise section, the distance disappears altogether—the pilgrim/observer is an active participant in the dialogue.[68]

The first-person form of dialogue also determines the momentum of the storyline, because the dialogue takes place at essentially the same time as the story itself. In *The Labyrinth* there is no stopping to take a breath, the actions follow one right after the other, and in every situation everything is at stake. The concept of "drama" by which Comenius identifies the *Labyrinth* in the Dedication is therefore proper, and not only for its scenic character.

The pace of the narrative slows down with the change of perspective in the paradise part. The narrative "I" is preserved, in the end we even hear the voice of God as if it's in the pilgrim's ears, but it's mingled with other voices and quite a new perspective. In chapter 44 for example, the pilgrim looks at how everyday life functions in "true" (the adjective is important here) Christians. In addition to unanimity, compassion, trust, and other

---

65. Kolár and Petráčková, "Komentář," 320.

66. The term "to correct" is appropriate, even though it wasn't yet in the emendational spirit of Comenius' later work. At this stage of his development of thought he had not thus far conceived his emendational projects in the true sense of the word. He rather sopke of the "expulsion" of the world. His emendational plans came later, based on the integration of some philosophical, theological and pedagogical initiatives. The satirical-critical wording of the *Labyrinth* prepared the way for the future "remedy." I deal with this more elsewhere (see *Lekce z lidskosti*). See also Patočka's observation: In the *Labyrinth* the question is not how to "fix" the world, but "what to do about it," in Patočka, *Komeniologické studie 3*, 45.

67. Doležel, "Kompozice."

68. The traditional division of the *Labyrinth* into two parts need not be in conflict with that of Doležel. It depends on the criteria for differentiation. Most interpreters (Škarka, Čapek, etc.) choose as their criteria the outward forms expressing the negative symmetry of the whole work. Doležel's criteria (the type of narrator) helps reveal new dimensions in its composition.

qualities he notices that these are not based on material possessions, houses full of furniture, clothing, food, gold or silver, but on the contrary they willingly shared their property with those in need. At that point comes some important (from the standpoint of perspective) statements: "Seeing this, I felt ashamed that with us it is often the opposite . . . ." Who is this "us?" For whom is he speaking? It can't be the pilgrim/narrator, for he is not an "us." So who is speaking? The answer is obvious. It is the empirical author speaking firsthand—Comenius himself. It is as if he couldn't contain himself and his voice drowns out that of his narrators. The plurals "we," "us" and "our" throw us into the actual, metatextual reality in which Comenius is confronted with false or fake, people and Christianity. These often "belch" with satiety, while others "yawn" with hunger. This is an embarrassment to Comenius and he cannot help but comment on it. I will lay aside these comments for now, though, because I am focusing on the literary aspects of Comenius's observations, not the social.

We meet the same phenomena in many other places in the second part of the book. For example in chapter 48 the distracting plural resounds again: "thus the ridicule, hatred, injury and harm meted out to us by the world shall be turned to our profit," or in another place: "It is true that the world is going from bad to worse, but will our fretting improve it?" Sometimes, even, the empirical author—as a speaker and preacher—can't resist abandoning the allegorical mode altogether and turning directly to the empirical readers with a rhetorical address. For example in chapter 47 we read: "Understand, you true servants of Christ, that we have a most watchful guardian and protector—the Almighty God Himself. Blessed are we!" And similarly in chapter 45: "Oh Christian, whoever you are . . . discover, experience and learn that the obstacles which your mind imagines are too small to be able to obstruct your will, provided only that you will be earnest!" It seems that Comenius resorts to this kind of authorial self-disclosure whenever he wants to say something urgent and important. It is as if he suspends the narration of the story, enters the scene himself and says: Dear readers, pay attention; let us put aside our allegorical games for a while and speak clearly, because everything is at stake now. And then when his speech is finished he returns again to the role of narrator. For example, he uses the phrase "and I saw" to make it clear that it is once again the pilgrim speaking.

In the Paradise of the Heart we are thus witnesses of changing perceptual and conceptual perspectives (in the terminology of Seymour

Chatman), as well as psychological and ideological ones (in the words of Boris Andrejevič Uspenský).[69] We could regard it as a narrative lapse, when the empirical author seems to have forgotten that he created the narrator and "jumps into his speech." But it is also possible to interpret this phenomenon as a particular strength of the narrative which, although perhaps not intentionally so on the part the author, gives the readers the possibility for both subjective identification and objective distance. On the one hand the reader can be immersed in the experiences of the narrator, on the other hand the reader can be led to the realization that there is also the real world, a real author, and a real reader, from whose points of view the narrative is inspected and evaluated. If the reader decides to listen to the instruction of the text, it is an invitation to specific epistemic walks—one is inside the reality of the text, the other is outside, leading to a questioning of extra-text reality.[70] This narrative dynamic is another factor contributing to what I call the magic of story.

NARRATIVE AND THE FORMATION OF IDENTITY

The telling of a story is a form of (self-) understanding, and the *Labyrinth* is no exception. From the outset of his story, Comenius warns us that it will be an almost therapeutic experience. Comenius himself described the therapeutic content of his writing in a letter to the Dutch publisher Petr Montanov:

> When the darkness of calamity deepened in 1623 and it appeared that there was no hope of human help or advice, tossed about by anxieties and temptations without end, I called in the deep of the night to God with unusual fervor; I jumped out of bed, grabbed my Bible and prayed . . . I opened randomly to the book of Isaiah, reading on and on with grief, and the moment I felt that my distress was dispelled I grabbed my pen and started to write—whether for my own future benefit if that terror should return again, or for others.[71]

---

69. See these classic works: Chatman, *Příběh a diskurs*; Uspenskij, *Poetika kompozice*. In addition to these perspectives we can also identify spatial, temporal, linguistic, etc. The terminology varies with the author; see for example, Schmid, *Narativní transformace*.

70. Kubíček, *Vyprávět příběh*, 138.

71. Translation by Julie Nováková.

In *The Labyrinth* then we are not reading some figment of the author's imagination (a "fable"), but a real episode that he himself experienced in "the few years of his life." And (I remind the reader again), the reason for his narrative is to get everything "more clearly in front of his eyes," in order to clarify things so he could better understand the world, the things that happened to him, and himself. Humans are beings who need to understand. One is, as Heidegger put it—a being stricken with care about the meaning of his existence. Or in still other words—he is "a being that cares about his own existence."[72]

Without wanting to psychoanalyze Comenius too much, the fact is that his goal approaches what contemporary psychology refers to as "narrative therapy." Stories help diagnose and heal. Narrative metaphors often function as catalysts for change of a client's self-understanding. The inherent power of reflection and verbalization is highly desirable. The client is led to questions of responsibility, of his own influence on (the authorship of) his life and also his ability to handle difficult (existential) situations and various life dilemmas.[73] According to Michael White and David Epston[74] the point of narrative therapy is a shift away from the problem-saturated story, towards an alternative story which both better reflects the lived experience, and makes sense.[75]

Questions of meaning, however, never appear in a vacuum. They take place within the background of the specific cultural tradition into which the questioner was born and in which she was raised—and a fundamental part of every culture is again, story. It is a large and important meta-story, around which the community is united, and which is shared, guarded, and bequeathed to the next generation. Milan Machovec noted that humanity always, one way or another, retains a vital relationship to something that is above the individual, which goes beyond it. This constitutes one of the fundamental needs of a human being—the need for transcendence. In narrative terminology, it's a meaningful plot to one's life that goes beyond the horizon of the individual.[76] Great stories (with a wide repertoire of sub-stories) have always been the intermediary for meeting this need. Narrative serves as a means of cultural identification. All of the elements, structures, concepts,

---

72. Heidegger, *Bytí a čas*, 220.

73. Compare Polkinghorn, "Narrative Therapy."

74. White and Epston, *Narrative Means*.

75. For more on this theme see Friedman and Combs, *Narativní psychoterapie*.

76. Machovec, *Filozofie*.

values, and institutions (including pedagogy) find their legitimacy precisely in their relationship to these universally shared meta-narratives (more on this later). In ancient cultures it was usual to codify exemplary models of human behavior in myths. In later traditions we find pictures of reality in narrative form, providing people with the basic reference points, incentives and appeals for forming one's self-image.[77]

Why exactly stories? The story is the only kind of discourse which, in the way it selectively presents, arranges, develops, and connects individual events, gives them special importance and makes sense of them. Stories, with their structure and wholeness, most resemble real life. Unlike scientific protocol, factual records, and other exacting genres, a story is set in a specific situation and time, it is organized, it has the twists and turns and dynamics of a plot, a denouement—and most of all, a beginning and an end. In this context Jiří Trávníček notes that, in addition to the possibility of identifying with the hero, a story also offers the possibility of an even deeper identification "with the story itself and its time, which in the story has a beginning and end that are not only the two endpoints but in particular function as its completion."[78]

All in all a story mirrors real life, and thus also even the life of the reader who can recognize himself in the story. This feature of story is, in terms of shaping the identity of the individual, irreplaceable. A story that is about me, in which I can see myself, interests me. I'm willing to listen to a story where I can play the central role. A story in which others listen to me through their imagination, calls forth that kind of empathy which is so desirable for gaining the reader's attention. In the story the characters through which we confront our own existence live, act, think, and are manifested with all their qualities and abilities. We compare and try to make sense of our lives. Thus engaged, the reader is prepared to allow her own life perspective to be changed by the perspective of the story, a key element in the process of self-understanding.[79]

77. Compare Hošek, "Proměňující moc," 88.

78. Trávníček, Vyprávěj mi něco, 52.

79. In view of the closeness to psychological themes, I am adding an observation from the pen of a psychologist who reflects Comenius's purposes well. In his dissertation Skorunka notes "that to find one's place in society it is necessary to form an adequately satisfactory connection between individual experiences and stories in a given culture and society. As long as one is unable to create such a connection, she is lacking something important and can feel isolated and lonely, especially if she cannot participate in the cultural narrative or the cultural stories that are dominant and in comparison to

In addition to this empathetic function stories provide their readers with even more possibilities. Consider imitation. Stories contain models of behavior which present a real option to imitate. "Stories give us the option of entering within ourselves and seeing ourselves objectively," says Jiří Trávníček.[80] The reader is thus invited to examine the many modes of his own actions. Through the configuration of the quantity of variables in an individual narrative a story can become to the reader a vision or revelation which serves as an incentive to imitate and eventually reconfigure or re-tell her own story. Some authors even speak of the heuristic potential of story.[81]

This is closely related to another function of stories—organizing. It is a very important yet not "innocent" function of every narrative, as Miller says. The events in any story are usually not told as they actually happened. The narrative's organization of the events serves to "confirm or reinforce, or even to create the most basic cultural assumptions about human existence, time, fate, one's own being, where we come from, what we are here on this earth to do and where we are going—about the whole story of human life."[82]

If someone asks me who I am, there arises in my mind a whole assortment of memories, passions, aspirations, beliefs, psychological states, and other particulars which have undergone significant changes over time. And because I don't have, in the words of David Novitz, a "wide-screen" perspective of myself, it is very difficult to answer the question.[83] A narrative, however, provides a unique organizational potential. If I am to understand who I really am, I have to organize the facts I know about myself into a meaningful storyline. "We understand events in terms of the events we already understand," Roger C. Schank said.[84] A story organizes the unstructured material of life experience into understandable frameworks, components, and patterns, or it functions as an organizing grid of fragmented experiences in the same way grammar coordinates meaning. According to the narrative structures we can reorganize, and often even transform, our life experiences to make sense; to find what we consider to be their true meaning. We emphasize some, criticize others, and at the same time put it

---

which the individual's experience is marginalized." See Skorunka, *Narativní přístup*.

80. Trávníček, *Vyprávěj mi něco*, 52.

81. In a reference to Paul Ricoeur, Hošek, "Proměňující moc,⊠ 89. Compare Ricoeur, *Reflection*, 135.

82. Miller, "Narativ," 34.

83. Novitz, "Umění," 28.

84. Schank and Morson, *Tell Me a Story*, 15.

all together into a meaningful whole. The way we tell the stories of our lives uniquely affects ourselves because there is a close connection between the way we view ourselves and how we will probably act.

There is another function of the story, which we can call performative. The question is, how is the story that I read or tell related to reality? Does the story shape reality, or only reveal it? I believe that the two are not necessarily mutually exclusive. The uncovering of reality is based on the assumption that reality (the world) has a pre-existing order which the story (or art in general), in one way or another, follows, imitates, or represents. On the other hand the forming of reality presupposes that reality is open to further organization or even a further creating—that there exists a kind of "pre-arranged harmony"[85] between reality and human imagination which enables the human spirit to create. And the purpose of this creation is to repeat one's understanding; as Katarína Mišíková noted, "Art transforms reality to reveal its inner meaning."[86] From the psychological perspective it is "performative"—as the theorists of speech acts say.[87] In this sense a story is a way of changing or influencing reality through words. It makes something happen in the real world. Or, in the words of Balderman, "the way a narrative presents the world determines its quality."[88]

Rami Shapiro expressed it concisely: "Attentive listening . . . to stories pulls us out of our own story and reveals an alternative drama that can offer us a greater understanding than any story we ourselves can tell. . . . And that is what makes great stories: they show us a different understanding of reality. Nothing has changed but our minds, and that of course changes everything."[89]

SUMMARY: THE MAGIC OF THE LABYRINTH

I have sketched a few selections of "magic" that came out of my reading of Comenius's work *The Labyrinth of the World and the Paradise of the Heart*—some literary strategies that have the power to so captivate the

85. This is a concept of C. S. Lewis (*Pilgrims Regress*, 169). Compare Hošek, *C. S. Lewis, Mytus*.

86. Mišíková, *Mysl a příběh*, 153.

87. See the classic works of Austin (*How to Do Things with Words*), Searle (*Speech Acts*) and Alston (*Illocutionary Acts and Sentence Meaning*).

88. Baldermann, *Úvod*, 88.

89. Shapiro, *Chasidské povídky*, 16–18.

reader that he or she is drawn in, engaged, and motivated. It is clear that the uniqueness of *The Labyrinth* is not in its originality. In terms of genre, literary devices, and the central motif (a pilgrim's journey and search for the true meaning of things), it is in keeping with the literary trends of his time. Suffice it to recall the utopian allegories of Johan Valentin Andreae, Tommaso Campanella, Thomas Moore and, in the English speaking world, the famous *Pilgrim's Progress* by John Bunyan.[90]

However, whenever Comenius took an idea from an older or contemporary work he used his own creativity to transform it. There emerged a very simple story, historically contingent, perhaps too allegorical, too didactic, or too moralizing, but still a story that has its own importance and magic. Analyzing magic usually means the death of it, so I have tried to tread carefully, preserving a methodical respect and rigorous desire to understand.[91] In doing this I have tried to show how the story gives birth to the reader and compels her to collaborate, feel, experience, think, and identify with it. We saw how Comenius's own story draws out the storyline, tantalizes the reader, and inspires her emotions—as he paints pictures and awakens the imagination, discloses through allegories and laughs at what is displayed, plays verbal games of language and words, speaks and evaluates through various narrative angles, and finally offers a way to (re)construct the reader's identity, which I consider to be the most valuable in terms of the theme of this book. Who am I? Who should I be? In the *Labyrinth*—as in his preceding stages—Comenius teaches the reader to distinguish between the ontological and moral dimensions of human nature. One should be a being of very specific moral character, and if one is not, one is going against one's ontological nature. And then it is necessary to do something

90. From the literary-historical perspective it is an interesting fact that one copy of Andrae's work *Peregrini in patria errors*, stored in the Nuremberg Museum, is mistakenly attributed to Comenius. Jan Skutil said that "even though we have to admit the possible influence of the above work on Comenius' *Labyrinth*, we also have to declare that the work is completely original, not only in its treatment of themes . . . , but also in its masterly adaptation of the contemporary Czech morality and conditions." See Skutil, "Comenius's Labyrinth," 126. Compare also Novák, *Labyrint světa*, 56–70; Kopecký, *Komenský jako umělec*; Čapek, *Několik pohledů*, 71–89; Balcar, "Theologické srovnání."

91. Jaroslav Vlček (*Dějiny české literatury*, 550) was aware of the need for a sensitive approach to the interpretation of Comenius' *Labyrinth*. He warned that if the reader is to understand it, "she cannot judge the book by the opinions of modern taste," because modern [and postmodern—my addition] tastes and thinking are subject to completely different goals and actualizations than those of Comenius.

about it. Comenius does not yet "rectify," he only describes, criticizes, allegorizes, satirizes . . . and in so doing, teaches.

I don't think this theme has been exhausted. I believe with this analysis I have only just begun the research into story. I'm sure that each future step along the narrative path will reveal new dimensions of its magic and give glimpses of new realities. The many dismantled layers of the story are preparatory to breaking down others for didactic purposes. If we ask what makes a good story good, it isn't enough to analyze the stated storyline, composition, perspective, etc. We know that their effect is based on their interconnectivity, compactness, and harmony. The fine web of a good narrative into which the reader is caught is the result of the polyphonic harmony (or disharmony in a bad story) of all its parts. The "organic unity" of the narrative, as Tomáš Kubíček said,[92] is thus difficult to understand and analyze, but that is precisely where its magic lies. When viewed from the didactic perspective, the activating power of the story does not lie only in the quality of its component layers, but is primarily in the quality of its interconnectivity as a harmonious whole. The specificity of the narrative genre thus corresponds to the specific nature of humanity. So just as a person isn't only a rational being but also emotional and physical, etc., neither does a story work in isolation, only in the mind, or only in the emotions, etc. A person exposed to the power of story is a being who goes through a holistic experience in which she thinks, feels, believes, endures, identifies with, receives information, evaluates, etc. A good story is a unique form of human art which can impact a person in her entirety and change her. Not every form of narrative succeeds in this, but it works in *The Labyrinth*. And in this lies its magic, and educational potential.

92. Kubíček, *Vypravěč*, 29.

CHAPTER 4

Didactics

Teaching and Learning from Nature

By the voice of nature we understand the universal Providence of God or the influence of Divine Goodness which never ceases to work all in all things; that is to say, which continually develops each creature for the end to which it has been destined. For it is a sign of the divine wisdom to do nothing in vain, that is to say, without a definite end or without means proportionate to that end. Whatever exists, therefore, exists for some end, and has been provided with the organs and appliances necessary to attain to it. It has also been gifted with a certain inclination, that nothing may be borne towards its end unwillingly and reluctantly, but rather promptly and pleasantly, by natural instinct.

Great Didactic, chapter V

BIOGRAPHICAL CONTEXT: EXILE, FAME, AND FLAMES

On July 31, 1627, the ingloriously famous imperial patent was issued by Ferdinand II, which set a six-month deadline in which all the "heretics" had to leave the country.[1] For Comenius and all Protestants it was a

---

1.. The privilege of either accepting the Catholic religion or leaving their homeland within six months was given to the aristocracy; ordinary people were not allowed to leave their homes, they were forced to change their religion. Compare Krofta, *Dějiny*

major turning point. In the spring of 1628, Comenius and a considerable number of Brethren crossed the mountains and found a temporary home in Lezsno, Poland.[2] Comenius didn't know that he would never again be permitted to return to his homeland.[3] For the next forty-two years, until the end of his life, he remained in exile. In Leszno, the Unitas joined the descendants of exiles from the previous century who had fled the country in order to escape persecution, and had found relative security under the tolerant local lord Count Rafael Leszczynski.

Comenius's fruitful, twenty-eight-year Leszno period (1628–56) was interrupted by three sojourns to other countries where he was invited to work, as his reputation of being an outstanding educator spread across Europe. The first invitation came from England (1641–42), the second from Sweden (1642–48), and the third from (today's) Hungary (1650–54). Before Comenius made these breaks, he had fully dedicated himself to work for his church and community. As a secretary and elder of the Unitas Fratrum, he was in charge of correspondence, editing, writing, and publishing. Comenius prepared a number of writings for the internal use of the scattered Brethren, which included defenses, polemics with opponents of the Unitas, as well as occasional papers of a varied nature.[4] He served as a pastor, taught in the Lezsno Gymnasium (High School), where he later became a rector. In addition he had family responsibilities, caring for his aged parents-in-law and his own young children. It is astonishing that, in spite of such busyness, Comenius still found time to study and develop his own philosophical ideas, sketching the first outlines of his corrective plans.[5] It was during this first Lezsno period that Comenius started to develop

---

československé; Polišenský, *Jan Amos Komenský*, 42 or Spinka, *John Amos Comenius*, 36.

2.. See Krofta, *Dějiny československé*, 458.

3. The year 1628 marked the end of the independent existence of the *Unitas Fratrum* both in Bohemia and Moravia. The Moravian Brethren sought refuge in Slovakia. Comenius—although Moravian—joined the group which went to Leszno mainly because of his family relations.

4. Eg., *Řád Jednoty bratří českých*—in both Czech and Latin; *Praxis Pietatis, Zpráva kratičká o morním nakažení; Otázky některé o Jednotě bratří českých.* The publishing of the documents was possible because the printing press from Kralice was moved to Lezsno.

5. During this period Comenius became acquainted in greater depth with Campanella and Bacon, whom he called "happy restorers of philosophy," and who further strengthened his notion of the general unity of all things. They brought him to see the need for a radical methodological revision of human knowledge, for "unified knowledge requires a unified method." See Comenius, *Předchůdce vševědy*, 288. For further details see Patočka, *Komeniologické studie 3*, 542–43, and 584.

his educational and pansophic concepts. Inspired by reading the works of Ratke, Bodin, and other contemporary didactitians, he began to realize the importance of education in the improvement of the overall human state of affairs. The term *pansophy*, meaning universal wisdom (pan-sophia), was in common use at that time, as Jean Piaget has noted.[6] Comenius borrowed the term and began to use it, Patočka said, "as soon as he realized the necessity of deepening the idea of the global order of the universe."[7] Similarly, Pavel Floss observed that at this time Comenius, "began to have in mind not merely the reformation of Czech education and the situation in general—as soon as the political circumstances allowed it—but he began to think in wider horizons. . . . It would not be enough to reform only the Czech situation, but the whole world would have to be radically reformed. Only a fundamental change of all human affairs could release the world from turbulence, wars, pain, and despair."[8]

Hints of his pansophic ideas could already be seen in the first of Comenius's didactic works.[9] Floss noted that he clearly planned the didactic endeavor to reform the school and educational systems only as a component of a greater goal, which was the improvement of human society—originally only of Czech society, and later of the whole of European society.[10]

The maturing of Comenius's pansophic-educational vision is closely related to the political circumstances of the time. As the Swedish and Saxon armies gained the advantage in 1631–32 and temporarily liberated Prague, Comenius worked eagerly and intensively on documents that would have contributed to the restoration of Czech society and its schools as soon as the country was freed.[11] In 1632, however, the advance of the anti-Habsburg

6. Piaget, *Jan Amos Comenius*, 173–96.

7. Patočka, Komeniologické studie 1, 405.

8. Floss, *Nástin života*, 11.

9. Eg., *Didaktika česká* was later reworked and translated into Latin as the *Didactica magna* (Great Didactic) *Informatorium školy mateřské* (School for Infants), *Janua linguarum reserata* (Gate of Languages Unlocked), *Navržení krátké o obnovení škol v království českém* (Brief Proposal for the Regeneration of Schools in the Kingdom of Bohemia).

10. Dagmar Čapková in the same way pointed out the pansophic background of Comenius' famous key didactic principle: *omnes, omnia, omneno*, meaning that *all people* (omnes) ought to learn and be taught *everything* necessary (omnia) in *every way* possible (omneno) in order to live in harmony. See Čapková, *John Amos Comenius*, 70.

11. *Navržení krátké o obnovení škol v království českém* [Short proposal for the restoration of schools in the Czech Kingdom], which was part of the *Heggeus redivivus* (Restoration of paradise).

armies was halted and the Swedish king Gustavus Adolphus, in whom the Czech and Moravian Brethren had put so much hope, was killed. Within the very same year the unfortunate "Winter King" of Bohemia also died.[12] He was, according to the prophecies, to stand up for the Protestant cause. As the hopes for the Czech exiles were literally dying one after another, "Comenius plunge[d] himself with a greater vigor into the work on the reform of the whole world," observed Floss. He continued, "The interest in didactics and other sciences was gradually more and more consciously only a part of Comenius's greater concept of 'improvement,' which gained clearer contours only at the end of the forties."[13] In agreement with Floss's observation, Jan Kumpera added that in this period, "Comenius began to write predominantly in Latin, clearly realizing that the remedy of his ill-fated homeland could be achieved only through a general universal reform . . . ."[14]

The success and subsequent fame of Comenius's pansophically conceived textbook *Janua linguarum reserata*,[15] aroused the interest of some influential figures in England, especially John Dury, a clergyman striving for the unity of churches and the general peace of nations. Also John Pym, a significant person in the English parliament, and Samuel Hartlib, an organizer of scientific life and educational reforms in England, were very influential.[16] They invited Comenius to work in London, where the conditions for the realization of his pansophic plans were supposed to be propitious. At first Comenius could not accept the invitation, for he was busy with his many responsibilities in Lezsno. But he sent some of his pansophic educational notes to Hartlib, who published them in 1637 under the title *Pansophiae praeludium*. From them an even greater interest in Comenius arose in England and elsewhere. Patočka said in light of the fact that Comenius considered the notes to be private, to outline the plans so boldy and openly called for special attention.[17]

12. King Frederick of the Palatinate ruled in Bohemia virtually only one winter, from 1619 to 1620.

13. Floss, *Nástin života*, 13.

14. Kumpera, "Comenius and England," 93.

15. Published in Lezsno in 1631. A plagiarized copy was published in London in 1632.

16. The correspondence with Hartlib began in 1633. Comenius knew Hartlib's brother George from his previous studies and journeys in Germany. Some contacts were probably also mediated by the Lezsno Scottish physician Jon Johnston, a friend of J. Dury.

17. Compare Patočka, *Komeniologické studie 1*, 406.

In 1641 Comenius finally managed to free himself from the Lezsno duties and travel to England, where he was met not only with an affirmative understanding of his pansophic ideas, but also with offers of material safety. These promises, however, were not made at the request of Parliament, as Comenius assumed, but at the request of "Comenians." These were his friends and supporters, who had some influence in Parliament and hoped that Comenius could contribute to a compromise between the King and Parliament.[18] But these promising prospects soon faded. The Civil War of 1642 divided his supporters into various political factions and prevented Comenius from carrying out his plans. Despite the failure of his "English" trip, the time spent in England was far from fruitless. Comenius worked intensively on preparations for the expected reforms to English schools. He prepared materials which were to be used for theoretic, didactic and methodological handbooks. This experience in England also awoke in him a new desire and inspiration for continuing work on his pansophic plans. Some of these ideas he formulated in the manuscript *Via lucis* (Way of Light), which in many ways anticipated his later great work *Obecná porada* (General Consultation).[19]

During this time an interest in Comenius's work was taken by some significant figures, including Cardinal Richelieu, the first minister of France under Louis XIII, the Transylvanian princely Rakoczi family, the Swedish court, and finally he was even offered the position of rector of the newly founded Harvard College in the New World.

When it became obvious that the realization of his projects in England was not feasible, Comenius decided to accept the Swedish invitation to help with the reformation of their education system. An important role in the negotiation between Comenius and the Swedes was played by the Dutch arms merchant and manufacturer Luis de Geer, who was the main supplier of the Swedish army. He was clearly sympathetic to Comenius's ideas, for he co-financed from his private resources the expenses of Comenius's work for Sweden. For Comenius, the decisive factor in his choice was political. As a Protestant he hoped that he could turn the attention of the Swedes towards

18. For more details on his English period see Kumpera, "Comenius and England," 93.

19. In *Via lucis* he outlined how to connect the reform of education with the larger reform of society, foresaw the importance of the social function of science, and presented the idea of an international board promoting education and world peace, which is virtually the founding idea of UNESCO, as Piaget recognized. See Piaget, *Jan Amos Comenius*, 173–96.

his homeland, which was still suffering under the counter-Reformation. The Thirty Years War was not yet over, and Comenius believed that Bohemia could still be liberated from the Habsburgs.

On his way to Sweden he met with a number of significant thinkers of the time but without any particular results. He had hoped to form an international circle of scholars from whom he expected an active contribution to the improvement of human affairs.[20] At the recommendation of the Swedish chancellor, Axel Oxenstjerna, Comenius settled at Prussian Elbing (today Polish Elblag) in 1642, which was then administered by Sweden. Here he worked with his assistants on the reformative assignment until 1648. He prepared a new edition of textbooks and theoretical writings on the methodology of language teaching for the Swedish school system.[21] But the work did not fulfill Comenius's expectations, as is evident from his correspondence and memoirs. For example, in his letter to Samuel Hartlib on January 21, 1647, Comenius wrote, "You asked me to copy everything [concerning pansophy] and send it to you, but it may not be done now, for all five of us are fully occupied by that didactic thorn, and thus I cannot bring my mind to anything else."[22] The overwhelming amount of didactic and editing work he had to do in the Swedish services prevented him from working on pansophy, which he more and more considered to be the main task of his scholarly endeavor.[23] Mathew Spinka commented on Comenius's difficulties during this period as follows, "His soul was afire with the pansophic ideals, the realization of which he considered the proper task of his life. Moreover, his English friends, especially Hartlib, never ceased urging him . . . not to waste his energies and talents on school books, which, they said, were beneath the proper dignity of his genius, but to devote himself to the pansophic studies alone." Later Comenius had to face the disfavor of the Swedes for his failure to meet the deadlines for submitting the textbooks. Still worse, he became personally involved in attempts at political and religious reconciliation in Poland, which were not in accordance with Swedish interests.[24]

20. In his autobiographical memoirs Comenius said that he even met with René Descartes to consult on the *Restoration of Human Affairs*, but without any result.

21. The most important work from this time was *Methodus linguarum novissima* (Newest Language Method).

22. Citation from Molnár and Rejchrtová, *J. A. Komenský*, 214.

23. See Spinka, *John Amos Comenius*, 99.

24. There was a controversial *Colloquium Charitativum* in Torun in 1645, which should have contributed to the reconciliation between the Catholic and Protestant sides.

When Comenius finally completed his assignment and delivered his textbooks to Sweden, he used the opportunity to personally plead with the Swedish Chancellor and the Queen for his nation and his church. His intervention was in vain. The conditions of the Peace of Westphalia, signed in Münster and Osnabrück on October 24, 1648, meant a definitive end of all hopes for both Bohemia and the Bohemian exiles. Tired and disappointed, Comenius returned to Lezsno with his family and assistants. There, soon after their arrival in late 1648, his second wife Dorota died, leaving Comenius with four children. Shortly thereafter came (in 1649) the death of Comenius's close friend and colleague Bishop Pavel Fabricius. This left Comenius as the last living bishop of the diminishing Unitas Fratrum.[25] He articulated his reflections on these events in his *Kšaft umírající matky Jednoty bratrské* (The Legacy of a Dying Mother Unitas Fratrum), published in 1650. In it his strong irenic desires were once again articulated as he urged the nations and churches to reconciliation and expressed his hope for the return of freedom to his nation.

In 1649 Comenius was married for the third time, to Jana Gajusová. Another light moment in his life was the happy marriage of his daughter Alžběta, who wed the best of Comenius's assistants and collaborators, Petr Figulus Jablonský.

A new hope appeared on the horizon when the Hungarian invitation was repeated by the Duchess Susan Lorántfy and her sons, the Dukes of Rákóczi. Comenius was asked to reform the schooling in Transylvania and, in particular, to establish a pansophic gymnasium (secondary school) in Sárospatak. Comenius, on the other hand, wanted to involve the Rákóczi family in the anti-Habsburg coalition. His hopes were once again stirred by the prophecies of his former school fellow, Mikuláš Drabík. He foretold, among other things, the early fall of the Habsburgs and designated Sigismund Rákóczi as the future king of the Empire. These expectations were further strengthened by the promising marriage of Prince Sigismund to Princess Henrietta Maria, daughter of the Bohemian "Winter King," Frederick of the Palatinate. The marriage took place in June 1651, and Comenius was asked to officiate at the wedding. He did so gladly, believing it to

---

Piaget commented on this, writing that Comenius "presupposed the displeasure of the Swedes, but nevertheless followed his goal, which was in accordance with his character." See Piaget, *Jan Amos Comenius*, 173–96.

25. See Říčan, *Dějiny*, 479.

be a privilege, for he had a very warm personal relationship with the whole family.

During the Sárospatak period Comenius wrote a number of outstanding books, mainly didactic in character.[26] Among the most important was his famous and successful *Orbis pictus* (The World in Pictures). It was basically a simplified and illustrated version of his *Janua linguarum* (The Gate of Languages Unlocked), revised to meet the Sárospatak needs. His main theoretical work of this period was *Schola pansophica* (Pansophic School). In it Comenius very thoroughly and systematically dealt with the issue of the relationships between all subjects in the educational process and proposed a way of harmonizing them into a unified whole. Another didactic invention, which he introduced in Hungary, was his *Schola ludus* (School as Play), representing dramatized selected subjects designed to animate the traditionally passive education by a theater performance. Unfortunately, Comenius's innovative didactic approaches became a source of conflict and malice between him and his Hungarian colleagues. In particular, the conservative rector of the Sárospatak School, John Tolnai, maintained a determined and overt opposition to his innovations. Comenius's stay in Hungary, which consisted in the introduction of reforms to the educational system, thus met with obstacles almost from the outset. At the end of his life, in his autobiography Comenius remembered exactly what he said to Susan Lorántfyová to explain the reasons for his resignation (apparently in the presence of his opponents). It was:

> because my presence here is superfluous. Rather, I suffer ridicule on account of my didactic endeavors and shall suffer even more if I stay longer. When they wanted me to speak openly I said, "My whole method is directed towards changing school drudgery into fun and games; and that is something nobody here wishes to understand. The youth, including the well-born, are treated altogether as if they were slaves, the teachers rest their esteem upon stern faces, rough words, and even in beating, and wish to be feared rather than loved. How many times I have pointed out both publicly and privately, that this is not the proper way; but always in vain![27]

26. As well as the most significant *Orbis pictus* and *Schola ludus*, Comenius also wrote *Leges scholae bene ordinatae* [The Laws of a Well-Ordered School] and *Gentis felicitas* [Happiness of the Nation], in which he outlined his view of a well-developing nation. Comenius also continued his preparatory work on his *General Consultation*.

27. See Molnár and Rejchrtová, *J. A. Komenský*, 238–39.

Faced with such circumstances, Comenius decided "to return rather than live in strife and waste his strength upon matters which led nowhere."[28] In addition, Comenius still desired to focus more fully on his "main" task—pansophy.

But there were also other reasons which expedited Comenius's return to Lezsno. First, there was the strong longing of his co-believers, countrymen, and kin, who persistently urged him to come back, appealing to Comenius as their pastor and elder of the Unitas Fratrum. Second, there was the international and political situation to consider. Not only was Sigismund Rákóczi not willing to respond to the appeal of M. Drabík's prophecy, but he and his wife died in 1653, and his brother George hesitated to take part in any anti-Habsburg action.[29] Therefore, after four years, Comenius returned to Poland.

His return was, among other things, motivated by new hopes which surprisingly shone again from the Protestant Sweden and England. In 1655 the new Swedish king, Charles X. Gustav, successfully launched a campaign against Catholic Poland.[30] All the Protestant nobles, including Bohuslaw Leszcynski, the Lord of Leszno, welcomed him gladly as their new king. Comenius himself expressed his pro-Swedish stand by writing the *Panegyricus Gustavo Adolfo*, which committed him and his Brethren irrevocably to the Swedish cause. Comenius apparently realized the possible consequences of such a stance and therefore hesitated to write such a treatise, only giving in after being urged a number of times by the Lezsno council to write it. The Polish Catholic majority, however, considered it to be a betrayal of Poland, and that turned out to be fatal for both Lezsno and the Brethren exiles.

When Denmark, the traditional enemy of Sweden, entered the conflict, King Charles suffered a series of defeats and was forced to withdraw from Poland. Thus, the city of Lezsno was no longer protected by the Swedish army, and the reprisal from the Catholic Poles was inevitable. On April

28. Molnár and Rejchrtová, *J. A. Komenský*, 237.

29. Matthew Spinka commented on this, writing "One might expect that this disappointment would have proven disastrous to Drabík's prophecies. But that was not the case. With an ease and elasticity . . . Drabík simply transferred the task expected of the pious Sigismund to his much less pious elder brother, the reigning Prince, George Rákóczi II," See Spinka, *John Amos Comenius*, 127. It is a matter of fact that George Rákóczi II eventually joined the Swedish forces in Poland in 1657, but we do not know whether it was a result of Comenius' or Drabík's exhortations. Further, the prophecy was not fulfilled, for George Rákóczi II died only three years later (1660) in a battle with Turks.

30. The reason for the invasion was the claim of the Polish king, John II Casimir (cousin of Charles X Gustav), to the Swedish throne.

29, 1656, a strong Polish contingent broke into the city and razed it with fire. Comenius and his family barely escaped with their lives, and all their property was lost. Comenius particularly regretted the loss of his and the Brethren's library, which included some of his important and personally precious manuscripts.[31]

FROM RESIGNATION TO DIDACTICS

In the beginning of the 1630s, several years after his emigration to Lezsno, we can discern a new shift in Comenius's thought. It was not a sudden change but rather a gradual process which led to a different attitude toward the nature of the world and the role of the human being in the world. This new attitude was first observable in his early didactic writings, namely in *Česká didaktika* (Czech Didactic) and *Velká didaktika* (Great Didactic). In these books Comenius showed a more positive view of the world with all its problems. He evidently abandoned his determination to merely bear the miseries of the world; on the contrary, he was determined to do something with them, to overcome them. He no longer renounced or turned away from the world but pointed to it, appealed to it; and, as we shall see, even drew didactic principles from its nature. The question which arises is: What brought about this substantial change in his thinking? And, likewise, what brought him to the concept of didactics at all?

The theme of education was not new for Comenius, for he had been pondering this area ever since he began to teach in 1614. We saw above that the teaching plans and handbooks were devised during the 1630s, when he consciously sought out and studied the pedagogical literature sources. While studying the available materials he came across the works of some of the famous contemporary didactic reformers,[32] such as, for example,

---

31. Especially painful was the loss of the *Thesaurus linguae Bohemicae* (Treasure of the Czech Language) and *Theatrum universitatis rerum* (Theater of All Things), on which he had worked for around 46 years. He also lost a number of pansophic manuscripts, some of which were almost ready for publication.

32. Comenius listed these authors as the sources of inspiration in the Introductions to both of his *Didactics* (Czech Didactic and Great Didactics).

Wolfgang Ratke,[33] Elias Bodin,[34] Eilhard Lubin,[35] Christoph Helwig,[36] Johannes C. Frey[37] and Johannes V. Andreae.[38] These authors ignited Comenius's interest in pedagogy, but they could not and did not provide the systematic philosophical framework that we observe in Comenius's *Didactics*, for they dealt with only narrow and specific didactic subjects. In the introduction to the *Great Didactic*, Comenius made it clear: "Some merely wished to give assistance towards learning some language or other with greater ease. Others found ways of imparting this or that science or art. . . . We venture to promise a Great Didactic, that is to say, the whole art of teaching all things to all men."[39] Where does this philosophical 'greatness' of the *Great Didactic* come from? Comenius let us know elsewhere that the decisive philosophical influence came not from 'handbooks' of mere didac-

33. Ratke was a German thinker who, in his *Memoriale*, boasted that he knew a method for teaching languages and sciences in a remarkably short time and with remarkable results. But when he was given an opportunity to prove his claims, he failed and was put in jail in 1619. Later he was given two more opportunities, but again the practical outcomes fell below his promises. It is an interesting matter of fact that Ratke kept his methodology secret, and his disciples were under oath not to reveal the method to anybody. Komenský tried several times to correspond with Ratke and consult with him about his pedagogical ideas, but Ratke did not respond. However, Komenský probably knew some of Ratke's handbooks developed for his 'experimental' schools and was able to infer some of Ratke's methodology.

34. Bodin was a German author. His *Didactica* is not a theoretical pedagogical system but rather a summary of instructions concerning language teaching. However, it was perhaps the first didactic book which Comenius had came across, and it ignited his interest and desire to write in the area of didactics.

35. Lubinus was a German professor of rhetoric, mathematics, and theology. He did not deal explicitly with didactics, but he wrote an introduction to a Greek-Latin-German edition of the New Testament with a rather long title: *Epištola, která vysvětluje, jak by se chlapci měli učit latinskému jazyku* [A letter that explains how a student should learn the Latin language]. Comenius was most likely acquainted with it.

36. Helwig was a professor of Greek and eastern languages in Giesen. The work which inspired Comenius was *Grammatica universalis, continens ea, quae omnibus linguis sunt comunia* [General grammar containing that which is common to all languages].

37. Frey was a German medical doctor who taught philosophy in Paris. Comenius calls his didactic work, published in 1629 in Paris, "milostná didaktička" [lovable little didactics]; it deals with teaching of rhetoric, sciences, arts, and languages.

38. Comenius valued Andreae above all in his *Czech Didactic*, with the explanation (in the *Great Didactic*) that he "excellently exposed the illnesses of the churches, states, and schools." Comenius already knew Andreae in his Fulnek period and was in touch with him via correspondence. The influence of Andreae was clear earlier in Comenius's *Labyrinth*, as we have seen above.

39. Komenský, *Didaktika velká*, 3.

ticians but from philosophers, most importantly, from Nicolaus Cusanus, Tommaso Campanella, and Francis Bacon.[40]

Cusanus helped Comenius to discover, among other things[41] the fundamental motif of the *world as a school*.[42] It was not a new idea in the history of philosophic thought. The idea of the world as the school of God's wisdom appeared in the writings of a number of church fathers, e.g., Gregory of Nyssa, Clement of Alexandria, Origen, and Augustine. And before that a similar idea occurred in classical platonic thought, where education was seen as essentially a way from delusion to truth, from darkness to light. Nor was it a new thought for Comenius, for the elements of this concept could already be seen in his early encyclopedic projects. But perhaps because of Comenius' life circumstances, he was not able to see the potential of this motif until this stage in his life. To what does the concept of the world as a school refer? Patočka understood Cusanus well, interpreting him as follows:

> The world and life are preparation for the future merging with God. . . . The whole of our daily life is focused on the individual things of the world, which are many and scattered. In the intellectual world there is only one object of the intellect, and that is truth itself. What we really seek in the school of this world is, therefore, something which the world cannot render us in a pure form: the absolute truth, the comprehension of it, to have the mastery of truth, to be the art of truth itself. . . . From the world itself we are to learn transcendence; we are to learn that the goal of each thing lies beyond itself; thus the goal of things is in human beings, and the goal of the human being is that which is beyond him.[43]

And Patočka elsewhere continued:

> If we grasp that the world in itself is not self-explanatory, that all of reality is structured in such a way that its every part and its every layer point beyond itself to the higher layers, but also the whole as such points beyond itself, then this wisdom in the world pointing

40. Comenius informed us of their influence in a letter written to Rafael Leszcynský in 1630. See Molnár and Rejchrtová, *J. A. Komenský,* 95–97. See also Patočka, *Komeniologické studie 1,* 151–52.

41. One of the other things was the idea of universal harmony, which I will discuss later in this chapter.

42. Comenius knew Cusanus through Pender's anthology. He found there a relatively large abstract from Cusanus's *De filiatione Dei,* where the motif was outlined.

43. Patočka, *Komeniologické studie 1,* 79.

beyond the world is going to be a school for everyone who allows the world to teach them."[44]

In other words, instruction lies in the actual nature of being. The nature of reality, as it is given, has an inherently educational character for "every being in its true form has received this self-transcending designation,"[45] said Palouš, when expounding on Comenius's newly discovered understanding of reality. In another place he added, "The world was not created as some accidental occurrence of something that runs according to an anonymous mechanism emerging from dark meaninglessness and heading toward empty indifference; on the contrary, the world is an intentional abiding of beings, called to be 'well,' beings called not merely 'to be,' but 'to be in order to,'" with an inherent purpose.[46] The world itself was and is, in Comenius's understanding, created and formed "*in order to* become the visible sign of God's intention, *in order to* prepare a space for the paramount role of human beings, *in order to* start the remarkable drama of a good world. . . . It is just this *in order to* which characterizes the nature of God's world."[47] Men and women enter the school of the world through birth and are immediately exposed to its education. "The particularities of this world prepare a human being for comprehension of the universal, undivided, and non-fragmented truth."[48] The world narrates the story of its own transcendence; thus the universe calls people to the same task—to fulfill their role in the drama. After all, they are part of the same story.

Note that this teleological understanding of reality was not in contradiction with Comenius's notion of *"nesamosvojnost"* (meaning that the universe and human beings do not have their goal and end in themselves), which he formulated in the previous (consolation) period of his life. This notion, as we have seen, viewed all the beings of this world (including human beings in the first place) as not self-existing and self-sustaining, but both ontologically and existentially dependent on God.[49] It was only after encountering Cusanus's idea of the world as school that the resigned dependence began to change into an active dependence in Comenius's thought. This is not to say that he stopped seeing the corruption and evils of the

44. Ibid., 182.

45. Palouš, *Komenského Boží svět*, 33.

46. Ibid., 18.

47. Ibid., 13.

48. Patočka, J. "Mezihra na prahu," 33.

49. Compare Patočka, *Komeniologické studie 1*, 182.

world. From this point, however, they did not prevent him from allowing the world to teach him.

This newly discovered educative dimension of reality was accompanied by impetuses from Campanella and Bacon. Campanella was a vigorous critic of the traditional Aristotelian approach to knowledge and strove for a fundamental reform. His project of a unified system of all the sources of knowledge included experience, reason, and faith. These, he hoped, would penetrate all branches of knowledge and would lead toward goals of emendation in the society. These goals strongly resonated in Comenius's mind, for he was similarly dissatisfied with the state of affairs and sought for a solution. That is why he considered Campanella to be one of the "happy restorers of philosophy."[50] Campanella's suggestions to Comenius fitted together well with thoughts he had come across in Cusanus. Patočka said that in addition to the idea of the world as a school, "Cusanus influenced Comenius by the idea of the fusion of contradictions, that is, the idea that every individual being is a particular explication of unity, which thus participates in universal harmony,"[51] which is the theme which Comenius revealed in his later works to be foundational.

The last source of inspiration to contribute to the further shifting of Comenius's thinking was Francis Bacon. Comenius's adoption of Bacon's method is quite peculiar and loose, as we shall see. Moreover, in the *Great Didactic*, Comenius gave no reference to Bacon, and that caused some dispute among the Comeniologists about whether or not Comenius knew Bacon when composing his early didactic writings. The quarrel was resolved when a letter written by Comenius to Rafael Leszcynski in 1630 was found. In the letter Comenius listed all the writers who inspired him, and after listing the didactitians (which he listed in the introduction to his *Great Didactic*), he attached today's well-known parenthesis: "addo Campanellam et Verulamium, felices philosophiae instauratores" [I'm adding Campanella and Verulam, happy restorers of philosophy]. It was quite an interesting and important discovery, for it not only revealed the fact that Comenius knew Bacon and studied him simultaneously with Campanella, but it also showed something about Comenius's systematic approach to study. Comenius added the two authors only at the end of the list as a separate group, because they were indeed separate; they were philosophers, not

50. In a letter written by Rafael Leszcynský in 1630. See Molnár and Rejchrtová, *J. A. Komenský*, 95–97.

51. Patočka, *Komeniologické studie 1*, 184.

didactitians, and thus for the composition of a didactic writing, they were in the category of auxiliary sources.[52]

Bacon's methodological reform of knowledge, which was to allow or even force nature to speak for itself, fit perfectly with the thinking of Cusanus and Campanella. The induction method promised to multiply human spiritual (intellectual) powers in the same way a machine multiplies human physical powers, and as a result of that, humans would be enabled to become the rulers of creation once again. In addition to Bacon as a source of methodological inspiration Patočka mentioned Vives, who is considered to be a predecessor of Cartesian methodology and who was linked to Comenius through their encyclopedic and educational interests. However, of the two it was Bacon who had the greater impact on Comenius. It must also be noted that Comenius did not adopt Bacon's method in its entirety. The special attention Comenius gave to nature "was not [based on] Bacon's research, but educationally based," as documented by Čapková:

> Comenius did not view nature as a machine which might be approached and observed externally. Even though he would use similar terminology such as *machina mundi* (world as machine), his approach was organic, that is, similar to that of neo-platonics and hermetics. . . . He was interested in the knowledge of nature on the one hand because people are surrounded by it and should become aware of the main things they can learn from it, so as to know what should be included in the school curriculum. And on the other hand it interested him because nature, as the closest and most easily accessible realm in the whole of the world, best reveals to people God's purpose and order as displayed in an upward structure from primitive to complex organisms to the most complex: man, and higher still to the spiritual. . . . Thus while Bacon sought via his induction method the key to the exploration of nature, and Descartes strove for the emancipation of the human mind, Comenius had in mind a new (scientific) method for the formation of human beings in their relation to the whole of life.[53]

Bacon's initiative was the last component in the mosaic of Comenius's foundation for a new educational philosophy: a) there exists a world which provides the educational material, b) there exists a knowledge which includes and harmonizes the whole (Comenius later called it *pansophy*), c) and there exists a method which enables the material to disclose its

---

52. For further details see Patočka, *Komeniologické studie 1*, 151–52.
53. Čapková, *Škola a utváření*, 557.

potential. Comenius's synthesis of these sources gave birth to a unique perspective first presented in his didactic writings, namely, *The Gate of Languages Unlocked* (1631), *Czech Didactic* (1632), and *Great Didactic* (1657).[54] I will focus on the *Didactics* in this chapter, for the method of teaching developed in *The Gate* is only part of the complex didactic system developed in the *Didactics*.[55]

Both of the *Didactics* have essentially the same structure.[56] The following four subchapters will follow Comenius's four basic sections:

1. Prologue and introduction to general pedagogy

2. General didactics and specific didactics of the arts, sciences, and languages

3. Moral and religious education

4. Organization of the overall educational system[57]

---

54. The *Great Didactic* wasn't published until 1657, as the first part of the *Opera didactica omnia*. But Comenious had already started to work on its translation into Latin and its improvement in 1633, when he began to realize that it was not only Czech affairs that needed to be remedied.

55. I will analyze the *Didactics*, even though the *The Gate* was much more successful and its fame overshadowed the other writings for a number of years. The exceptional success of *The Gate* surprised even Comenius himself, because it was based on the same theoretical foundation as the other didactic writings. It can be explained by the more immediate and specific results that *The Gate* brought about in language learning. Another likely factor was the urgent need for a better method of foreign language teaching and learning.

56. As I mentioned above, the *Czech Didactic* was written for Czech readers who knew nothing about the subject, while the *Great Didactic* was written later (in Latin) for the educated circles. The slightly different emphases and formulation, however, complement each other well; therefore, I will found my analysis on both *Didactics*. To indicate the source I will use the following system of abbreviations in this chapter: *Czech Didactic*, Chapter 1, paragraph 2 (CD, 1.2); *Great Didactic*, Chapter 3, paragraph 4 (GD, 3.4). Only the citations from the *Prologue* will be noted differently, because they are not sequenced by chapter and paragraph.

57. Although Comenius did not divide his *Didactics* in this way, the fourfold organization of the book was hinted at in the title page of the *Great Didactic* where he announced the four main themes of his plan: foundations, truth, approach, way. I am following the formulation of the divisions as given by Jaroslav Havelka in the introduction to the *Czech Didactic* (1937) and Jan V. Novák in his introduction to the *Great Didactic* (1905).

PROLOGUE: THE STARTING POINT OF HUMAN(E) EDUCATION

A reader of the *Didactics* might be tempted to skip the Prologue (literally, the *Appeal*) as "merely" a prologue, but in fact it is one of the most important parts, testifying to the substance of Comenius's anthropology. On the title page of the *Great Didactic* Comenius indicated that the first part of his book would deal with "foundations." A careful reading shows however, that it would not be about fundamentals in the sense of the most important trivia, but rather the fundamentals on which the entire educational structure would stand. The opening words reveal how broad and thorough Comenius's objectives were:

> In the beginning God created human beings out of the dust of the earth and placed them in a paradise of pleasure which He had planted in the East, not only for them to tend and care for, but also that it would be a garden of pleasure for God Himself. For as Paradise was the most delightful place in the world, so was humankind the most magnificent of all creatures . . . created in the image of the One whose going forth was from the beginning, from eternity. (CD, Prologue)

After an exposition of the Creator's wisdom and outlining the beauties of the original state of creation, Comenius continued:

> But alas! We have lost the paradise of the physical pleasures which we inhabited, and likewise we have lost the paradise of the spiritual pleasures. To the wasteland of the earth we have been driven, and in our hearts we have become wastelands. We did not appreciate the paradisal arrangements, we coveted something more both for our bodies and for our minds, and thus we lack both, both our bodies and minds are weighed down by the burden of wickedness. (CD, Prologue)

And still elsewhere he added:

> For what is in relation to people as it ought to be? What stands in its proper place? Nothing. Everything is upside down, everything has gone wrong, for all the order, all the government, all the noble features are scattered. Instead of the wisdom by which we were to resemble angels, there is foolishness and dullness . . . resembling dumb beasts. Instead of prudence, which leads one to prepare for eternity, for which we have been created, there is a forgetfulness of both the eternal nature and the mortality of man. . . . Instead of

DIDACTICS

mutual candidness and truthfulness, there is slyness, deceit, and
falsity everywhere. Instead of grace, there is envy, instead of confidence, there is deception. . . . Instead of unity, there are discords,
quarrels, and rages, secret malice as well as open hostility, fights
and wars. Instead of righteousness, there are injustice, robberies,
thefts; everyone greedily amasses only for himself or herself. Instead of purity, there is lechery, both internal and external; there
is adultery, infidelity, misconduct, and lewdness, both in the mind
and in speech. Instead of truthfulness, there are lies and gossip
everywhere. Instead of humbleness, there is arrogance and pride,
preening and boasting; one rising against the other. Woe to you,
miserable generation, how deeply you have sunk into wretched-
ness! (CD, Prolog)

Such a woeful condition of human affairs did not, however, lead
Comenius to a renunciation of the world or his generation. He saw a way
out—or rather a way toward—the world, toward a remedial engagement
with the sick world. The solution was related to his eschatological hopes,
which once again provided motivational power. Comenius knew two "joys"
in the midst of all the above described miseries: 1) "That God is preparing
the paradise of eternity, where there will be everlasting perfection. . ." 2)
"God will restore his paradise and his church at a certain time and will
turn the wasteland into a delightful garden" (CD, Prolog). According to
Comenius's reading of Scripture and history, God did such things a number
of times in the past: after the flood, when bringing his people out of Egypt,
and later out of Babylon; in King David's time; and, of course, when send-
ing his Son, the Savior.[58] And Comenius added a conclusion which seems
to be one of the key moments in his "didactic turn": "It is highly important
that we would understand well the foundation of God's glorious and joyful
restoration and thus know how to contribute to the merciful work of God"
(CD, Prologue). Notice that Comenius was no longer determined to merely
put up with the miseries of the world as he had been in his "resignation" period, but he was ready to participate in the restoration of the world, which
was indeed a significant shift in his thinking.

The idea of didactics, which played an essential role in the process of
restoration, needed to be explained to the reader because the concept was
a new one, especially for Czech readers.[59] Comenius presented didactics

58. In the *Czech Didactics*, he also mentioned Jan Hus and Martin Luther as the servants of restoration, for these figures were clearly familiar to the Czech readers.

59. That is why the introduction to the *Czech Didactic* is longer and more detailed.

as the "art of arts"; that is, the "artful teaching" of youth (and people in general) in the arts. He further explained that all the confusions and mazes of contemporary schools show the urgent need of such an art. He acknowledged the didactic reformers who inspired him and in whose footsteps he wanted to follow, but he humbly suggested there was a need for far greater and more substantial reform. In his judgment, Comenius's predecessors formulated their didactic handbooks "only as guidelines for how to teach "this or that . . . by means of unconnected precepts, gleaned from a superficial experience, that is to say, *a posteriori*" (GD, Prolog), and their advice covered merely external and partial aspects of education. But he ventured:

> to promise a Great Didactic, that is to say, the whole art of teaching all things to all men, and indeed of teaching them with certainty, so that the result cannot fail to follow; further, of teaching them pleasantly, that is to say, without annoyance or aversion on the part of teacher or pupil, but rather with the greatest enjoyment for both; further of teaching them thoroughly, not superficially and showily, but in such a manner as to lead to true knowledge, to gentle morals, and to the deepest piety. (GD, Prologue)

In contrast with his predecessors this grand project was to be derived "*a priori*, that is to say, from the unalterable nature of the matter itself, drawing off, as from a living source, the constantly flowing runlets . . . ." In the very next paragraph Comenius admitted the greatness of the things promised and invited all readers to evaluate his project very carefully, encouraging them to contribute to it.

In the following paragraphs of the Prologue Comenius further explained the importance of education in general, and in particular, the education of youth, elaborating on the general benefits of a better educated society. He spelled out the teleological foundations of his pedagogy. The ultimate goal of all education is to bring human beings to the fulfillment of their purpose for existence. Comenius naturally developed his understanding of this purpose from the Scriptures and expressed it in the following words as: "being united with God, the culmination of all perfection, glory, and happiness, and of enjoying with Him absolute glory and happiness for ever" (GD, 2.1). If one wants to understand this goal, one must first understand oneself (CD, 1.1), that is, one must know:

a. That human beings "are the greatest, strangest, and most glorious of all creation" (CD, 1.2–4).

a.i Human beings are the greatest, because only humans possess all the attributes of being: life, senses, and reason. For example, a stone has being but does not possess life; plants and trees are given life, and even the ability to multiply, but do not sense things; all the animals, beasts, birds, fish, reptiles, etc. possess life and the senses but not reason (CD, 1.2).

a.ii Human beings are the strangest of all creatures, for only in them "the heavenly with the earthly is merged; the visible with the invisible, the mortal with the immortal. To embed a rational, immortal, and eternal soul into a piece of clay and make it to be one personality, that is a mighty act of God's wisdom and artistry" (CD, 1.3). It was only the human being to whom God related personally (nexus hypostaticus),[60] and thus united His nature with human nature (GD, 1.3).

a.iii The greatest glory of human beings lies in the fact God himself in Jesus Christ became a human being in order to "recreate what has been corrupted." No other creature in the whole universe has been so gloriously honored by the Creator (CD, 1.4).

b. The ultimate goal of human life is not in this life (CD, 2). This is made known to people in the Scriptures, but also it is observable in human nature and life:

b.i The composition of our nature shows that what we have in our lives is never sufficient. For human beings have a threefold life in themselves: vegetative, in common with plants; animal, in common with beasts; and spiritual or intellectual, which is specific for people. From the fact that we tend to grow and develop toward perfection on all these levels, though we reach perfection on none of these levels, Comenius concluded that "there must be something greater cherished for us" (CD, 2.2).

b.ii "We do not attain our ultimate end here, but everything connected with us, as well as we ourselves, has another destination" (GD, 2.5). "Everything that happens with us in this life happens on levels on which we ascend higher and from which we always see yet higher levels. . . . Similarly, our efforts are first smallish, thin, and feeble, but gradually they grow greater and

---

60. For the most recent Latin edition see Comenius, *Didactica magna*, 53.

reach further. But as long as we are alive . . . we always have something to do, something to desire, something to strive for. Nevertheless, we can never fully satisfy or fulfill our efforts in this life" (CD, 2.3).

c. Earthly life is but a preparation for eternal life. Comenius saw the evidence of this in three things:

   c.i   People. "If we examine ourselves, we see that our faculties grow in such a manner that what goes before paves the way for what comes after. For example, our first life is in our mother's womb. But for the sake of what does it exist? Of the life itself? Not at all. The process that here takes place is intended to form the embryo into the suitable abiding-place and instrument of the soul, for convenient use in the life on earth which follows. As soon as this preparation is finished we burst forth into the light. . . . In the same way is this life here on earth" (GD, 3.2).

   c.ii The world. "The visible world itself, from whatever point of view we regard it, bears witness that it has been created for no other end than that it may serve for the progeneration, the nutrition, and the training of the human race. . . . Thus the world is nothing but our nursery, our nurturing place, and our school, and there is, therefore, a place beyond, whither we shall be transferred when we are dismissed from the classes of this school and are sent to that university which is everlasting" (GD, 3.3)

   c.iii The Holy Scriptures. "Although reason shows it, the Holy Scripture also affirms most powerfully that God, having created the world and everything in it, made man and woman a steward of it and commanded him and her to multiply and to replenish the earth and subdue it. Hence the world is here for man and woman. God speaks about this clearly in Hosea, that the heavens are for the earth, the earth then for corn, wine, oil, etc., and those things are for people (Hos. 2:21,22). All things, therefore, are for humans, even time itself. . . . After all, the Scripture speaks about this world almost always as about preparation and training, a way, a journey, a gate, an expectation; and we are called foreigners, pilgrims, and guests, who are awaiting another place, which is everlasting" (CD, 3.7).[61]

d. The ultimate goal of every human being is "eternal happiness with God" (GD, 4.1). To reach this goal a person needs to fulfill his or her human vocation, which Comenius derived from the Scriptures, specifically from the account of the creation of human beings (Gen 1:26). There are, according to Comenius, three main tasks given to people as a life assignment:

   d.i To be a rational being, which means "to name all things, and to speculate and reason about everything that the world contains" (GD, 4.3).

   d.ii To be the master of creation, which means "subjecting everything to his own use by contriving that its legitimate end be suitably fulfilled; in conducting himself royally, that is, gravely and righteously, among creatures . . . and thus will he preserve the dignity which has been granted to him. He should enslave himself to no creature, not even to his own flesh and blood." In other words, "to be able to control with prudence his own movements and actions, external and internal, as well as those of others" (GD, 4.4).

   d.iii To be the image of God. That is, "to constantly turn one's heart, desires, and efforts toward God, both externally and internally . . . and thus reflect the perfection which lies in human origin" (CD, 4.9).

Before proceeding further I want to emphasize the anthropology which Comenius was expressing here. What he only indicated or suggested allegorically in the preceding stages, here he speaks of explicitly. The quotations capture traditional Brethren teaching on "the creation and fall of man." That Comenious based his anthropology in the biblical narrative is not surprising. What is important is that using this source enabled the distinguishing between the ontological and moral components of human nature. As in his works of previous stages, here also Comenius saw human beings as "the most magnificent of all creatures" because they were created

---

61. To support his argument, Comenius gave the following biblical references: Gen 47:9; Ps 39:13; Job 7:1–2; Luke 12:34.

as the *Imago Dei*,[62] but also as "a wasteland, vile and unclean." In our ontological potential we are almost like angels, but in our moral actualization of
that potential we are often more like demons. The question is, how education can respond to this anthropological reality.

In the following chapter, Comenius further explicated the three tasks
in order to show they are rooted in human nature. Human nature has a
"natural" tendency toward *learning* (d.i), *virtue* (d.ii), and *godliness* (d.iii).
In the explanation, Comenius made it clear that by nature he understood
"not the corruption which has laid hold of all men since the Fall . . . , but
our first and original condition, to which, as to a starting point, we must be
recalled" (GD, 5.1). To support his view he quoted Ludwig Vives and Seneca, recognized authorities of the time. Vives said: "What else is a Christian
but a man restored to his own nature." Which is similar to what Seneca
expressed in this quote: "This is wisdom, to return to nature and to the
position from which universal error . . . has driven us" (GD, 5.1–2). To
further strengthen his argument Comenius related his concept of nature
to the doctrine of common grace (*universalis providentia Dei*), which was
quite familiar to his readers (GD, 5.2).[63] The sign of God's wisdom, which
secures the continual functioning of everything, is that:

> He does nothing in vain, that is to say, without a definite end or
> without means proportionate to that end. Whatever exists, there-
> fore, exists for some end, and has been provided with the organs
> and appliances necessary to attain to it. It has also been gifted with
> a certain inclination, that nothing may be borne towards its end
> unwillingly and reluctantly, but rather promptly and pleasantly
> (GD, 5.1–2).

It is similar with human beings, according to Comenius, who are
"naturally fitted for the understanding of facts, for existence in harmony
with the moral law, and above all things for the love of God (GD, 5.2). Comenius admitted that "the natural desire for God, as the highest good, has
been corrupted by the Fall . . . so that no man, of his strength alone, could
return to the right way," but God had His tools, "the Word and the Spirit,"
which "illumine those who are His." And therefore, "while we are seeking for the remedies of corruption, let none cast corruption in our teeth.
For God will remove it through His Holy Ghost and by the intervention

62. For a more detailed interpretation of this concept see Pelcová, *Vzorce lidství*,
40–41.

63. For the most recent Latin rendering see also Comenius, *Didactica magna*, 60.

of natural means. . . . Did not God, soon after the Fall, and after the exile was threatened to us (the penalty of death), sow in our hearts the seeds of fresh grace (by the promise of His blessed offspring)? Did He not send His Son to restore us to our former estate?" (GD, 5.21–22) This "raising up" or restoration of the original state of human beings given by the Creator, then, constitutes the overall goal of all Comenius's didactics.[64]

After defining the general goals of education, Comenius turned to the actual subject of education. From all that has been said, it follows that education is (and is to be) general, or universal; that is, it concerns all people. Comenius first affirmed that every human being is not only an educable being but also one in need of education, for "if a man is to be produced, it is necessary that he be formed by education" (GD, 6). Without education a person becomes "the most intractable thing in the world" (GD, 6.6), and in the end a "non-man," Comenius said later in the *Pampaedii* (2:8). Therefore it is necessary to educate all people, whether smart or dull, rich or poor, boys or girls, rulers or serfs (GD, 6.7–9). This was a truly revolutionary proposal, and Comenius, being aware of it, anticipated his opponents' objections:

> If any ask, "What will be the result if artisans, rustics, porters, and even women become lettered?" I answer, If this universal instruction of youth be brought about by the proper means, none of these will lack the material for thinking, choosing, following, and doing good things. All will know how the actions and endeavours of life should be regulated, within what limits we must progress, and how each man can protect his own position. Not only this, but all will regale themselves, even in the midst of their work and toil, by meditation on the words and works of God. . . . To sum up, they will learn to see, to praise, and to recognise God everywhere, and in this way, to go through this life of care with enjoyment. . . . Does not such a condition of the Church represent to us the only paradise that it is possible to realize on this earth? (GD, 9.8)

Education should begin as soon as possible in early childhood, according to Comenius, for the youth are "most easily formed" (GD, 7). Educating

64. The paragraph explaining what is meant by *human nature* was added only in *Great Didactics*. Perhaps some of his colleagues or critics pointed out to Comenius that the concept of "natural tendency" needed such clarification. It seems that part of Comenius's argument attempted to respond to some implications of the Calvinist doctrine of *total depravity*, which is the first of the five traditional points of Calvinism (TULIP); the others are: Unconditional election, Limited atonement; Irresistible grace, and Perseverance of the saints.

children is the solemn task of all parents, but Comenuis realistically recognized that parents often do not know how to do that or do not have time for it, and therefore, it is helpful to have schools where children might be educated together.[65] In addition to these practical reasons, Comenius saw another advantage of institutional training, which in today's terminology could be classified as socio-psychological:

> Nevertheless it is better that the young should be taught together and in large classes, since better results and more pleasure are to be obtained when one pupil serves as an example and a stimulus for another. For to do what we see others do, to go where others go, to follow those who are ahead of us, and to keep in front of those who are behind us, is the course of action to which we are all most naturally inclined. . . . Young children, especially, are always more easily led and ruled by example than by precept. If you give them a precept, it makes but little impression; if you point out that others are doing something, they imitate without being told to do so. (GD, 8.7).

In the following chapter Comenius further developed the theme of the universality of education from the content perspective. Comenius put it briefly and plainly: "Everyone ought to receive a universal education" (GD, 10.1). But that does not mean that "we demand from all men a knowledge of all the arts and sciences. This would neither be useful of itself, nor, on account of the shortness of life, can it be attained by any man" (GD, 10.1). Comenius had in mind such an education as that of "the principles, the causes, and the uses of all the most important things in existence that we wish all men to learn; all, that is to say, who are sent into the world to be actors as well as spectators. For we must take strong and vigorous measures that no man, in his journey through life, may encounter anything so unknown to him that he cannot pass sound judgment upon it and turn it to its proper use without serious error" (GD, 10.1). In the *Czech Didactic*, Comenius elaborated this theme in greater detail and related the content of education to the previously set goals: a) the goal of rationality refers to the knowledge of the created being (that which is); b) the goal of virtuousness refers to the knowledge of morality (that which ought to be); c) the goal of godliness refers to the knowledge of God's grace (that which is to be enjoyed). These three areas of knowledge then constitute the content of education, which

---

65. It should be noted that the reasons for parental busyness were significantly different than those of today.

enables humans to understand why they were given life: to serve God, other creatures, and themselves (CD, 10).

Such schools, then, would be the "forging-place of humanity."[66] This famous phrase has become a motto in modern Czech schools, but it should be stressed that behind the phrase lies: a) a theological definition of humanity which shapes the general goals of education: a being having a personal relationship with God, a rational being, a self-controlled master of creation, and a being reflecting the glory of God; b) specific reasons for the universality of education: all have fallen into sin and, therefore, all are in need of restoration through education; c) the specific content of education: foundational knowledge of all things necessary for properly serving God, others, and oneself.

In the next chapter Comenius lamented that although there already existed a number of schools and academic institutions, none of them were the kind he proposed and urged. He anticipated that many of his colleagues in the field of education would take such a claim as a personal criticism of their pedagogical performance, therefore he provided a comprehensive warrant for his claim: a) there were not enough schools, b) the existing schools were neither designed for nor intended for everyone, but only for a few, c) the method of teaching resembled "torture" and turned children away from learning, d) the important things were not taught, as evidenced by the loose morals of the pupils despite harsh discipline, e) a verbal approach leading to "parrot-like loquacity" predominated everywhere; pupils were given merely external shells, without an understanding of the core of things and were forced into mindless repetition, f) the problem was most evident in the method of teaching Latin (GD, 11).[67]

METHODOLOGY: GENERAL AND SPECIFIC DIDACTIC

In the following chapters Comenius went on to argue that the situation was not completely lost. The schools could be reformed, and it was both necessary and possible to do so. Comenius was convinced that the reform

66. In the Latin version of the *Great Didactic* Comenius used the phrase "humanitatis officinae."

67. Here Comenius very sharply and colorfully criticized the current method of teaching Latin in the schools, to which he undoubtedly had a right because his famous Latin textbook, comprising his own new methods, had already proven to be extremely successful and effective.

would succeed if it was based on the *natural order of things*. He wrote: "It is now quite clear that that order, which is the dominating principle in the art of teaching all things to all men, should be, and can be, borrowed from no other source but the operations of nature" (GD, 14.7) Therefore, Comenius deduced, if we carefully observe nature *sub specie educationis* (from the educational point of view), it will tell us everything we need to know for proper teaching: a) the order of arranging the educational materials, b) the order of speed and timing, c) the order of method (GD, 12–14). These orders or principles derived from nature constituted the core of the actual didactics which Comenius elaborated in the second part of the book. He arranged the principles into three sets of twenty-nine didactic fundamentals, as he called them (chapters 16–18). The first set is entitled: How to make education certain. The second: How to make education easy. And third: How to make education thorough.[68] Each fundamental was outlined according to the same pattern. For example, in Set 3, Fundamental 7:

1. Comenius first set out the principle of nature, for example: "Nature . . . never begins anything fresh at the expense of work already in hand, but proceeds with what she has begun, and brings it to completion."

2. Then he demonstrated the principle with an example from nature: "For instance, a chicken is not compelled to quit the egg before its limbs are properly formed and set; is not forced to fly before its feathers have grown; is not thrust from the nest before it is able to fly well, etc. A tree, too, does not put forth shoots before it is forced to do so by the sap that rises from the roots."

3. Then Comenius showed how the principle had been broken or neglected in the traditional schools: "Now the faculties of the young are forced: i) if boys are compelled to learn things for which their age and capacity are not yet suited. ii) If they are made to learn by heart or to do things that have not first been thoroughly explained and demonstrated to them.

4. And finally, Comenius proposed a better alternative derived from the first principle: "It follows i) That nothing should be taught to the young unless it is not only permitted, but actually demanded, by their age and mental strength, ii) That nothing should be learned by heart that has not been thoroughly grasped by the understanding . . . iii) That

68. Instead of "thorough" (education), in the *Czech Didactic* Comenius used the term "powerful" explaining that it was "in order to bear abundant benefits."

nothing should be set boys to do until its nature has been thoroughly explained to them, and rules for procedure have been given" (GD, 17.36–38).

In a similar way Comenius deduced all the rest of the principles under the common theme of the teaching methods consistent with the *a priori* character of nature, as he also expressed with his famous motto *omnia sponte fluant, absit violentia rebus*[69] on the title page of his later work, *Opera didactica omnia.*

Before Comenius began to apply his principles and rules in concrete areas, he summarized all the didactic principles in six basic points: "You can easily enlighten someone so they can understand even the most hidden things if:

1. you prepare—with gusto, appeals, and a careful approach—every learner to see things,

2. step by step you lead him from the closer things to those farther away, from the more well-known to the less well-known,

3. you paint before his eyes everything he has to learn (if it is not possible to have the actual living thing), for him to touch, smell, taste, hear, to get to know them with his own senses,

4. and only after that you talk about them, what they are, where they are from, what and when they are for; how, why, and for how long they can be used, and so on, always speaking briefly, simply and understandably,

5. you ask often whether you are understood, and to refresh his spirit commend him; where he didn't understand correctly, explain more fully and repeat a second and third time, asking (always in a friendly, courteous and homey manner) the source.

6. Finally, if you always lead from the general to the particular, first summarizing the whole thing and then analyzing in more detail part by part to the end, or as needed" (CD, 20.6).

Miroslav Cipro has translated these principles into modern language in the following terms: 1) interest, 2) gradualness, 3) clarity, 4) verbalization, 5) feedback, 6) application. The individual principles essentially correspond to the pedagogical attributes of procedural, psychological, empirical

---

69. "Let everything flow naturally (spontaneously), let there be no violence."

and practical. The fact that Comenius was able to capture these patterns long before Herbart and all of modern pedagogical science, Cipro regarded as "remarkable."[70]

However archaic, flowery and poetic are the formulations of the didactic fundamentals, it is clear that Comenius was an excellent observer of nature. His pictures are didactically pertinent, functional and timeless. It is evident that he was able to identify the principles that modern pedagogy only much later has experientially discovered and verified.

The three sets mentioned previously are further supplemented by eight principles of conciseness and rapidity in teaching, which are structured somewhat differently. Comenius did not offer fundamentals here, but raised eight problems put into questions, to which responses were provided. The problems were, for example, How can one teacher teach a number of boys, no matter how many, at one time? How is it possible for all the scholars to be taught from the same book? How can many things be explained in just a few words?

It is both unnecessary and impossible to describe all the fundamentals in detail, for they constitute about one-third of the book.[71] However in summary it can be said that all the fundamentals are based on the same principle of analogy to nature, and they have three characteristics in common:

a) Consistency in the correlation of things and their names—the senses (as many as possible) must be involved in the process of learning; the things themselves must be learned together with their names.

b) Appropriateness of the phasing and the progression of teaching, which are determined by the individual aspects of a child's development.

c) Suitability and pleasantness of the teaching method, which is determined not only by the proper choice of the learning matter, but also by the proper (nonviolent) methodological treatment of the matter.

In the following chapters, 20, 21, and 22, Comenius applied these general didactic principles to the specific methodology for teaching arts, sciences, and languages.

70. Cipro, *Prameny výchovy*, 410.
71. For an outline of all the principles, see Appendix 2.

INSTRUMENTS: MORALS, PIETY, DISCIPLINE

At the beginning of chapter 23 Comenius explained that everything which had preceded was only the "beginning," and not the main work. The main work was "that study of wisdom which elevates us and makes us steadfast and noble-minded . . . and draw nigh to God Himself" (GD, 23.1), which are the goals that the author announced at the very beginning of the book. In chapter 10 Comenius wrote that an education which is not held together by the "unbreakable union" of morality and piety, is a "wretched" education. "For what is literary skill without virtue?" Comenius raised the rhetorical question and immediately answered with a reference to the old proverb: "He who makes progress in knowledge but not in morality . . . recedes rather than advances." And thus, what Solomon said of the beautiful but foolish woman, holds good of the learned man who possesses not virtue: *As a jewel of gold in a swine's snout, so is a fair woman which is without discretion*" (GD, 10.17). The importance that Comenius attached to moral education calls for a detailed examination.[72]

Comenius started by presenting the so-called "fundamental virtues" that should be taught at school. Without them, the "building" would be "without a foundation." There are four traditional virtues: prudence, temperance, valor, and courage (*prudentia, temperantia, fortitudo, iustitia*). They have been passed down as the cardinal virtues since antiquity.[73] Comenius clarified and expanded individual virtues, but mainly explained the didactic method of their acquisition, which is dealt with in the ten principles. For reasons of brevity and clarity they are summarized here:[74]

1. Virtue is cultivated by deeds, not speeches. For mankind is given life "to spend it in contact with people and in activity." Without virtuous

72. Comenius dealt with the question of morals and ethics as such mainly in the *Moral World* (Mundus moralis), the sixth level of his Pansophy. Detailed notes are spread throughout many of his other works, for example *Informatorium, Cesta světla* etc. The didactic side of morality is thoroughly discussed in the *Didactics*—both *Czech* and *Great*, and briefly also in the *Analytics*.

73. Komenský, *Didaktika velká*, 23. Comenious dealt with this subject more broadly in the *Czech Didactic* than in the *Great Didactic*—here he listed all the individual virtues and gave attention to each one separately. For the question of virtues see also Kreeft (*Ethics*, or *Making Choices*), or MacIntyre, *After Virtue*.

74. The following summary is a compilation of both the *Czech* and the *Great Didactics*. The original six principles that Comenius presented in the *Czech Didactic*, he separated and re-categorized in the *Great Didactic* into ten principles. The questions is whether the re-classification is clearer—some of the principles are overlapping.

actions a person is nothing more than an "unnecessary burden on the earth."

2. Virtue gains strength by being often in communion with virtuous people. An example of this is the education of Alexander, given to him by Aristotle.

3. Virtuous conduct is cultivated by active perseverance. For an appropriately moderate and continual occupation of the mind and body becomes diligence, and thus idleness becomes unbearable in such a person.

4. At the core of all the virtues is service to others. Human nature was spoiled by the terrible self-love that causes "everyone to want all the attention to be devoted almost exclusively to them." Therefore it is necessary to carefully instill the knowledge that "we are not born into this world only for ourselves, but for God and our neighbor."

5. Cultivation of virtue must begin at the earliest age, before "bad habits and vices can begin nesting." As wax and plaster are easy to shape when soft, but when hard "in vain one tries to modify them," so with people most everything depends on the "first skills" that are learned "by the smallest children."

6. Virtue is learned by virtuous conduct. As one learns "to walk by walking, to speak by speaking, to write by writing" etc., so a person learns "to obey by obeying, temperance by delaying [gratification], "truthfulness by speaking the truth" etc.

7. Virtue is learned by example. "For children are like monkeys: what they see, whether good or bad, they immediately want to imitate even when they are told not to, and thus they learn to imitate before they learn to know." Therefore, the teachers must be "living examples."

8. Virtue is also taught by the "preaching" that accompanies the example. Preaching, or instruction, in this case means making sense of the given virtue so the learners understand what they should do, why they should do it, and why they should do it in that way. In the same way "as the barb goads an animal to pull or run, so gentle speaking not only successfully affirms but even goads the mind to run towards virtue."

9. It is necessary to protect children from bad people and influences. Inasmuch as children's minds are easily infected, it is necessary to

remove them from "evil society." We must also, however, avoid lazy people, for one who is idle "learns to do evil, because the mind cannot be empty, if it isn't filled with useful things, it will fill itself with empty, vain and wicked things."

10. Virtue requires discipline. Since fallen human nature reveals itself to be constantly [wandering] "here and there," it is necessary to systematically thwart and discipline it.[75]

It is worth noting Comenius's insight that a tender age is suitable for education to begin. He expressed this principle in the seventh chapter of the *Great Didactic*: "Everything that comes into being, . . . while tender it is easily bent and formed, but . . . when it has grown hard, it is not easy to alter." He goes on to say, using almost developmental-psychological language, that it is also true with people, whose brains, muscles, arms, as well as other members, are best "fit" for "shaping" at an early age.[76] Where piety and morality is concerned Comenius spoke clearly: "If piety is to take root in any man's heart, it must be engrafted while he is still young; if we wish any one to be virtuous, we must train him in early youth" (GD, 7.5).

An important aspect of Comenius's concept of moral education is the relationship between knowledge and virtue. Unlike the holders of the later, modern concept, which, under the Enlightenment paradigm assumed that the development of science and knowledge would be automatic factors in the process of the moral refinement of humankind,[77] Comenius wasn't convinced that knowledge alone could lead one to virtue. Just the opposite. Precisely because knowledge is not guaranteed to bring morality, it must be accompanied by moral education. When that does not happen, it goes against human nature, an "unhappy tugging," because people are not only given to "be knowing beings" but also to use their knowledge for good (and thus also worship their Creator). A person who doesn't use their knowledge in a moral way is not truly educated; one might know a lot, but without

75. Comenius provided a closer analysis of the methods of discipline later in chapter 26.

76. For more on the concept of "shaping" compare the section with the subtitle *formare* in *Mundus moralis*.

77. After all, *scientia potentia est* (knowledge is power), as we already know from Francis Bacon. However, within the Enlightenment paradigm, this idea changed somewhat and they began to believe that someone who knows properly will also act properly. Several authors have criticized this approach; see for example Bauman, *Individualizovaná společnost*, 147; Wilson, *Classical Christian Education*.

morality one is a "useless burden on the land," even a "disaster"—to oneself and to others, for the more knowledge one has, the worse it is when it is used for evil. Therefore Comenius said that a humanity which is learned but immoral marches "to the rear" instead of going "forward," and thus degenerates. In contrast, the "workshop of humanity" consciously strives for regeneration, i.e., a rebirth of all dimensions of humanity—intellectual, character, and spiritual (that is, knowledge, morals, and piety).

I argue with Peter Menck's interpretation of the relationship between knowledge and virtue, when in his treatise on the formation of conscience he suggested that Comenius believed in "moral automatism by which conscience follows knowledge—provided that the knowledge is true." Menck arrived at this conclusion from his interpretation of Comenius's illustrations in the *Orbis Pictus*. However, I believe this is a hasty conclusion which does not take into account others of Comenius's didactics writings. If Comenius believed that morality came automatically with right knowledge, it would be logical that his *Didactics* focus only on the level of cognitive education. But the fact that alongside intellectual education Comenius insisted on moral education and wove into it his most thorough methodological principles, speaks against Menck's interpretation.[78]

The interdependence between morality and piety cannot be overlooked in Comenious's moral education. What he presented only implicitly in the preceding chapters, in chapters 23 and 24 he makes explicit. The chapter on morals is immediately complemented by the following chapter whose subject is "the imparting of piety." Comenius stated that piety is a special, supernatural "gift from God," but added that God also uses "regular" (natural) means for His grace. In such cases He uses parents, teachers, and the clergy as His helpers. Guidance towards true piety should be an integral part of scholastic education. Comenius reiterated that by piety he meant the ability of the heart "to seek God everywhere . . . and when we have found Him we should follow Him, and when we have attained Him should enjoy Him." He further reminded us that "the first we do through our understanding, the second through our will, and the third through the joy arising from the consciousness of our union with God" (GD, 24.2). There are given to us three sources of piety: *The Holy Scriptures, the world, and ourselves*: to draw piety from these sources we have to dedicate ourselves to careful reading, observation and meditation (GD, 24.3–5). To grow in piety we are given *contemplation, prayer and temptation* (understand that

78. For more information see Menck, "Formation of Conscience," 261–75.

as refining), by which, according to Comenius, believers become "true Christians" (GD, 21.6–9). Piety, however, may not be merely "a matter of the lips and words," it must be based in a "living faith," which is testified to by appropriate actions (GD, 24.23), for true *prudence*—one of the cardinal virtues—consists rather in actions than in knowledge. It isn't difficult to know what one should do, but it is difficult to do it," Comenius added in one of his later works.[79]

It is also worthy of mention that Comenious considered it to be utterly obvious that morals and piety can be taught. He stated it clearly in the *Pampaedia*: "it is manifestly evident that even piety itself is teachable" (GD, 3.47). At the same time, for Comenius "natural" teachability in no way rules out a "supernatural" action of God. Comenius recognized the necessity of a spiritual rebirth, which is a prerequisite for any piety and which is given to humanity by grace alone.[80] He also assumed that true grace "does not disturb nature but renews, improves and completes it."[81] Therefore according to Comenius it is quite legitimate to use natural tools for teaching morals and piety. The educational process, however, must not be "violent" or "rough," but is rather to be carried out in the spirit of "prudence," "kindness" and "freedom."[82] For this is the same way in which the Creator Himself relates to His creation."[83]

One of the key sources for cultivating morality and piety is, according to Comenius, the Scriptures (as has already been noted), and therefore he dealt with that in the very next chapter, chapter 25. Here Comenius recommended using the Bible in education rather than pagan books (the ancient classics). It does not mean that he would refuse the classics altogether, just that they shouldn't be the first influence to which a youth is exposed. He admitted that pagan literature contains much wisdom, which in many ways agrees with Scripture. This wisdom should be looked for, gathered and used, as Comenius often did in his writings. But at the same time this literature contains much "immorality, wickedness and blindness" (CD, 25.7)

79. Comenius, *Mundus moralis*, 2.5. One of the seven books of the *Obecná porada* is Pansofie [Pansophy], which is divided into several sections, one of which is Mundus moralis.

80. With this statement Comenius professed his commitment to the reformist tradition of orthodoxy. See Comenius, *Mundus spiritualis*, 7 (another section of the Pansofie book in *Obecná porada*).

81. Comenius, *Mundus spiritualis*, 7.6.

82. Comenius, *Pampaedia*, 3.46.

83. Compare Comenius, *Mundus spiritualis*, 7.2.

which only a trained spirit can recognize, so this literature is not suitable for young people.[84]

The final chapter (26) in this part of the book deals with school discipline, which was already mentioned in chapter 23 in connection with the cultivation of morals. There is no dispute about the need for discipline in schools. Comenius stated this fact by beginning his treatise on discipline with the following old Czech proverb: "A school without discipline is like a mill without water." But it does not follow that the school should be "full of shouting, wounds and stripes, rather it should be full of attentiveness and care on the sides of both teachers and pupils. The basic didactic motto still applies: "Let everything flow naturally (spontaneously); let there be no violence."

In his book *Analytic Didactic*, then, Comenius applied this principle with the words: "We wish that beatings and anger were far from such a sacred thing as the education of the spirit."[85] An educated spirit is a disciplined spirit and at the same time, if teachers are to help the students to attain this desired goal, it is necessary that they themselves thoroughly understand a) the purpose, b) the substance and c) the method of discipline; that is, that they know why, when and how to discipline.

Comenius regarded discipline as very important, if the educator wants to reach the educational goal. An educator must have clearly in mind why discipline is needed and what the goal is in using it. That children often misbehave and "it is necessary to discipline those who sin" is without debate for Comenius. However the reason for disciplining is not "because they sinned," he emphasized, "but so that they will not sin later." With such a goal as this, then, discipline is to be used "without passion, anger or hatred, but with such honesty and sincerity that the one being disciplined knows it is for his good and it is being done with a fatherly love . . . and therefore accepts it as one receives any bitter medicine from a doctor." The purpose of discipline should therefore, according to Comenius, be primarily a

---

84. Some of Comenius's statements concerning the classics, such as Ovid, Lucianus, Diogenes, and Aristotle, led some interpreters (e.g., F. X. Šalda) to the conclusion that Comenius was an "enemy of the antique" as such. That, however, is a very artificial reading of Comenius, for throughout all his work, there are virtually hundreds of quotations from the classics used as validations of his arguments. The same attitude can be observed also in Comenius's late *Věječka moudrosti* [Pinnacle of wisdom], where in paragraph 38, he shows in contemporary examples how pagan literature turned a number of people, including the Swedish queen Christina, away from the truth. For more details on this subject, see Kumpera, *Jan Amos Komenský*, 183–84.

85. Comenius, *Didaktika analytická*, 42.

preventive measure, and its use is to be understood by both sides. Both teacher and student must understand why the discipline is being used.

It is worth noting Comenius's pschological insight, that awareness of the ultimate goal of discipline dampens the temper of the educator. The impulsiveness, anger or sudden rage which disciplinary situations usually bring about, the teacher or parent can manage better if it is clear what the educational aim is. The rage called forth by injustice, humiliation or the decimation of the child is a manifestation of the failure of the educator, and leads nowhere. The goal of discipline is to help the child be better—to be a better person. It is not about the teacher, nor in a certain sense is it about the student either. Comenius was neither teacher-centric nor pupil-centric. It is about education itself, namely, about humanity. The awareness of such a goal significantly influences the means of achieving it, as well as the teacher herself. The ultimate goal of Comenius's education, and thus also discipline, is the formation of authentic humanity. Let us remember Comenius's dictum that "if a man is to become humane, it is necessary that he be formed by education" (CD, 6).[86] Discipline towards humanity then, must always be humane and a good educator is aware of it.

The second aspect of discipline is the subject of disciplining itself, and it can be two-fold:

1. If the disorderly student in question has no interest in studies, Comenius advocated restraint in discipline. A student's lack of interest in studying is, in Comenius's view, not a problem with the student but with the teacher. "For if learning is properly arranged, that is in itself an attraction to the spirit and its sweetness attracts and captivates all (with the exception of a human monster). If it is otherwise, it is not the fault of the student, but the teacher. If we don't know how to artificially lure the spirit, we surely use force in vain. Wounds and beatings don't help instill a love for learning, but are the very cause of a dislike for it."

2. If, however, it's about moral wrongdoing, Comenius advised more vigorous action. Examples of such misbehavior include: obscenity, defiance, stubborn malice, pride, arrogance and other evidences of wickedness. Why is it necessary to come strongly against these offenses? Because moral transgressions "offend the magnificence of God and

---

86. Be careful not to confuse this statement of Comenius with the somewhat deterministic one of Kant, which comes out of a different intellectual context: "One can become a human only by education. People are nothing other than what their education makes them." See Kant, O výchově, 34.

uproot the foundation of all virtues." Comenius knew that without virtue or moral standards, not only schools but all of human society would become like a mill without water. It wouldn't work. Therefore he advised the "reconciliation" of these offenses by the "strictest punishment." What did he mean by that? Comenious provided the answer in the following paragraph where he discussed the third aspect of discipline, which is the method.

Comenius distinguished three, or four, means of discipline, which basically reflect what today we would call progressive penalizing. As an illustration he used the sun, "which gives to everything that grows a) light and heat, continuously b) rain and wind, frequently, c) thunder and lightning, but seldom."[87]

Similarly a teacher will best hold the youth to their work if she a) herself is a continual and living example to show what it requires, b) frequently uses instructive words to admonish and sometimes even chasten them so none would become corrupt, c) seldom uses the harshest means, physical. For these extreme methods Comenius used the Latin term "violentia remedia" At the same time, however, he noted that it is necessary "to beware to not use those extreme methods for any and every insignificant reason, or they will be worn out before an extreme case is encountered." In addition Comenius again emphasized that when a teacher must resort to extreme measures, he should "remove every bitter tone from his voice, every angry expression from his face and every bit of cruelty from each blow, so the student will be convinced that the teacher isn't behaving out of angry resentment, but has the student's good in mind."[88]

As the very last stage of discipline for those who have "such an unfortunate nature that no milder method is enough," Comenius allowed removal of that individual from the school, so they wouldn't corrupt the others or be an obstacle for them. A child excluded from the educational process was, however, Comenius's greatest sorrow, because for him education has soteriological, that is, salvific, significance. Education is part of the "emendatio rerum humanarum," that is, the remedy for human affairs, as Comenius wrote later. Everyone needs an education which will discipline their human tendency to sin. The one who is the least disciplined is precisely the one who needs education the most. They need to be made nobler, better, more

---

87. The natural philosophy underlying Comenius' pedagogical principles is clearly conditioned by the climatic zone in which he lived.

88. Comenius, *Didaktika analytická*, 42.

humane.[89] Therefore, Comenius urged teachers to "try everything rather than leave someone like dirt, unfit for education and consider them lost."

In conclusion, Comenius emphasized that every method of discipline must be such that pupils "can also know how to love and respect their teachers, and to not only enjoy being taken to the place where they can be taught, but also ardently desire it themselves." In summary, "discipline must strive to ensure that in everything and through everything is awakened a reverence for God, a willingness to help one's neighbor and a vibrancy and liveliness in doing their work, and that all of these qualities be strengthened by their continual use and application."

STRUCTURE: THE SYSTEM OF EDUCATION

The last part of the book (chapters 27–31) deals with the organizational aspect of education. It is interesting, but not surprising, that for the formal complexity of his educational system Comenius again drew inspiration from nature. Based on observations of physical growth he distinguished four main developmental stages of young people, and proposed four types of schools: a) nursery school—for those up to age six, b) basic or grammar school—from six to twelve, c) secondary (Latin) school—from twelve to eighteen, d) academia (university) from eighteen to twenty-four.

As for curriculum, Comenius proposed a very innovative concept:

> These different schools are not to deal with different subjects, but should treat the same subjects in different ways, giving instruction in all that can produce true men, true Christians, and true scholars; throughout graduating the instruction to the age of the pupil and the knowledge that he already possesses. (GD, 27.4)

In other words, Comenius suggested that pupils are to be taught essentially the same content or forms of knowledge at each of the four school stages, because these correspond to both human nature and pupils' continuing needs. The difference between the stages lies mainly in the amount of and the way in which the knowledge is mediated (presented) to the learners. In the first stage, things must be learned primarily via the senses. In the second, the training of senses ought to be complemented by practical educational activities ("manual training"), such as writing, reading, counting, measuring, singing, memorizing; all is to happen in the mother tongue. In

---

89. Compare Palouš's conception of *e-ducatio* in Palouš, *Čas výchovy*, 63–64.

the third stage, abstract thinking ought to be taught, together with Latin. Lastly, the university studies should provide a scholarly (scientific) education, including also the gaining of experience.

Piaget's observation that Comenius's division of schools according to level of knowledge, previous knowledge and individual qualifications very well anticiplated the findings of modern developmental psychology, which has established that learning actually occurs through a gradual reconstruction of the same information corresponding to individual developmental stages. Comenius's proposal to proceed from fundamental cognitive activities to simple representations to conscious reflection was ahead of the theory of consecutive development.[90]

In concrete terms his curriculum covered twenty areas and subjects, which were to be studied at each of the four stages: 1) Metaphysics, 2) Physics, 3) Optics, 4) Astronomy, 5) Geography, 6) Chronology, 7) History, 8) Arithmetic, 9) Geometry, 10) Statics, 11) Mechanics, 12) Dialectics, 13) Grammar, 14) Rhetoric, 15) Poetry, 16) Music, 17) Economy, 18) Politics, 19) Ethics, 20) Religion. It may sound curious to teach, for example, metaphysics in a nursery school, but Comenius explained that children encounter the foundations of metaphysics as soon as they "begin to understand such general expressions as: something, nothing, is, is not, the same, contrary, where, when, similar, dissimilar, etc." Thus parents and teachers, even in the early stage, quite naturally introduce children to the basics of metaphysics by showing, naming, and relating things. As the child's capability to comprehend the concepts grows in the following stages, the treatment of the subject ought to deepen and go into greater detail.

At the end of the chapter (GD, 31.15) Comenius proposed the interesting idea of founding a "school of schools," where the best scholars could dedicate all their time and energy to studies for the sake of the rest of society, which is, in fact, a description of the foundational objective of the contemporary institution called the Academy of Sciences.[91]

In the Conclusion of the book the author showed how his *Didactic* could be used for the good of the whole society. He compared his invention to that of the printing press. The old method was slow, time-consuming, inaccurate and ineffective, while the new method had the exact opposite

90. Piaget, *Jan Amos Comenius*, 173–96.

91. Comenius further developed this idea in his *Via lucis*, written in England. Interestingly, the idea was first implemented when The Royal Academy of Sciences was founded in England in 1668, which was still during Comenius' lifetime.

characteristics. However in order to implement his project the cooperation of the key leaders of the nation was required. That is why Comenius addressed the learned, the theologians, and the politicians, whom he encouraged towards restorative action.

CRITICAL SUMMARY

Before moving to the final phase in the development of Comenius's thought, we must conclude this "didactic" phase with several analytical observations related to the anthropological questions. To summarize the main points of Comenius's didactic project, we have seen that he outlined four key pedagogical issues: 1) the foundations of the educability of human beings; 2) general and specific didactic methodology; 3) instruments for the implementation of educational goals; 4) the organization of the educational system.

The first part is the result of the synthesis of Brethren theology with the ideas of Cusanus and Campanella. From the Brethren tradition came Comenius's notion of the human being as both ontologically "noble" and teleologically "nesamosvojný," meaning that they are part of God's created reality: not self-existing or self-sustaining and not having their ultimate goal within themselves. Further, soteriologically humans are in a fallen condition; they were originally perfect, "the most perfect of all creation," but they turned away from their Creator; they lost their "nexus hypostaticus," their personal relationship with God, and consequently lost their harmonious state. The original harmony of human nature is, however, not completely destroyed; it is revealed by "general revelation"—the natural human tendency and desire for harmony. Moreover, it is confirmed by "special revelation," the Scripture: Jesus Christ came to provide restoration and salvation for lost humanity.

Comenius found such a theology perfectly consistent with Campanella's idea of the unity and harmony of the universe, and with Cusanus's concept of the world as a school. Thus Patočka commented that in Comenius's anthropology "a human being appears to be an unfinished being, a being that is constantly developing and self-transcending, . . . who is never content with anything partial and particular."[92] For Comenius a human being is a learner in the school of the world, in which "the particularities of this world prepare him for comprehension of the universal, undivided, and

92. Patočka, *Komeniologické studie 1*, 48.

non-fragmented truth."[93] Thus, the universal character of his educational project was revealed; it was not to produce a method which would more easily equip individuals with specific knowledge or skills, but to contribute to the "restoration of paradise," a united harmonious universe, which required recovery of the corrupted condition of humankind caused by their turning away from God.[94] In other words, pedagogical teleology is determined by anthropological teleology.

The actual didactic methodology, which was outlined in the second part of the book and then applied to all other aspects of education (the teaching of specific subjects and school organization), was derived from "the operations of nature," as we have seen. The influence of F. Bacon's inductive method is evident here. However, Comenius adjusted Bacon's method to his understanding of a harmonic universe. "The harmony is not just a contingent accident of being, but a transcendental attribute, without which no existence can be. It is God's deposit of his idea which enables the fellowship of all beings to bear witness—each being in its own way—about the same thing, and thus find God's message everywhere," as Palouš interpreted him.[95] Holding the notion of the unity and harmony of the universe, Comenius strove for a unified system of knowledge that would integrate all three sources or "books" of knowledge available to human beings—the world (cosmos), the human being (micro-cosmos), and the Scripture (faith).[96] Providing the whole universe rests on common principles, things which cannot be known directly (by induction) might be derived by comparison and analogy from the other sources, which is exactly what Comenius did in his formulation of both the general and specific didactic principles. He brought the parallel sources into line with each other—in one source (nature), which is endowed with an educative character, he found—via analogy—instructions for the other source, the world of human beings. "What

---

93. Patočka, *Mezihra na prahu*, 33.

94. Hence we can understand why Comenius considered all his work to be primarily theological, not pedagogical. In his *Opera didactica omnia*, Comenius said: "Ego quae pro Iuventute scripsi, non ut Peadagogus scripsi, sed ut Theologus" [Whatever I have written for the youth, I wrote not as a pedagogue, but as a theologian.]. See *Opera didactica omnia*, vol. 4, 27.

95. Palouš, *Komenského Boží svět*, 24.

96. The concepts of macrocosm and microcosm refer to the old Zoroastrian conception of the world as one organic whole. It was brought into the Western mind through Neoplatonism. Comenius became acquainted with it through Cusanus, Paracelsus, Böhm and others.

nature writes in capital letters is written in human beings in small letters," summarized John Darling and Sven Erik Nordembo.[97]

It is clear then, that Comenius adopted Bacon's induction as only one component of a wider synthetic method. He recognized its strength, but on its own he considered it too partial, since we have three reliable sources of knowledge which complement each other. Patočka rightly inferred that Comenius did not comprehend the actual meaning of Bacon's method; he did not fully grasp that Bacon wanted to allow the things themselves to speak independently of any human presuppositions or speculations.[98] Nevertheless Bacon helped Comenius to see that a new unified science, which he strove for, would require a unified method. The new method, which Comenius developed and called syncrisis, was a synthetic adaptation of Campanella's concept of the three sources of knowledge, together with Cusanus's concept of general harmony.[99] Thus, according to Patočka, Comenius's method is, in effect:

> A method of discovery, meant as a technical demonstration which explicates what has been proven or established as true; it is a posteriori and a priori at the same time because it relies as much on factual experience as on the antecedent inventory of the mind. It is made possible by the foundational idea of general harmony, which explicates itself in all reality, in the objective nature as well as in the human subject. The method is essentially synthetic, but it includes an analysis and induction as its dependent component.[100]

In other words, Comenius's "scientific" methodology wasn't truly scientific in the modern sense of the word. Comenius did not fully understand Bacon's forward looking, methodological requirement. Rather he incorporated it into his—original—but otherwise wholly speculative system that was typical of pre-modern thought.

The fact that such a "backward" foundation gave rise to so many "progressive" ideas, even to the timeless pedagogical system, is both confusing and fascinating at the same time—and we will therefore return to it at the end. At this point suffice it to note that Comenius's non-modern philosophical base gave rise to very modern didactics. Modern Comeniology has thoroughly dealt with the "modernity" of Comenius's pedagogy, from

97. Darling and Nordembo, "Progressivism," 291.

98. Patočka, *Komeniologické studie 1*, 187–88.

99. For further details on syncretism, see Kyrášek, *Synkritická metoda*.

100. Patočka, *Komeniologické studie 1*, 188.

a variety of perspectives: psychological, literary, linguistic, sociological, political and others. The characteristics of Comenius's system for which he is traditionally praised and admired can be summarized into several basic areas:[101]

1. Systematic thoroughness. Darling and Nordembo state that Comenius found inspiration for all aspects of education in nature, namely, for its phases, progression, manner, and matter.[102] Thus, he covered the key areas of pedagogical science, which in itself is considered to be one of the greatest contributions to pedagogy. Vlastimil Pařízek affirmed this when he said that

> the didactic system, which was founded on the defined role of education, included all the basic issues of educational work: there are both the goals and the elements of education as such, the choice and content of education are elaborated, the conditions and the process of learning and teaching are analyzed, the school system and organization of learning are worked out, and the methodology of teaching is developed. Thus Comenius created an entire and unified system of education and elucidated its main interrelations. In doing so he founded pedagogy as a scientific discipline.[103]

J. Patočka saw Comenius's didactic project in a similar light:

> In spite of the fact that the educational instruments are not derived from an objectively exact causal analysis of the educational process, there is delineated a complete conceptual program of the pedagogical discipline: there are developed all its basic categories, relations, and relevant problems. In this sense, he is indeed a founder of pedagogy as a science, that art of teaching all people all things.[104]

2. Psychological integrity. The truthfulness of Comenius's psycho-didactic insights fascinated a number of scholars. Jean Piaget, for example,

---

101. Please note that the following paragraphs are merely summaries of significant amounts of material. For more information about Comenius's system from the pedagogical perspective see for example Schaller, *Die Pädagogik*; Čapková, *Některé základní principy*; Patočka, J. *Komeniologické studie 1*, 164–78; Pařízek, "Pedagogická soustava"; Srogoň, *Comenius's Basic Principles*, 107–11; Marklund, *School Stages*.

102. Darling and Nordembo, "Progressivism," 291.

103. See Pařízek, "Pedagogická soustava," 53; Compare Tichý, "S J. A. Komenským," 12–13.

104. Patočka, *Komeniologické studie 1*, 282.

observed that "if we go into the details of [Comenius's] theory of education based on spontaneous development, we are struck by the modern sound of a whole series of statements, despite the absence of a clear-cut theory of the relationship between action and thought."[105] Comenius did not cover the field exhaustively of course, but with "remarkable intuition," according to Piaget, he formulated a number of principles enhancing the educational process from the psychological point of view, such as the dependence between cognitive functions and activity, the principle of positive and affective motivation, the principle of consecutive development, aspects of the facilitation/inhibition of the educational process, and the principle of teacher/learner cooperation.[106] Piaget even regarded Comenius as "the predecessor of the idea of developmental psychology and the founder of the system of progressive instruction adjusted to the stage of development the pupil has reached."[107] J. Patočka also said that he could not deny the didactic timelessness of the following: the principle of realism, the principle of things before words and words as helpful tools, the principle of visual instruction, the principle of learning with understanding, the principle of proceeding from the concrete to the abstract and also from the whole to the parts, from the simple to the complex and from easy to difficult, the fundamental principle of periodicity, etc.[108] Václav Kulič spoke similarly when he observed in Comenius's didactics "much [that is] stimulating, which anticipates and confirms some of the current tendencies and approaches in the sphere of the psychology of learning and its management.[109] And in the same way, when studying Comenius's instructions for leading the actual learning process Cipro found the individual elements of the process to be "logical and psychologically integral."[110] Still other Comeniologists have described Comenius's psycho-didactic principles as an example of "timeless pedagogical realism."[111]

105. Piaget, *Jan Amos Comenius*, 173–96.

106. See also Srogoň, "Comenius's Basic Principles," 107–11; Marklund, *School Stages*, 55–63; Čapková, *Impact of J. A. Comenius*, 11–28.

107. Piaget, *Jan Amos Comeniu*, 173–96.

108. Patočka, *Komeniologické studie 1*, 48.

109. Kulič, *J. A. Comenius*, 177.

110. Cipro, *Prameny výchovy*, 410.

111. See Kratochvíl, "Pedagogický realismus," 123–31.

3. Democracy. This is, of course, a term Comenius would not have used, but the universal aspect of his system brought about practical implications which many contemporary scholars have called "democratic." Dagmar Čapková interpreted Comenius's well-known didactic motto, *omnes, omnia, omneno,* as the foundation of his democratism, for *omnes* stands for all people, who ought to learn and be taught *omnia,* that is, everything necessary, in all possible ways (*omneno*), in order to live in harmony.[112] Moreover, Čapková saw the roots of Comenius's democratism already existing in the Hussite and Brethren traditions: "The characteristic feature of the Hussite and the Brethren movement was the conviction that the corruption of human beings might be restored and that humans are able to participate in the process of restoration. . . . That is naturally related to the social and widely democratic character of the remedial endeavor."[113] Piaget further observed that the democratic inclusion of all people went even deeper: Comenius was not merely pleading for the girls and the poor, but for everyone—indeed, for the "naturally dull and stupid." They must not be excluded; on the contrary, "The slower and the weaker the disposition of any man, the more he needs assistance. . . . Nor can any man be found whose intellect is so weak that it cannot be improved" (GD, 9.4), which is an approach that Piaget found to be "astonishingly prophetic."[114] A number of other Comeniologists, both Czech and foreign, and interestingly, both communist and non-communist, have similarly marveled at and appreciated the democratic character of Comenius's didactics.[115]

4. Organizational complexity. "The architecture of a system in which a parallel is established between man and a perpetually formative nature inspires not only a functional system of education but also a conception of the general organization of education,"[116] said Piaget. One of the practical outcomes of Comenius's didactic work, at a time when education had neither stable institutions nor general programs of study, was his confident proposal for both. As we saw in the fourth

112. Čapková, "Demokratizmus," 19–22.

113. Ibid, 16.

114. Piaget, *Jan Amos Comenius,* 173–96.

115. See for example Patočka, *Úvod do prvního svazku,* 16; Karšai, "Democratizmus," 3–5; Čuma, *Vztah ruskej;* Cipro, *Prameny výchovy,* 410; Tichý, "S J. A. Komenským," 10.

116. Piaget, *Jan Amos Comenius,* 173–96.

part of his *Didactics*, he outlined a complex rational administrative structure, together with the fourfold curricular program. From an organizational point of view, the system was based on a twofold unity: horizontal unity in respect to curricula at a given educational level and vertical unity in the hierarchy of stages of education.[117] Cipro considered such a "systematic approach" to all details of the organizational aspects of education to be "far ahead of its time."[118] Sixten Marklund viewed it likewise, saying that "the organization Comenius proposed was implemented in the national basic school systems about 200 years later, and with slight variations it continues to be applied in the majority of school systems."[119]

117. Ibid.
118. Cipro, *Prameny výchovy*, 404.
119. Marklund, *School Stages*, 55.

CHAPTER 5

Pampaedia

Teach Everything, to Everyone,
Using Every Possible Means

Pampaedia, or universal education, is the universal refinemenet of the whole human race. . . . It is for the purpose of educating πάντες, πάντα, παντώς [all people, in all areas, broadly]. That desire is divided into three parts. The first thing we wish is that not only one person, or some or many of them could be educated fully and to full humanity, but all people together. . . . Secondly we wish that every man should be integrally educated and properly trained not only in a single thing or a few things or even many things, but in everything which completes the essence of humanity. . . . And do that broadly, so that every person would be made as similar as possible to God (in whose image they are created), that is, to be truly reasonable and wise, truly active and alert, truly moral and honest, truly pious and holy, and thus truly happy and blissful, now and forever.

Obecná porada o nápravě věcí lidských, Pampaedia

BIOGRAPHICAL CONTEXT: DYING MOTHER UNITAS FRATRUM AND PANEMENDATION

After the destruction of Lezsno in 1656 Comenius had to once again see a new refuge both for himself and for the scattered "dying mother" church, the Unitas Fratrum. There came a number of invitations from friends from all over Europe.[1] The dispersed remnants of the Brethren had found new homes in Upper Silesia, Hungary, Lusatia and Brandenburg.[2] Comenius himself accepted the invitation of Lawrence de Geer, the descendant of Comenius's old friend and former patron Louis de Geer, to settle in Amsterdam. At the decision of the city council, which recognized the significance of the new citizen, Comenius received a regular income and a subsidy toward the completion of his didactic and pansophic works. Encouraged by such support, by the end of 1658 Comenius had published his famous *Opera didactica omnia* [Complete Didactic Works]. It represented a lifetime of his reform thought and activity spanning thirty years of his educational experience. Concurrently with the work on the *Opera didactica omnia*, Comenius continued to labor on his most extensive pansophic masterpiece, the *General Consultation*, which, however, remained unfinished.

Aside from his writing and editorial work Comenius was very active in the service of his dispersed church. He continued to conduct extensive collections for the benefit of the exiles while he also ministered to their spiritual condition. In 1658 he published *Manuálník aneb jádro celé Biblí svaté* [A Manual or The Kernel of the Holy Scriptures], in 1661 a *Hymnal*, and in 1662 *Vyznání víry* [A Confession of Faith], which was an updated reprint of the Confession of 1535. The remainder of his time and energy was dedicated to reworking and editing his previous writings. The purpose of most of them was to make political and religious appeals for peace and universal reform to the European countries, especially Holland, England, Germany, Poland, Hungary, and Bohemia.

The close of Comenius's life was clouded by numerous disputes which prevented him from focusing on his major work. Perhaps the most disappointing controversy for Comenius was the criticism of Samuel des Martes

1. He even received an offer from the members of Oliver Cromwell's circle to settle the exiles in Ireland, but Comenius refused it, being aware of the unstable situation in the British Isles.

2. Comenius was very committed to taking collections for aiding the exiles in various countries where he had some influence or fame. See Spinka, *John Amos Comenius*, 137.

(Samuel Maresius), a French Calvinistic theologian and former student of Comenius, who not only criticized Comenius's pansophy and chiliasm but also unjustly accused him of wheedling money from trusting patrons. This unjust and painful accusation spurred Comenius (fortunately for us) to write a self-justifying autobiography, in which he recounted the details of his life and the motives for his conduct in many historically extremely important details. Further criticism came, for example, from Nicholas Arnold, a former student of Comenius in his Leszno period, which denounced his faith in prophecy. Another was a written conflict with the Polish socianist Daniel Zwiker, who misinterpreted Comenius's irenism and incorporated him into Zwiker's socianist camp. Comenius understandably felt the need to respond to the unwelcome interpretation of his theological position.

Comenius died at work at the age of seventy-eight, on November 15, 1670. On his deathbed he solemnly urged his son Daniel and his closest assistant, Christian Nigrinus, to publish his collection of pansophic works on the improvement of human affairs. I believe that Comenius's biography significantly illuminates his literary work. Faced with lifelong suffering, armed conflicts, religious conflicts and personal tragedies, Comenius did not fall into negative bitterness or revenge, but on the contrary aimed at finding peaceful solutions to the problems of "human affairs." He believed that by such efforts he was participating in God's great restoration plan, which would lead to a positive final outcome of history.

"OMNES, OMNIA, OMNENO": THE PEDAGOGY OF EMENDATION

The final stage of Comenius's thinking is usually referred to as his pansophic or emendational or universal remedy stage.[3] The shift toward pansophy came about as soon as he realized the universal dimension of education. It is true that the universal element was already present in his *Didactics*, for it was built on the idea of the harmonization of various levels of the universe, but its actual application was limited merely to the reformation of

3. The meaning, scope and depth of Comenius' pansophist-emendational work is immense. The aim of this study is not to cover all the works of this period exhaustively. My intention is only to capture the shift in Comenius' anthropological thinking. Thus the brevity of this chapter. The universal dimension of Comenius' masterpiece has been thoroughly dealt with by others: see for example the many texts of Dagmar Čapková, see also Sadler, *J. A. Comenius*, or the relatively recent interesting and thorough study of Comenius by Daniel Murphy, *A Critical Reassessment*.

schools. It took Comenius some time to fully realize the universal potential of his method.[4] In fact, we can observe an overlap of the educational and pansophic phases in Comenius's thinking. It is clear that the purpose of the didactic writings was to remedy the disorders of society, but originally it was only Czech society. Then, during the '30s—because of external political changes and the internal maturing of Comenius's pansophic ideas—the addressee of his writings gradually changed. It was no longer only Czech society but society in general. This shift is apparent in the fact that in 1633 Comenius began to translate (and slightly rework) the *Czech Didactic* (and other writings) into Latin.[5] In the words of Patočka, Comenius's didactic works from this period gradually "yielded to the process of pansophization," which ended in a clear awareness of the "necessity of deepening the idea of the global order of the world."[6] In a letter to Samuel Hartlib in 1638, Comenius indicated he already directly understood education as "an instrument for the pansophic method."[7] Thus the concept of the universal restoration of human affairs was born in Comenius's mind.[8] It was a shift from a latent universalism (in the *Didactics*) to an explicit one, fully elaborated, in his magnum opus *General Consultation*, on which Comenius worked (with several interruptions) until the end of his life.

The focus on universal harmony, expressed in the systematic use of the "pan" prefixes (meaning all), did not mean, however, that education would be put aside in this new phase. On the contrary, education lies in the center of the Consultation; it is even visualized in the way Comenius structured the contents of the work; it has seven parts, with the Pampaedia as the

---

4. Perhaps one of the stimuli was a devastating critique of the *Great Didactics* by Joachim Hübner (1611–63), who belonged to the intellectual circle of Samuel Hartlib. His criticism was aimed at two main concerns: first, all the art of teaching is limited solely to schools, as if outside of school it was of no use; second, since the didactic principles are self-evident, it is unnecessary to derive them from nature. It seems that because of this criticism, Comenius postponed the publication of the *Great Didactics* for more than 20 years.

5. Schaller, *Die Pampaedia*.

6. Patočka, *Komeniologické studie 1*, 405.

7. See Ryba, *Sto listů*, 32.

8. It seems that his stay in England was of great importance in Komenský's development. There he met with acceptance and encouragement from his friends. As a result, he wrote *Via lucis* (The Way of Light) in 1641 and *Consultationis brevissima delineatio* (A Very Brief Description of the Consultation) in 1642, in which he first outlined his pansophic plans.

center of a triad, opened and closed in turn by a threefold introduction and a threefold conclusion. This is how Comenius schematized it:[9]

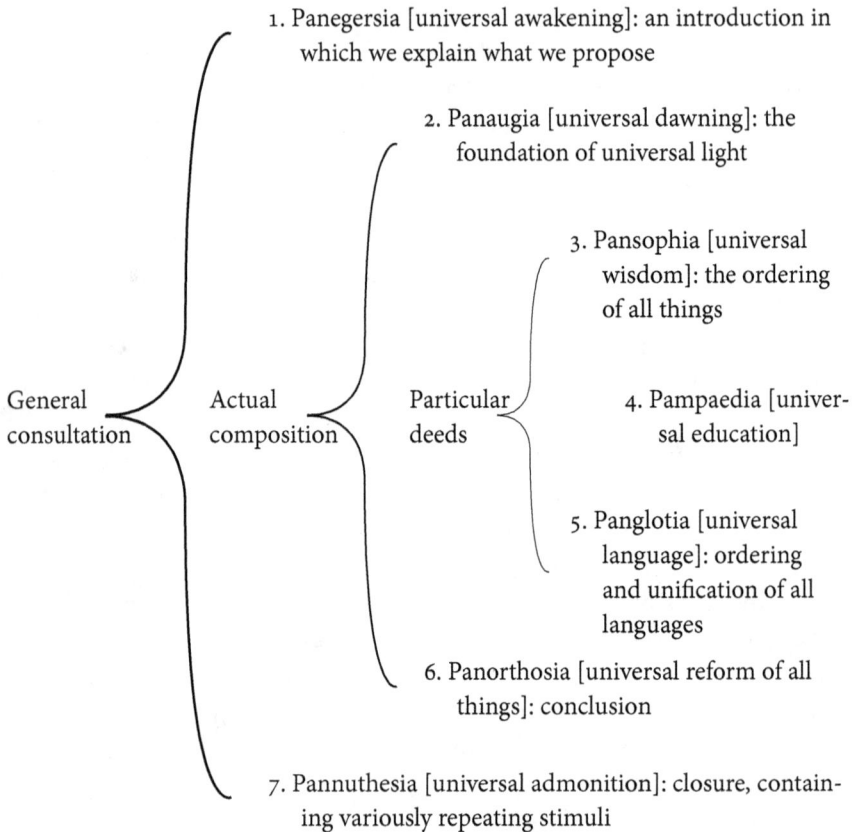

General consultation → Actual composition → Particular deeds →

1. Panegersia [universal awakening]: an introduction in which we explain what we propose

2. Panaugia [universal dawning]: the foundation of universal light

3. Pansophia [universal wisdom]: the ordering of all things

4. Pampaedia [universal education]

5. Panglotia [universal language]: ordering and unification of all languages

6. Panorthosia [universal reform of all things]: conclusion

7. Pannuthesia [universal admonition]: closure, containing variously repeating stimuli

One of the practical results of a method based on the requirement of universal harmony was the art (*ars*) of handling things in accordance with their natural character; it means that human activities should not undermine their basic natural function and designation. Comenius's basic didactic motto expressed it well: *Omnia sponte fluant, absit violentia rebus* (let everything flow spontaneously, without violence).[10] Patočka saw in this notion of *ars* the creative (synergetic) role of human beings, which until Comenius had had no parallel. He did not separate the human being from

9. See Comenius, *Obecná porada*, 69.

10. This motto is written on the first page of Comenius' *Opera Didactica Omnia*. See also *Didaktika analytická*, 42.

the whole. The starting point of his concept was not an isolated human individual, or even the human mind, as it was with Descartes, but universal harmony. If Comenius was up-to-date in anything it was precisely in this, said Patočka, because on the threshold of the modern age Comenius proved almost prophetic in seeing a common danger arising in the subject-object splitting of reality: "fragmentation, self-centeredness, undervaluation of service and overvaluation of control and power, a lack of harmony."[11]

The subject of the *Consultation* is *mundus sub specie educationis* [the world from the educational point of view].[12] Comenius developed the idea of the world as school one step further—nature is endowed with educative keys not merely for the reformation of schools but for the whole of human society. The foundational idea of education as outlined in both *Didactics* remains, but in the *General Consultation* education became pan-education and emendation pan-emendation. The remedy must be universal in every aspect and every area of human endeavor:

> If the human classes are to be restored, the individual people that constitute the classes must be restored; if the individual people are to be restored, the workshops of humanity, the schools, must be first restored; to restore the schools, books, which are to be the appropriate tools of formation, must be first restored; to restore books, it is necessary to restore the method of writing and handling of the books; and finally, if the method is to be fully restored, it is necessary to take heed of the order of things themselves. . . . Thus the foundation of all hope for true restoration of human disorders is the order of things. . . . For in accordance with the laws of things (I repeat), the method of learning things must be reformed, so that books might be reformed through method, school through books, people through schools, human societies through people, so that the whole human generation might be reformed. And thus light and peace with abundance of God's blessing will return to schools, churches, and states.[13]

One of the interesting pedagogical results related to the pansophic shift was the fusion of the idea of *world as a school* with the idea of *life as a school*. We have seen that in the *Didactics* (both *Czech* and *Great*) Comenius outlined four stages of education, ending at age twenty-four. In the *Pampaedia* he added and quite thoroughly elaborated four more schools: the school of

11. Patočka, *Komeniologické studie 2*, 133.

12. Ibid., 199.

13. Comenius, *Obecná porada 3*, 367.

youth, the school of adulthood, the school of old age, and the school of death. The description of the complementary school phases sounds very consistent with previous ones:

> The whole of life is a school, as we have seen in the preceding chapters. Thus also is its middle period, which is characterized by full strength. In fact, this period is the most important part, for the previous ones were but steps on the way to this point. Not moving ahead would mean to decline, especially when there remains so much to be learned, and not only through some preliminary games but through serious behavior. Much might have been received from the schools, but no school could give what this one can, that real touch with things and people throughout the whole life. Certainly they spoke the truth who said: I have learned much from my teachers; more from my schoolfellows, but most from my pupils. For through forming we form ourselves, and only through work do we become masters of work.[14]

Similarly, Comenius considered old age to be very educative. At anytime before, "people might die, but here they have to," which fact gives human beings the opportunity to turn away from the vanishing things, give thanks, and prepare for "embracing death and entering into a new, everlasting life." Comenius recognized that of all fearful things, death is the most fearful, but in faith and full reliance on God, there is no need to fear: "You had no fear when being born; why should you have any fear of dying? In neither of the cases does the decision lie in your hand but in God's."[15] The whole of our earthly life is a lower planting, where we are preparing for "the eternal academy."[16]

The changes observable in Comenius's system during this final period were of "a peculiar kind," wrote Patočka: "it is not a complete replacement of older concepts by new, radically different ones, but rather it is a placement of old schemes into a new context, a context that is to be in principle holistic, general, and unifying."[17] There were some interesting practical implications of the universal shift,[18] but from the anthropological point of

14.. Komenský, *Obecná porada* 3, 123.

15.. Ibid., 135.

16.. Ibid., 141.

17.. Patočka, *Komeniologické studie* 3, 30.

18.. One such implication was the proposal to organize the so-called *Collegium lucis*, which was to be a kind of international ministry for education, for the purpose of overseeing the implementation of the restorative plans for the world.

view, it did not bring about much substantial change in comparison to the previous stage. Human beings were still teleologically rooted in God; men and women were learners in the school of the world (and life) given by God with an educative purpose. What had 'merely' changed was the scope of human activity or engagement within the world. The ultimate goal of all education was still the restoration of fallen human nature, but what was added here was a regard to the whole, for all human affairs are mutually interdependent. The harmony of an individual cannot be attained without the harmony of the whole—as Comenius often expressed in an apropos motto: *Homines omnes sumus, eiusdem mundi cives.*[19]

19.. We are all citizens of one world.

CHAPTER 6

Conclusion

And now, you gathered heads of the world, set this one goal: that your holy congregation would truly be the beginning of a better world! . . . Demonstrate the acts which have already begun to be shown in the whole Consultative work: that it is possible as a whole to care more appropriately and beneficially than as a part. It will happen if you manage (and you certainly can), to unite for the common salvation of the whole human race.

Obecná porada o nápravě věcí lidských, Pannuthesia

THE CURE FOR INCURABLE THINGS

The intention of this book was to show how Comenius's anthropology established and determined his pedagogy of humanization. Based on an analysis of Comenius's key works and their biographical contexts I have identified five stages in the development of Comenius's thinking, each of which was characterized by a specific anthropological accent.[1]

The first, the encyclopedic stage, was dominated by the motif of wonder and amazement. The human being was essentially an observer, a spectator of life, which led to wonder, because reality is a testimony of the

---

1. The number of stages depends on the method of periodization. The stages are defined only relatively; some Comeniologists consider the encyclopedic, consoling and critical periods as only one stage—a preparatory or pre-pansophic one, while others made a distinction between these stages.

Creator's wisdom, justice and power. Who sees well, is educated. "If one cannot see beauty in the world, he sees little . . . ." In this stage, then, a person becomes "truly human" through contemplation and wonder.

As a result of difficult life circumstances there was a shift in Comenius's thinking. In the face of suffering he found solace in "resignation," which was, however, characterized by attributes such as hope and peace, for it flowed from the awareness that we are not left at the mercy of a meaningless fate, but in the care of a good God. In a world of "labyrinths" and "confusion" in which people stray because they are blinded by their sinful self-centeredness, Comenius comforted, taught, and encouraged (himself as well as others) that the centerpoint or the depths of human safety is only in God.

The resignation-consolation phase was largely overlapped and complemented by the allegorical-narrative phase. Here too Comenius sought solace for himself and others, although the methods for attaining his goal were different. He taught through story; that is, by means of narrative allegory he led a person to a "proper soothing of the mind" and the discovery of the "highest good," which is essentially the same as the concept of *resignare*. The form or genre that Comenius used here to communicate his "curriculum" was exceptional. We saw that narrative allegory is a unique didactic tool for a holistic experience of activation, or even transformation, of the reader.

Under the influence of the writings of thinkers like Cusanus, Campanella, Bacon, and others, Comenius's anthropology deepened further. Comenius discovered the educational potential in the nature of the created reality, and subsequently tied it together with human nature. For Comenius the world was the macrocosm and human nature the microcosm. Between the two there is a specific relationship: both are parts of one harmonic universe given in order to educate. A human being is a learner in the school of the world, which teaches her everything necessary for both a good earthly life and a good life to come. Armed with syncrisis—a Bacon-inspired methodology for deriving didactic principles from the operations of nature—Comenius developed his own pedagogical system, whose goal was to recover the corrupted character of humanity as well as society.

The didactic stage somewhat overlapped again with the final stage of development in Comenius's thought, the emendation stage. In this time Comenius came to realize the universal dimension of his educational project. He realized that education had emendative implications not merely for an individual human being or an individual nation but for all humankind, for he understood that the harmony of an individual cannot be attained without the harmony of the whole. Universality and integrity play an important role in the concept of emendation—it is necessary to educate the whole person, the whole of humanity, in every thing that needs correction, by every means available, etc. Through eschatological glasses humanity is also seen as a participant in the historical cyclical process of restoring the original state. The perfect world was thrown into disarray as a result of human actions (Paradise lost), and so also human activity is needed for the remedy (Paradise regained). At this stage therefore, there is not merely a toleration for the filth of this world, but active participation in the remedy. Human beings are and must be not only observers and students of the order of being, but they themselves have become the organizers, that is, those who bring order to the world and thus both continue and complement God's creative activity.

A key finding and contribution of this work is that the anthropological positions include (as a common denominator) the ambivalence of ontological nobility and moral depravity. At every stage Comenius was always peering at humanity as a being who in essential design is excellent because of having been created as *Imago Dei*, but has dubious morality because of falling into "samosvojnosti," that condition in which one finds one's ultimate goal and purpose only in oneself (and as a result, missing one's purpose in life). All of Comenius's emendational and humanizing efforts arose from this basic anthropological assumption. The need for the pedagogical "workshop of humanity" flows from the fact that human affairs are corrupted (morals), but not completely lost (ontology). The goal, content, and method of his humanization flows out of this assumption about human nature.

Before I close this chapter and go to the final exposition of those elements of Comenius's work which are considered relevant to the current debate on educational humanization, I will present some critical remarks arising from my own anthropological reading of Comenius's work.

It is evident that Comenius's notion of the human being, as well as his work in general, arose and was conditioned by the historical circumstances of his time. His *General Consultation* in particular was a monumental attempt to respond to the problematic social, political, and religious situation in which he lived. Nevertheless the general concept of his pan-emendation project was quite ahistorical and static. Comenius did not believe the source of the dismal condition of humankind lay in the changes to the social and cultural structures of society or other similar historic phenomena, as is common in modern interpretations,[2] but in the corruption of the ideal state of things from a metaphysical standpoint. Therefore the remedy would lie in an equally non-historic act of restoration of the original, *a priori*-assumed ideal state of the world. It would restore the connection (*nexus hypostaticus*) of a personal relationship with God. Some commentators consider this the most problematic and unrealistic part of Comenius's work, while others see it as edifying and inspiring.[3]

Another issue is Comenius's "exuberant optimism,"[4] as Jan M. Lochman called it, which no reader can miss. It is expressed not only in his staggering objectives, but also in the ease of their implementation. The truth is that Comenius's optimism "did not spring from the simplistic generalization of a humanistic or rationalistic faith in the potential of natural man in the style of the modern spirit of the age," added Lochman,[5] but rather from his "teleologically motivated orientation," said Molnár. It is therefore an optimism of "grace and hope."[6] In Comenius's defense Lochman further added that his own life story, full of tragic twists and experiences "was itself a sufficient protection against any superficial optimism of a naïve emotional sort."[7]

However, it must also be admitted that Comenius's work contains elements, and not only peripheral ones, which are best described by adjectives such as *unrealistic, utopian, naïve,* or even *fantastic.*[8] Examples of such elements can be found, for example, in the numerical (often triadic) speculations and analogies concerning the order of the universe, mystical explanations of the harmonic nature of reality, the chronological analogies, the chiliastic prophesies, a so on. Another element that belongs here is Comenius's intention to unite all human learning into a set of rules and regulations which would—after approval by a global council of scholars— bring about universal and lasting reconciliation between peoples and reli-

2. See for example Chlup, *Zhodnocení*, 53.

3. To compare the antithetical positions see for example Červenka, "Úvod," 5–53, and Palouš, *Náboženský myslitel*, 7–12.

4. Cited in Lochman, J. M. *Comenius as Theologian*, 45.

5. Ibid.

6. Ibid.

7. Ibid.

8. Compare Patočka, *Komeniologické studie 2*, 271–82.

gions. Consider, for example, what bold and salvific effects (besides other almost miraculous results) Comenius hoped for in the conclusion of his *Pampaedie,*[9] a key part of the *Porada*:

1. The cleansing of Augeias' barn.[10]

2. The opening of the right way to God's paradise.[11]

3. The invention of the spiritual printing press: not impressing wisdom onto paper, but onto people's hearts.

4. The discovery of the true perpetual mobile.[12]

5. Solving the quadrature of a circle, which would stabilize the unstable and put into motion the motionless.[13]

6. The ignition of the unquenchable educational light that will proliferate indefinitely by each pupil gradually becoming a teacher who will in turn teach other pupils.[14]

The fact that Comenius meant none of these outcomes metaphorically nor, in addition to optimism, does Comenius lack self-confidence, is evident from these words which state the expected result: "If anyone has any divergent opinions, let them speak and disprove them. If it doesn't happen

9. See Komenský, *Obecná porada* 3, 143.

10. This allusion refers to the myth about Heracles, who extremely quickly accomplished the impossible task of cleansing Augeias's stable by redirecting the flow of the Alfeus and Peneus Rivers into them. Comenius also used the same analogy in *Panorthosia* 3, 31, 35, 40.

11. Here Comenius alluded to the title of one of his earlier works, which he intended for youth: *Paradisus juventuti Christianae reducendus* [Christian youth restored to paradise]. In the same way, the *Pampaedia* opened paradise to adults.

12. Comenius dealt seriously with the "physical" problem of spontaneous motion and was acquainted with the attempts to construct a self-propelled mechanism. His perpetual mobile concerned the education of human hearts and minds which—once set into motion—continue to function forever.

13. Here Comenius referred to the unsolveable problem of squaring the circle, proposed by ancient geometers and mathematicians. It is the challenge to construct a square with the same area as a given circle by using only a finite number of steps with a compass and straightedge. Comenius was convinced that the problem is solvable; see Comenius, "Geometria," 15–16. Here he used the issue analogously—the problem of human restoration through education is possible.

14. Comenius referred here to God's wisdom, which King Solomon desired and which is compared to "the light that never goes out" in the apocryphal Book of Wisdom (7:10).

we will be boastful in God by these realities."[15] At the same time it must be emphasized that the emendation project was presented as a "consultatio." That is, a public invitation to consult or discuss the reformation of human affairs, but never as a final or definitive result, as Radim Palouš helpfully observed.[16]

Comenius's optimism did not worry only philosophers and pedagogues, but also theologians. Molnár, for example, spoke of Comenius's optimism as a "theologically tricky question."[17] How can we explain the ease with which Comenius hoped to overcome the consequences of the human fall through his pansophically conceived education? Did he reduce the weight of sin by placing it "too close to ignorance," as René Voeltzel wrote?[18] Or did his optimism arise from the eschatological hope related to the redemptive role of Christ, as J. M. Lochman[19] and Molnár[20] affirmed? Or did Comenius's soteriology here approximate to the Roman Catholic notion of justification, as Stanislav Sousedík,[21] a Czech Catholic thinker judged? Apparently Comenius's categories of natural theology are not easily classifiable by denomination.

A further problematic question is the so-called "scientific quality" of the method by which Comenius constructed his pedagogical system. If it is possible to talk about any kind of "scientificity" in his work, it is certainly not in the modern sense of the word. Bacon's principle of induction, which could have brought it closest to modern scientific discourse, was not well understood by Comenius and he merely adapted it for his own purposes. Comenius treated the works of other authors similarly, adapting and sythetically working them into his own—albeit original—but entirely speculative system.[22] Piaget was right, writing that the grandly conceived

---

15. Comenius, *Obecná porada 3*, 143.

16. Palouš, *Čas výchovy*, 79.

17. Molnár, "O Komenského," 8.

18. Taken from Molnár, "O Komenského," 9.

19. See Lochman, *Comenius as Theologian*.

20. Molnár, "Eschatologické naděje," 88–89.

21. Sousedík, *Comenius chiliastische Rechtfertigungslehre*, 174–83.

22. Evidence of the speculativeness of Comenius' science is, for example, his *Physics*, written around the same time as the *Didactics* (1632). It was based on qualitative Aristotelian cosmology, despite Comenius' open opposition to Aristotelianism. His cosmology was essentially a unified system of cosmic principles having an upward three-part structure connected by teleological parallelism and analogies. For example Comenius assumed that motion is the first product of the combination of the three basic cosmic

apriority which he promised in the introduction of his *Didactics*, was rather a kind of "quasi-sensualistic empiricism," on top of the construction of a metaphysics that dwelt somewhere between "Aristotelian scholasticism and the mechanism of the seventeenth century."[23] Piaget's judgment is perhaps harsh,[24] but the fact is that Comenius (sometimes deliberately)[25] went in a different philosophical direction than the newly emerging schools of modern thought.

Therefore we can agree with Patočka that Comenius did not grasp the essence of modern science. At the same time it is true that "he didn't need it" for his philosophy of education, as Patočka went on to say. His concept of nature as a school of wisdom, combined with the assumption of universal harmony and the parallelism of the universe gave him enough material for a very effective education project. Moreover, if it is about wisdom in the complete sense of the word and not only about the specific knowledge appropriate to technical control of natural forces, then it could be obtained without the achievements of modern discourse. Patočka says: "[Comenius] understood how a harmonic universe which is controlled by

----

principles of matter, spirit and light; from motion arises the quality of things, and from quality, changes to things, which is origin, continuing, growth, change, and decay. The material world is composed of three basic qualities: salt, sulphur and mercury; matter exists in three basic states: solid, liquid, and gaseous. There are three mental forces acting in human beings: vegetative, sensitive and rational, as well as a triad of spiritual forces: action, reason, and volition, and so on. Such speculative concepts prevail throughout Comenius' *Physics*. He did not know experimentation as a starting point for the formulation of scientific principles. Nor was there any trace of the mathematical aspects of nature or quantitative expressions of natural laws and facts in his cosmology. This does not mean that Comenius was not interested in contemporary physics; in fact, the opposite was true. Think of Copernicus's treatise on the Revolutions of Celestial Bodies. Comenius also knew about the invention of the telescope, studied the writings of Tycho Brahe, and corresponded with Johannes Hevelius, one of Brahe's biggest followers. See Komenský, *Přehled fyziky*, chapter 3.

23. Piaget, *Jan Amos Comenius*, 173–96.

24. Admittedly, it is true that Comenius recognized the importance of the senses in learning, as he referred to Bacon's "there is nothing in the mind that was not first in the senses." Piaget knew that and quoted it. Yet a thorough reading of the *Didactics* shows that for Comenius sensory knowledge was a sub resource, necessary to be complemented by other sources. It is also true that Comenius spoke about his "didactic machine," as he was impressed by Bacon's idea of a machine that multiplies human strength, but further research reveals that Comenius's educational system was far removed from the mechanistic tendencies of the time. From that came the "inconsistency" that Piaget saw in Comenius. For more see ibid.

25. See Comenius's famous discussion with René Descartes.

general parallelism is extremely useful for didactic purposes, because in such a world everything forms a whole, and therefore everyone learns everything, by every possible means."[26] That is the powerful new "organon"[27] whose goal is "that the minds of the students be as open as possible to things themselves in their originality, so they can deal with them as directly as possible and so their knowledge would not be only some dead possession, but become part of the student's being so that the light of things would join and connect with the light of our spirit."[28]

THE RELEVANCE OF COMENIUS'S ANTHROPOLOGY FOR CURRENT PEDAGOGY

In the introduction I promised to present an argument in favor of the relevance of Comenius's anthropological concept for the contemporary discussion on educational humanization. The accents of a time change with the time. What was relevant in the recent past is not necessarily relevant today.[29] František X. Šalda captured it well when he said about Comenius, that he was "a great man who was strangely ahead of his time, and yet also behind it."[30] The question is: In what ways was Comenius ahead and in what ways behind? So ahead of his time as to approach ours? What is relevant for us and what is not? Jaroslava Pešková answered succinctly—Comenius "isn't great for his answers to the questions of the time, he is important for raising the right questions, by which he was able to express the key issues of his day."[31]

We have seen that Comenius's system, including his anthropology, was built on the foundations of a broader philosophical and theological whole. As a theologian he saw nature and the entire natural world as a creation, as the work of the Creator who created everything effectively and

26 Patočka, *Komeniologické studie 1*, 265.

27. Comenuis called this method *syncrisis*. For further details of his inclination to combine faith and reason see, for example, Lášek, "Der Bekenner."

28. Patočka, *Komeniologické studie 1*, 48.

29. The period of the national revival, for example, regarded as relevant different aspects of Comenius's work that the post-modern period. We can make a similar distinction between the modern and post-modern periods. For further information about which periods of Comenius's work were valued and considered relevant, see Appendix 1.

30. Šalda, "O literárním baroku," 302.

31. Pešková, "Aktuální aspekty," 5.

meaningfully. As a philosopher he explored natural existence "under the guise of education,"[32] in order to discover the educational potential in its essence. Recall that in the introductory part of both *Didactics* it says that "whatever exists, exists for some end." The natural world is not a random occurrence of things or the result of events which took place haphazardly, coming out of nowhere and going nowhere, but a purposeful existence capable of meaning. Everything has some purpose. Every thing, every being is characterized by its teleological nature. It has a goal lying outside of itself, beyond itself; there exists a "coming out" of oneself, because that is what each one was intended and created for. As Comenius put it, nothing exists for itself. On this divine deposit rests the pedagogical bent of the natural world. The world is imbued with an educational spirit. From birth a person enters the school of the world, which by its very nature educates a person towards the true essence of humanity.

That a person needs such an education was evident to Comenius. In all of creation there is only one being which is able to make itself the final goal of its existence, to make itself "homo mensura" (humankind as the measure of all things). This is something that, unlike either antiquity or modernity, Comenius did not view as positive, but as the core of the human tragedy, the source of all human confusion and bewilderment. Those for whom the meaning of life is to be found within themselves are annoyingly sticking out from the order of creation and universal harmony of all creation, for their purpose is unnatural, non-native and out of order. The separation of human beings from God, from whom flows all "breath and life itself," separates them from each other, because it "forces man to make himself the goal of his existence, that is, to love himself, to pay attention to himself, and care for himself first."[33]

Comenius's explanation of the source of the ambivalent nature of human beings comes from the traditional biblical narrative of the creation of humankind as *Imago Dei*. Humans are ontologically clothed so that their character mirrors God's character, in their being is a reflection of the greatest conceivable good (*summum bonum*). All of the unique capacities of a person to think, to choose, to experience beauty, to feel, to know oneself etc., have their ontological basis in the creative act. Yet as a result of the archetypical fall of humanity, caused by the human desire for equality with God, human beings have lost the aforementioned "nexus hypostaticus,"

32. Compare Patočka, *Komeniologické studie 2*, 133.
33. The citation is given in Kožmín and Kožmínová, *Zvětšeniny*, 60.

that deep, personal relationship with their Creator. In considering themselves equal with God, humans have lost or "bent" themselves, alienating them from their natural pre-ordained authority that was to enable them to transcend their own selves. As a result of the moral distortion, all of one's ontological capacity for humanity is also affected so that we are not able to fulfill our human calling, and require help and salvation. Thanks to the salvific action of Jesus Christ that is not only possible, but—given the miserable state of humanity—also supremely desirable. All inhumanity needs to be done away with, guilt can and must be confessed and forgiven, which is the key spiritual principle, through which comes the important "rest for humanity," i.e., the reconciliation of humankind with God, with others and with themselves.

Such theologizing of reality was by no means unusual in Comenius's time.[34] However, out of Comenius's creative synthesis of various philosophical sources arose a unique system of thought. Comenius's distinction between the ontological and moral nature of the human being realistically captured the complexity and ambivalence of humanity. Humans are endowed with both positive and negative potential. The ontological value of a person (humanity) is firmly anchored. The moral nature (humaneness) is open. It is not pre-determined as, for example, an earthworm its earthworm-ness or a triangle its triangle-ness. A triangle cannot do anything about its triangle-ness; it cannot become more triangular or less triangular. But a person can. A person is capable of both humanity and inhumanity. Every human potential, each piece of knowledge or skill (including what is acquired in school) can have a positive or negative realization. They can be used for good or for evil. *Usus* and *abusus*, said Comenius. In the end the greater the potential, the greater the danger for "corruptio optimi pessima."[35] Humanity is not okay; but it isn't lost.

Therefore, according to Comenius, a "workshop for humanity" is necessary, schools and education whose primary task is the cultivation of the negative human tendencies. All education consists in overcoming the tendency to live life only for ourselves, that is, in coming out (e-ducatio) away from the twisted self-centeredness and isolation. Thus conceived, pedagogy by its very nature implies the ascendancy of humanity, or an upward movement which is very desirable because it leads one to the sought-after

---

34. See for example the anthropological insights in Pascal's *Myšlenkách*. Pascal, *Pensées*, fragments 613, 206.

35. "The corruption of the best is the worst thing."

transcendent relationship. In practice this reaching out means that a person learns to act, decide and be responsible not only for herself. Learners are led to the recognition that within the order of being is subordinated the authority which fundamentally transcends it. Here we can see the basis for the treasured universalism or holism, with very significant social and ethical consequences.[36] Comenius did not intend the cultivation and reparation of humanity only for individuals, but holistically, globally, as indicated by the prefix *pan*, which at the height of his work was prefixed to every human effort. For a proper relating (reconciling) to the final authority implies properly relating to others, and thus to the whole of creation. What lay on Comenius's heart was not merely partial existence, but the whole being. His school was not just about humanizing individuals but "the restoration of human affairs," because Comenius knew that the welfare of the individual could not be achieved without the welfare of the whole: "We all stand on the one great stage of the world, and whatever happens here happens to everyone."

From what was said it follows that the anthropological assumptions determine the concept of pedigogical humanization. Comenius's anthropology leads to an entirely different kind of humanization than what we encounter in the modern conception. For Comenius, educational resources are not adapted to the demands and needs of the individual because an individual is neither autonomous nor is her end purpose within herself. Both the individual and the didactic means by which the individual is to be cultivated are submitted to requirements which transcend them. I believe that here lies the core problem of the modern concept of humanization. Human nature is in reality not clothed as non-problematically or positively as modernity used to imagine. If human nature is more problematic, as Comenius proposed, that is, if it is endowed with both positive and negative potential, then simply complying with the demands of the individual does not guarantee humanization, because an individual can have needs and demands which not only do not lead to the development of humanity but can even go in the opposite direction, towards total inhumanity. For example, towards indolence, superficiality, malice, greed, dishonesty, etc. Therefore humanization operating from a romantic image of human beings as basically good doesn't work. It is essentially a tautology, as Rýdl correctly noted, because to humanize what is already human makes no sense; it would be

---

36. See for example Patočka, *Komeniologické studie 3*, 30.

like naturalizing nature.[37] However well-intentioned is the modern pursuit of educational humanization, its nonfunctionality over time has revealed it as an empty "slogan" or "cloak"[38] under which it is possible to "promote virtually anything" that is in some way nontraditional, innovative, alternative or fun.[39] But it does not bring about the humanization of humanity.

Rousseau's conception can serve as a good example. Unlike Comenius, Rousseau believed that human beings are basically good, both ontologically and morally.[40] Out of that came his romantic (non)education. His representative boy, Emil, was only watched and accompanied by the teacher, who in fact was no longer a teacher, but merely an assistant. Rousseau believed that education should simply let the good that dwells within a person blossom on its own. All liberalizing approaches to minimal education stand on this premise.

But the opposite assumption, which is at the opposite end of the anthropological spectrum, also results in a problematic pedagogy. If we assume that human beings are both ontologically and morally "nothing but"—the typical phrase of modern reductionism—for example, nothing but an animal, a machine or even just matter, we will treat them accordingly. We will teach, form, tame, indoctrinate or condition them, but never humanize them.[41] All totalitarian and authoritarian approaches tend to this type of pedagogy.[42]

I am convinced that it is just here that the relevance of Comenius's anthropology as well as his entire system of thought, can most clearly be seen. The main contribution lies not so much in his didactic principles

37. Rýdl, "Didaktické perspektivy," 351.

38. Rýdl's concept; ibid.

39. Ibid.

40. Wolfgang Röd was right when he said that "Rousseau's thinking constantly circles around the concept of nature and the concept of human nature in particular, without ever defining those concepts or at least describing them clearly enough" (Röd, *Novověká filosofie*, 488). However the attentive reader cannot miss Rousseau's anthropological presumption—human nature is fine, "sinless," the only thing that corrupts a person is the world, society and "culture." Where the corrupt society came from when every individual was born good, Rousseau never explains (compare Hessen, *Filosofické základy*). See also primarily Rousseau, *Emil*.

41. There is no doubt that human (not only that of children) nature sometimes needs the kind of education which these concepts approach, and not only in pathological cases. Pedagogy knows the "regime methodology," authoritarian approaches, directives, and so on, but if it knows nothing more than that it is no longer pedagogy.

42. Compare Thiessen, *Teaching for Commitment*.

and propositions, as fascinating as they are,[43] but mostly in his ontological and moral presumptions, which have proven to be realistic and functional. His teaching on humanity as *Imago Dei* provides for the essential dignity of humanity while at the same time functions as a very refined anthropological teleology. The teaching about the violation of humanity that Comenius's system includes, on the other hand, works as a preventative against an over-romanticizing of human nature. This realistic anthropological configuration creates the space for a meaningful cultivation of all human potential—which is neither over- nor under-valued, but truly taught. The dimension of responsibility towards the transcendent creates the functional moral framework so important for the proper handling of the school-acquired arsenal. Knowledge and virtue are in the closest association here because Comenius knew that knowledge alone does not guarantee humanity. An educated but immoral person is a threat, a "burden" to him- or herself and others.

Comenius's metaphysics as the anchor of humanity is clearly non-modern or pre-modern. I believe, however, that that is its greatest value. If we take into account the fact that it is the modern paradigm which is currently in crisis, Comenius's "old-fashionedness" no longer appears as a weakness but rather as an advantage.[44] Moreover, together with his "old-fashioned" anthropology it has proven to be very fruitful and effective not only in pedagogy but also in everyday life. That is why I have allowed Comenius to speak in his own words and own intellectual integrity. To the modern or postmodern[45] ear it can sound strange, but if it is the modern

43. Patočka with his own subtlety uncovers the typical modernist Comeniology, which strives to derive from Comenius some pseudo-modern psychological, pedagogical, linguistic, etc., doctrines, is merely a cover for its own self-admiration. What is the point of constantly—through Comenius—applauding what is already well known from modern empirical science?

44. Stephen Toulmin illustrated the crisis of modernity with the help of a picture. He suggests the trajectory of modern philosophy is like the shape of the Greek letter "Ω." It means that despite achievements in experimental and technical areas, the philosophical questions about the meaning of the final order of things are still unresolved. About three hundred years later we are once again at the beginning; we didn't get very far. See Toulmin, *Cosmopolis*, 167.

45. In this work I have not dealt with the problem of modern and postmodern philosophy and culture per se. Others have already discussed it thoroughly and well. See for example Eagleton, *Illusions of Postmodernism*; Erickson, *Truth or Consequences*; Grenz, *Primer on Postmodernism*; Greer, *Mapping Postmodernism*; Greer and Lewis, *A Brief History*; Harvey, *The Condition of Postmodernity*; Lyotard, *The Postmodern Condition*; Murphy, *Beyond Liberalism*; Murphy and McClendon, "Distinguishing Modern

paradigm that has alienated human beings from their humanity, then Comenius can best serve us by his very foreignness, because it shows us the limits of our spiritual universe.[46]

---

and Postmodern"; Murphy, *Anglo-American Postmodernity*; Murphy, *Theology*; Wright, *Religion*,.

46. Compare Patočka, *Komeniologické studie 1*, 21. Jiří Pospíšil came to similar conclusions based on an analysis of modern Noetics. See Pospíšil, *Filosofická východiska*, 117–18.

APPENDIX 1

Comenius in the Course of History

Brief Notes on Comeniological Studies

COMENIUS AND HIS TIME: FAME, CONTROVERSY AND DISREGARD

Comenius's work met with a variety of responses during his lifetime. He attempted to write approximately 200 books.[1] Unfortunately, a large number of them seem to be irretrievably lost. Comenius's international fame was brought about by the publication of his *Janua linguarum reserata* [The Gate of Languages Unlocked] in 1633, and he began to be recognized as an able teacher of languages. The Jesuits, whose pedagogical approaches were so antagonistic to Comenius's pedagogical universalism, recognized and used his *Janua* as their textbook, and in 1667 (still in Comenius's lifetime), the Jesuits published it themselves. The fame of Comenius's textbooks was so great that it even reached the royal courts; Douphin the Great, son of Ludwig XIV, and Kristina Augusta, the Swedish queen, for instance, learned Latin from Comenius's textbooks. In 1658 his educational fame

---

1. In addition to his didactic writings Comenius researched and wrote about irenic, religious, political and other issues. For an overview of Comenius's writings see for example Hendrich, *Jan Amos Komenský*, or Floss, *Poselství*.

increased even more when his *Orbis sensualium pictus* [The Visible World of Pictures] was published.

Comenius's idea of the encyclopedic organization of the material as well as the interconnection of real things, sense experience, and language terms proved to be very effective in language learning. Comenius's didactic inventions were so well thought of that the appreciation of them has tended to overshadow other aspects of his work. Some areas most frequently missed were his pansophic and emendation programs, which dealt with the central problem of humankind. According to Comenius, that problem is the alienation of human beings from God, the author, source and center of life and universal harmony.[2] The specific didactic methodology did play an important role, but it was, however, only a means to a greater end. It seems that the brilliance of Comenius's didactics prevented many from seeing the whole picture of his thought. Radim Palouš observed that "Komenský's didactic tools were readily received and employed in various areas and for various purposes, but their original intention and function were neglected." He continued:

> Education and its concrete instrument—school—were intended to bring about the restoration of affairs, not to become a factory producing functionaries properly tooled and shaped in order to carry out the functions of a given production regime. . . . Komenský first of all seeks to provide both a critique and the instruments for the improvement of existing affairs. Educational and didactic rules are not his primary scholarly issues; they are to him an important way of realistically overcoming the religious schisms in the beginning of modern times, the ravages of the thirty-years European conflict, and the spiritual fractionalism of existing knowledge. Education functions here as a tool that is to bring humankind to the age of universal harmony.[3]

Even during Comenius's lifetime there were many who recognized that a greater concept was behind his didactic inventions. A list of the most significant of them includes men such as Laurence de Geer, the open-minded Dutch businessman; John Jonston, Comenius's close friend; and Samuel Hartlib, who headed a group of English social reformers. They encouraged Comenius to develop and publish his pansophic philosophical

---

2. Comenius addressed this problem previously in *Centrum securitatis* (The Center of Safety).

3. Palouš, *Komenského Boží svět*, 5–6.

concepts.[4] Others, however, were suspicious of his pansophy. Among the educated, the reasons were usually theological: for example Hieronym Broniewski and the Swedish chancellor, Axel Oxenstjern, who charged him with undue rationalism.[5] Nikolas Arnold and Samuel Maresius discard all pansophic projects from the position of reformed theology; René Descartes and Marin Mersenne viewed Comenius's demand for the unity of theology and philosophy just as skeptically.[6] Some of Comenius's ordinary uneducated co-believers were jealous of his philosophizing and complained that it dragged him away from his pastoral and episcopal responsibilities.[7] Most of Comenius's patrons and benefactors placed his didactics above his pansophy.[8]

After his death, the influence of and the interest in Comenius's work faded for a time.[9] Jaroslav Pánek observed that at the beginning of

4. But many other "unnamed" friends hailed Comenius's broad philosophical thought, and they played an important role in his life. For biographical details see for example Říčan, *Jan Amos Komenský*. Or Říčan, *Dějiny*.

5. Thanks to Comenius's autobiographical notes, we have a record of his conversation with the Swedish chancellor Oxenstjern, which perfectly sketches the situation Comenius faced with his views: "'It seems to me that you hope in some kind of enlightened, godly, peaceful, or as they say, golden age. Is that so?' I, not knowing his intentions, responded with brightened face: 'Yes, it is, my majesty.' Suddenly he put on a strict expression and said: 'I beseech you as a man learned and a theologian to tell me, do you mean that seriously or are you jesting?'" For the full account of the conversation, see Molnár and Rejchrtová, *J. A. Komenský*, 162–69. See also Urbánek, "Konflikt ortodoxního," 149–57.

6. Comenius actually met with Descartes in 1642, but no particular result came out of this meeting, for Descartes refused to "step outside of the circle of philosophy," while Comenius saw philosophy as merely a part of the "whole," as Comenius said in his autobiographical memoirs. They separated after four hours of discussion with a diplomatic disagreement. See Molnár and Rejchrtová, *J. A. Komenský*, 155–56.

7. Comenius oftentimes felt the need to let his readers know that all his work was primarily theological. See, for example, *Didaktika velká*, Praha 1905. Molnár commented on this, saying that such apologetic allusions were to respond to those who doubted his orthodoxy. See Molnár, "O Komenského," 3.

8. Especially the Swedes and Hungarians, who invited him to reform their schools. In fact, they showed open displeasure toward Comenius's occupation with his pansophy at the expense of work on particular school reforms.

9. There were some exceptions, who exercised a continual interest in Comenus, such as Robert Boyle in England, Gottfried Wilhelm Leibnitz in Germany, and August Hermann Francke from Lusatia, who most significantly contributed to the promotion of Comenius's ideas. While serving as a teacher in Halle, he became acquainted with Comenius's ideas through Count Nicolaus Ludwig von Zinzendorf. The count later founded Herrnhut, which was the famous settlement of the exiled Unitas Fratrum, where the legacy of Comenius was not only kept alive but spread throughout the world, for the

the eighteenth century, most people accepted the influential judgment of Pierre Bayle, the French encyclopedist, who described Comenius as "an impractical visionary, if not a dangerous fanatic."[10] The reason for such a wide acceptance of Bayle, as Pánek saw it, was his ability to "make his statements impressive through seemingly unsubjective objectivism."[11] This kind of statement seemed to be in fashion at that time.[12] Palouš also pointed out that Bayle was not able to see Comenius as anything more than a "grammarian."[13] Similarly, German thinkers of the Enlightenment period, such as J. F. Reimann and J. C. Adelung, criticized Comenius for mixing up theology and politics. Thus Comenius was put aside, and John Edward Sadler correctly observed that "apart from the textbooks which continued the memory of his name, there was little direct influence of Comenius for over 100 years."[14]

COMENIUS AND THE CZECH NATIONAL REVIVAL: A REDISCOVERED HERO

The rediscovery of Comenius at the beginning of the nineteenth century was closely related to the Czech national revival. The decisive moment proved to be the so called Toleration Patent of 1781, which ensured religious freedom for non-Catholic believers. In spite of some difficulties with the implementation of the newly declared freedom, the Patent encouraged a number of national revivalists, most of whom passionately cared for the Czech language, to publish some of Comenius's works written in Czech in order to promote the native language.[15] Thus, by 1757 Comenius's great

---

Herrnhut Brethren were exceptionally active in missions on a worldwide scale.

10. Pánek, "Heritage of the Czech Humanist," 14. Compare Bayle, Dictionnairie Historique, 882–87.

11. Pánek, "Heritage of the Czech Humanist," 14.

12. There were not many who were able to break away from Bayle's traditionally accepted point of view. Among those who were able to do so I would name the well-known Czech historian Bohuslav Balbin (1621–88), a non-orthodox member of the Jesuit order who appreciated Comenius's pedagogy and unique religious tolerance. Also Johann Gottfried von Herder (1744–1803), a German thinker who pointed out, as Marta Bečková has reminded us, that in Comenius's works only his didactic understanding is against his original intention. See Bečková, *Das Werk Komenský*, 216.

13. Palouš, *Komenského Boží svět*, 5.

14. Sadler, *J. A. Comenius*, 28.

15. For example, Jan Nejedlý published Comenius's *Labyrinth* at his own expense in

work, the *Labyrinth*, the so-called Berlin edition (3rd), had already been published by V. Toužil. The fate of the *Labyrinth*, as the most famous of Comenius's work, reveals a lot about not only Comenius, but also the Czech and emigré circumstances, and therefore deserves special attention here.

It was at the request of the dispersed "Brethren of the Czech Church" that the *Labyrinth* was published, "for the lack of examples," along with *Kšaft* [Testament] and *Smutný hlas* [A Sad Voice]. Professedly this was done "not sparing our own cost . . . so that, what our ancestor (a lover of truth and the pious life) wrote in this book towards the putting off of worldly vanity and the encouragement of a true heart desire for a steady inner pleasure and rest in Christ, would be given again to you as a people, wherever you dispersed in this world." Around this time there was also in circulation a complimentary critique of the Jesuit thinker Bohuslav Balbín, who wrote in his *Učené Čechy* (*Scholarly Bohemia*, first published in 1777): "How excellent was the man . . . who exposed with an abundance of flawless expressions, apt vocabulary, depth of thought; for his statement of the groundlessness of the world and his very rare and deep scholarship he deserves the highest praise, and it is the most worthy of reading."

Antonín Koniáš, also a Jesuit, saw Comenius's work otherwise. Equipped with his famous *Klíče kacířské bludy k rozeznávání otvírající, k vykořenění zamykající* [Keys of the heretical delusion to the opening of discernment, to the locking up of extermination] (1729), he found *The Labyrinth* "worthy of destruction." Similarly the strength of the metanarrative presupposition became apparent in the judgment of the regional Catholic chronicler František Jan Vavák. An otherwise excellent self-taught farmer, in his *Paměti* [Memories][16] he discussed the *Labyrinth* as something "strange," from "Jan Comenius a fiction in which he wants to proudly show off his execrable wit, resembling mucking dung out of a cow barn."

A non-dogmatic perspective was taken by Jan Samm, also a Catholic, who in 1782 arranged for the publication of the fourth, so-called Prague edition of *The Labyrinth*. It was the first post-Toleration Act printing. In his Preface he responded to František Jan Vavák's comments: "The beauty and value of the famous books of Comenius . . . remain a mystery to Vavák,

---

1809. However it should be noted that not all Czechs were thrilled with Comenius. Josef Dobrovský, for one, regarded him as a "mystic and hunter of innovations in language." František Jan Vavák called Comenius an "anti-Habsburg rebel." For further details, see Kumpera, *Jan Amos Komenský*, 162.

16. The whole name is: Paměti Františka J. Vaváka, souseda a rychtáře milčického z let 1770–1816.

as is shown by his acrimonious and unfair judgment." The ambivalence of the relationship of the Catholic thinkers to the *Labyrinth* literally calls for a deeper examination—whether in terms of psychology, religious studies, history, or otherwise. Such an investigation is, however, beyond the scope of this study.[17]

The Patent of Toleration of 1781 also opened the way to the publication of others of Comenius' works. In a relatively short period there came forth several of them: *Smutný hlas* (The Sad Voice, 1782), *Hlubina bezpečnosti* (The Depth of Safety) and *Boj Michala s drakem* (The Fight of Michael and the Dragon, both in 1785), *Praxis pietatis* (The Practice of Piety, 1786), *Dvojí kázání* (Two Sermons, 1790) and others. However, the Metternich Censorship soon put an end to the relative heyday of publishing. Admittedly there was another printing of *The Labyrinth* in 1809, but it wasn't without problems. "For the excellence of the Czech and delightful variety of content"—was how Jan Nejedlý justified his publishing plan. But his first request in 1808 was denied by the Prague censors, and later accepted only with reservations.

The Bishop of Hradec Králové again warned of the "negative" influence of *The Labyrinth* in 1823 when, in his report on sects in the Hradec diocese, he complained that many "have read and circulated J. A. Comenius's *Labyrinth*" and that it was a "satire of every situation, disturbing all spiritual and secular order, criticizing the church, its servants and its endeavors." He continued that "it is completely incomprehensible" that the work was again published in 1809 in Prague. "Short-sighted publishers"—the bishop warmed to his theme—"who go after purity in the Czech language yet tear down faith in the morality of their fellow citizens." The complaint of the Bishop was accompanied by a message from František Müller, a local priest from Radhošť, who confirmed the pernicious influence of this book. Müller lamented that earlier the sectarians had been held back, but now (dated October 20, 1822) they are said to be raising their heads and hoping for "universal freedom." The whole situation was worsened by the fact that the work "The Labyrinth of the World and the Paradise of the Heart" was

17. An appropriate example of such an examination might be the memoir of Pavel Hošek, *Cesta ke kořenům*. This is a study dealing with the fate of the once famous knightly Milner family from Milhausen. Their ancestors escaped execution in Old Town in 1621. Their descendants—both Protestants and Catholics—were seeking their identity in the midst of complex historical events. It is evident from Hošek's study how crucial was the way in which the family story was told in individual historical eras. In other words, *narrative* is here the key to self-understanding.

being circulated with official authorization and was widely read among the sectarians. So apparently the authorities were undermining the "strenuous work" which he—František Müller—was performing by trying to bring back the lost sheep into the fold of the church. Müller further provided that it would be more easily tolerated if the work were published "in the language of the intellectuals," that is, in Latin, which few understood, but in Czech it would only strengthen the obstinacy of the Czech farmers. In reaction, at the Bishop's request, in 1823 *The Labyrinth* was again censored, and after prolonged negotiations further publication was totally banned—by a ministerial decree dated October 16, 1825.[18]

The revolutionary year of 1848 brought a certain freedom to publish, and with that the next—coincidentally, the "Hradec" edition—of *The Labyrinth* was published by Jan Hostivít Pospíšil in Hradec Králové. But then came the absolutism of Bach. Therefore no further editions came until the end of 1862—in Litomyšl and in Prague. The "National Awareness-raising" efforts that followed quickly on its heels brought a sharp increase in publishing. Within a relatively short period of sixty years came no fewer than eighteen further editions. At the initiative of "wise and experienced educators," who in 1886 met together in the first Congress of Czech Professors, came the first edition designed specifically for educational purposes. In the adaptation by František Bílý, then a professor at Přerov High School, based on the 1887 edition of the *Labyrinth*, he left out everything "that could in any way be a stumbling block or that isn't appropriate for schools." From the historical and didactic perspective all these omissions are research-provoking; they apply to the following parts: chapter 8 on marriage, chapter 13 on Rosecrucianism, chapter 18 on the Christian religion, chapter 25, section 7 on sexual pleasure, and chapter 32, sections 15–16 on the complaints of both sexes. Bílý also left out a significant portion of text in chapters 39–49, which he considered to be "mystical-pietistic chapters," in which the pilgrim is transfigured, conversing with Christ, and seeing the true nature of things. It is important to note that Bílý's truncated version was both favorably received by some and heavily criticized by other experts of the day.[19]

The highlight of the Revivalist efforts was the edition by Jan Václav Novák, who in 1910, as part of an extensive project to publish all works of J. A. Comenius, prepared a critical edition of *The Labyrinth* including

18. Compare Švankmajer, "K zákazu Labyrintu."
19. Compare Souček, "Komenského Labyrint," 36.

variant readings of the first two editions from 1631 and 1663. In addition
to many others, the edition of Josef Brambora in 1941 deserves special
mention, with its excellent epilogue by Jan Blahoslav Čapek, as well as the
editions by Vladimír Šmilauer in 1940 and 1958, and by Antonín Škarka in
1950 and 1970, which excel in the quality of footnotes and detailed com-
mentary. A major publishing achievement in recent years is the 2010 edition of *The Labyrinth* by the Poutníkova Četba publishing house, which
offers Czech readers a "translation" of the text into the language of the
twenty-first century by Lukáš Makovička.

"Our native sons," in the words of Stanislav Souček, are responsible
for most of the foreign language editions; that is, emigrants who sought
"to introduce readers unfamiliar with Czech to the works of the revered
teacher of nations."[20] Thus Jan Gaius's Dutch translation appeared even earlier than 1661. However, a translation by a relative of Comenius' third wife
was never published.

Another descendent of an exiled Czech family was Johannes Petroso-
linus Corvinus, an evangelical pastor in Gdansk, whose translation of *The
Labyrinth* into Polish (*Labirynt swiata y dom pociechy*) was published in
1695. But it was not "a special success." Souček explained that it was due
on the one hand to modifications the translator made to the text, and on
the other hand to the political situation at that time in Poland, where the
subject matter of *The Labyrinth* was unable to "find favor" in the dominant
Counter-Reformation Catholicism.[21] Other Polish translations were produced later, of varying quality.

The motivation for the first German translation (Übergang aus dem
Labyrinth der Welt in das Paradis des Hertzens), by Ondřej Macher in
1738, was so that Christian souls would be "encouraged to serious attention
to what would in time come from all manner of wickedness and futility in
the world, and through Christ seek true peace in God." But his very free
translation of the book bore signs of significant "distortion," in Stanislav
Součka's judgment.[22] Later came many other German translations, of which
the most successful seems to be that of Zdeněk Baudník in 1906.

The first Hungarian translation was published in 1805 by István
Rimány. Exactly one hundred years later, in 1905, László Stromp published
another Hungarian translation, but although it was in up-to-date language,

20. Ibid., 49.

21. Souček, "Komenského Labyrint," 50.

22. Ibid., 51.

it was abridged. At about the same time two Russian translations appeared; the first in 1896 by F. V. Říha, and the second, better in Souček's opinion, in 1904 by N. P. Stepanov. The first French translation was done by Comenius admirer Eduard-Henri Robert (1833–91), but his work, carefully annotated and with excerpts from other works by Comenius, remained as a manuscript. Thus, the French reader was unable to become familiar with *The Labyrinth* until 1906, when Marguerite de Crayencour translated the text from the English version by Count Francis Lützow (*The Labyrinth of the Word and Paradise of the Heart*). That Austrian diplomat and politician was an ardent scholar of Bohemia, who among other subjects devoted himself to Czech history. His English translation was published three times in a row within a short period of time: in London in 1901, in New York in 1901, and again in London in 1905.

Other important personalities who contributed to the popularization of Comenius's work in this period included Karel Ignác Thám, F. V. Hek,[23] Josef Jungman, František Palacký, and Jan Evangelista Purkyně.[24] The publication of Comenius's works was interrupted several times and at times even banned, and those responsible for spreading the ideas of Comenius had to face various forms of persecution. The battle over Comenius thus became part of the overall political and cultural efforts of national liberation. First Comenius was hailed only as a patriotic symbol of the Czech National Revival; later, in the second half of the twentieth century, some of the deeper aspects of his work were gradually discovered and appreciated by a number of researchers (often secular) from Bohemia, Moravia, and Slovakia.

In 1870, after more than 250 years, the Unitas Fratrum had returned to the Czech lands, which yet further increased the interest in Comenius's legacy.[25] The 300th anniversary of Comenius's birth in 1892 proved to be similarly significant; it was organized by the Czech intellectual elite in spite of a direct ban by the Vienna Ministry of School Affairs. The bans and restrictions only stoked the national emotions and intensified the attraction

23.. F. V. Hek was popularized by writer A. Jiráskem in a well-known historical novel under the pseudonym F. L. Věk.

24. It was Purkyně who very systematically searched with his friend J. Kačer in Lešno for Comenius's works, and progressively managed to gather number of precious lost manuscripts—among which were the *Czech Didactics* and Comenius's extensive correspondence.

25. The first Brethren church was reestablished in Potštejn in eastern Bohemia, not far from Kunštát, the original birthplace of the Unitas Fratrum.

of Comenius. As result of the growing interest in Comenius in the beginning of the twentieth century, a new scholarly discipline was developed, called Comeniology (or Comenius studies), which brought together thinkers from various fields such as history, linguistics, pedagogy, and politics.[26]

As a result of the initiative of these men, in 1910 the publication of a specialized scholarly journal was begun, called *Archiv pro bádání o životě a díle J. A. Komenského* (Archive for Research into the Life and Work of J. A. Comenius). It is now published under a new title, *Acta Comeniana* (renamed in 1969). The pioneers of Comeniology were mainly interested in the pedagogical and linguistic (and occasionally religious) aspects of Comenius's work, but the philosophical, theological, and sociopolitical side of his legacy was left unnoticed at the time—mainly because a significant number of Comenius's manuscripts were still unknown.

Gradually Comenius (together for the most part with Jan Hus) became a symbol of the national revival and was given the special attention he deserved. Sadler, however, called this new attention "compensation for previous neglect."[27]

IMPACT OF THE GREAT FINDS OF THE 1930S: COMENIUS THE PHILOSOPHER

The new interest led to the discovery and appreciation of various aspects of Comenius's work. The real breakthrough in Comeniological research came about through the famous discoveries of Comenius's pansophic manuscripts in the 1930s. The three big finds were: 1) Stanislav Souček's so-called "Leningrad discoveries," which he found in 1931 (and published the results) in the Saltyk-Ščedrina library. The discovery was an outcome of Souček's long-term explorational endeavor. The six very important manuscripts included, among others, Comenius's *Prima Philosophia, Geometrie,* and *Cosmographiae compendium.* 2) In 1933 G. H. Turnbull found quite a large number of manuscripts in Hartlib's written estate. Some of them were originals of works already know, but there were also a number of works, documents, and letters that were completely new. 3) The third find

---

26. Jan Patočka in his helpful overview of Comeniological history listed names like Karl Gustav von Numer, František Boleslav Květ, Gustav Adolf Lindner, František Jan Zoubek, Jan Václav Novák, Tomáš Garrigue Masaryk, Ján Kvačala, and others. Patočka, *Komeniologické studie 1,* 164–76.

27. Sadler, *J. A. Comenius,* 31.

is considered to be the most significant one. After a long period of focused research in the area of Slavic studies, D. Čižévskyj found, in the archives of the Francke Orphanage in Halle in 1934 (on Christmas Eve), a great manuscript of 2,000 pages. It was four (out of seven) parts of Comenius's magnum opus, the *General Consultation*.

These finds revealed some new facts concerning the philosophical foundations of Comenius's work. According to Patočka, with few exceptions[28] the Comeniologists of the period believed that "Comenius's ideas were identical with the ideas of the modern period. Comeniological research, both historical and systematic, rested on this hidden assumption."[29] Prior to these discoveries Comeniological research had a tendency to isolate Comenius's *modern* pedagogy from his *premodern* philosophical-theological concepts, which they considered to be obsolete and, therefore, unimportant.[30] Ladislav Kratochvíl, for example, disclosed his modernist prism when expounding on Comenius's theological assumptions as an *a priori* current in his otherwise realistic pedagogical system:

> The problem isn't that Komenský knows little of the natural sciences; the main deficiency is that in science he considers the Scripture as equally reliable a source of knowledge as experience or reason. . . . Therefore he constantly seeks analogies between nature and education, and between nature and a human being, for their relationship to God.[31]

With this presupposition of Comenius's theology, Kratochvíl elsewhere made a definitive judgment: "The pansophic and pan-enlightening intentions which stand in the background of his work interfere disturbingly with his otherwise realistic pedagogical principles."[32] Červenka had a similar observation:

> The activity of Comenius-the-didactician was separated from the activity of Comenius-the-pansophist, while at the same time the main emphasis was laid upon the didactics. The pansophy thus remained somehow only peripheral, being spoken about with a

---

28. Patočka mentioned K. B. Štorch and C. F. Kraus. See Patočka, *Komeniologické studie 2*, 7–8.

29. Ibid.

30. Ibid. Patočka calls this group The Comeniologists of "Kvačala's and Novák's epoch."

31. Kratochvíl, "Pedagogický realismus," 130.

32. Ibid., 127.

certain reservation; it was rather considered as at least a detour from his didactic activities, if not his life's error.[33]

But the new finds seem to show that such an approach to Comenius violates the integrity of his thought. Comenius was not an essentially modern thinker with a few minor old-fashioned ideas which could be easily put aside. In fact, the finds revealed it is exactly the opposite. Palouš commented on this, saying that "the modern period characterized by its split of the universe into the subject and object, *res cognitas* and *res extensa*, turns out to be foreign to Comenius."[34] A careful analysis of the works that have been found enabled Comeniologists[35] of the twentieth century to realize that Comenius was not a servant of the modern enlightenment agenda.[36] Pavel Floss, for example, rightly drew our attention to "four heresies"[37] that Comenius mentioned in his newly-found diary which (Floss said) identify him as a non-modern, even "anti-modern" thinker. These heresies, with which Comenius struggled the whole of his life, were in a certain sense the pillars of the modern period: Cartesianism, Copernicanism, socinianism, and atheism.[38]

Thus, Comenius can no longer be viewed merely as an author of a helpful methodology equipping human beings (as subject) to dominate or rule over the world (as object). The goal of all Comenius's methodological principles, precepts, laws, and all of his pedagogical efforts, was not the effective teaching of what is needed as a preparation for life—or in modern words, for successful self-promotion in the marketplace. For him it was completely opposite; it was about educating a person away from the idea that one's ultimate meaning and goal is to be found within oneself. It was about *educatio* in the true sense of the word, that is leading out, away from oneself, from one's own submerging into the self and closed-ness to others and the outside world—because Comenius knew that the welfare of the

33. Červenka, *One Hundred Years*, 43.

34. Palouš, *Komenského Boží svět*, 6.

35. Especially Jan Patočka's *Komeniologické studie 1, 2, 3*; Schaller, *Die Pädagogik und die Anfänge*; Geissler, "Das Christus-Verständnis"; Neval, "An Approach," 215–28; Palouš, *Komenského Boží svět* and others.

36. Compare Pešková, "Jan Amos Komenský," 21–28.

37. Comenius's use of the term "blud" (heresy) is significant, for he never used the term "kacířství" (also heresy—English does not have an adequate distinction here). "Blud" for Comenius meant the result of lack of knowledge, while "kacířství" was a term characterizing those who were usually executed.

38. Floss, *Poselství*, 14. Compare Komenský, *Clamores Eliae 40*, 238.

individual cannot be achieved at the expense of the welfare of the whole. This all flowed from his holistic-universal prefix *pan-*, which by the end of his thought development permeated almost every human activity. It is possible therefore, to conclude along with Patočka, that the major findings revealed that "what Comenius gave the world as a didactician, methodologist, educator, writer, humanist, and author of pansophic projects was only a fraction of what he had planned . . . ."[39]

COMENIUS IN THE COMMUNIST INTERPRETATION: GREAT DIDACTICIAN, FORGOTTEN METAPHYSICIAN

The Communist post-war period formed a specific chapter in Comeniological research. In the Communist interpretation, Comenius was presented as "a great radical thinker affirming the possibility that human nature could be changed by education."[40] Comenius was linked with socialist reformers and revolutionaries like John Lilburne the Leveller, John Bellers the Quaker, and Robert Owen the Socialist. Despite the new discoveries of the 1930s and the excellent analysis of the above-mentioned scholars, the Communist prism prevented the interpreters from appreciating Comenius's work in its fullness. In 1957 Patočka bravely stated[41] that Communist interpreters like Otakar Chlup,[42] Robert Alt,[43] and Archip Alexejovič Krasnovskij[44] "emphasize Comenius's connection with Bacon's inductive realism and assume that this connection affects his pedagogy. However, they usually do not provide sufficient warrant for their theses, but simply affirm that

---

39. Patočka, *Komeniologické studie 1*, 91.

40. Sadler, *J. A. Comenius*, 34. Jiří Pospíšil similarly noted that in this time Comenius's work was subjected to a not very adequate "modernization." See Pospíšil, *Náboženská pedagogika*, 1.

41. Patočka was persecuted by the Czech totalitarian regime for his non-conformist views. It is quite instructive to read M. Bečková's review of Comeniological research from 1982, where she lists extensively all the authors dealing with the subject since the War, but Patočka's studies, clearly not fitting to the socialist ideology, are not mentioned at all (see Bečková, *Development of Comenius Research*, 143–50). It is a matter of fact that Patočka's scholarly honest and excellent studies were banned and today are available to us only because certain brave people hid and protected them from the well-known STB (State Secret Police) who strove to destroy them. In Radim Palouš's study, I saw the cabinet with a secret case where the original manuscripts used to be kept.

42. See Patočka, "Nový obraz."

43. See Alt, *Pokrokový charakter*.

44. See Krasnovskij, *Jan Amos Komenský*.

Comenius belongs to the materialistic and sensualistic traditions."[45] Such an approach might—in the words of C. S. Lewis—be identified as "chronological snobbery," which without proper reasoning considers everything that doesn't agree with its own philosophical agenda as outdated.[46] In 1966 Sadler identified the problem of reductionism in the Communist interpretation in a similar way as Patočka (although from a safer distance from the totalitarian regime): "[Comenius's] educational methodology is seen as an expression of his educational philosophy and as something which could be detached without great loss from its religious framework."[47] The following citation from Jiřina Popelová perfectly represents the enthusiastic tradition of Communist-influenced interpretation:

> The joining of cognitive optimism with sensualism is a feature that allies Comenius with the great Renaissance thinkers. The value of such epistemological optimism, as well as democratism in education, is not degraded by the fact that Comenius's justification of it is based on the idea that a human being is in the image of God. Such a residue of feudal thinking is more a residue of form, which does not disrupt the otherwise modern content of Comenius's concepts.[48]

At the same time it must be said that not all of the Comeniological scholars working with the totalitarian regime complied with it and produced only ideological interpretations. But nor am I suggesting that the Communist interpretations had no value. The erudition of a number of Communist scholars is indisputable and needs to be recognized. Nevertheless, the fact remains that the ideological starting point of the Communist world view—often dogmatically enforced—produced a specifically reduced view of Comenius's thought, which was often motivated by "looking for justification for its cultural-political goals," as Kumpera put it.[49]

45. Patočka, *Komeniologické studie 1*, 168. See also Patočka, *Komeniologické studie 3*, 18.

46. The exact definition of Lewis's term *chronological snobbery* is "uncritical acceptance of the intellectual climate common to our own age and the assumption that whatever has gone out of date is on that account discredited." See his autobiography, *Surprised by Joy.*

47. Sadler, *J. A. Comenius*, 35.

48. Popelová, *Cesta k všenápravě*, 143.

49. Kumpera, *Jan Amos Komenský*, 171.

THE POST-TOTALITARIAN OPPORTUNITY: COMENIUS IN HIS INTEGRITY

The post-totalitarian period opened up opportunities to tackle the problem from a new perspective: the historical experience of various misinterpretations and even abusive interpretations has made it impossible for interpreters to ignore the danger of interpretative biases.[50] The contemporary post-totalitarian circumstances seem to be inviting an approach that would strive "to take hold of Comenius in his entirety and seek out the neglected and forgotten aspects of his personality and work," as Palouš remarked.[51]

Some contemporary scholars have also taken this approach, for example Jan Kumpera, Aleš Prázný, Věra Schifferová, Vladimír Urbánek, David Krámský, Tomáš Kasper, M. Šístek, Jiří Pospíšil and many others.[52] Their studies have clearly exhibited a concern for preserving the legacy of Comenius in his own intellectual integrity. Rýdl has explicitly expressed himself on the theme of humanization in Comenius's conception. He refers to the fact that Comenius was not aiming at the welfare of the individual in the sense of an easier and more comfortable life with regard to its individual specifics, but rather at exceeding one's own individuality. Respecting the needs of the individual does not guarantee her humanization. Comenius knew this, and today we are rediscovering it. In the meantime a number of well-intentioned attempts at "humanization" have been attempted, that were rendered completely ineffective because they understood human beings in a reductive way—as a resource—without any idea what the humanity of this "resource" consists in.[53]

50. For a detailed review of Comeniological research in the twentieth century, see Čapková, "K obrazu," 203–41.

51. Palouš, *Komenského Boží svět*, 6.

52. See for example the author's team monograf *Idea harmonie v díle Jana Amose Komenského*, which came out under the guidance of Věra Šifferová, Aleš Prázný and Kateřina Šolcová.

53. Rýdl, "Jak vlastně," 207–14.

Outline of Comenius's Didactic Fundamentals from the *Great Didactic*[1]

1. The universal requirements of teaching and of learning; that is to say, a method of teaching and of learning with such a certainty that the desired result must of necessity follow.

    1.1. Nature observes a suitable time.

    1.2. Nature prepares the material before she begins to give it form.

    1.3. Nature chooses a fit subject to act upon, or first submits one to a suitable treatment in order to make it fit.

    1.4. Nature is not confused in its operations, but in its forward progress, it advances distinctly from one point to another.

    1.5. In all the operations of nature, development is from within.

    1.6. Nature, in its formative processes, begins with the universal and ends with the particular.

    1.7. Nature makes no leaps but proceeds step by step.

    1.8. When nature commences anything, it does not leave off until the operation is complete.

---

1. Taken from the English version translated by M. W. Keating.

1.9. Nature carefully avoids obstacles and things likely to cause hurt.

2. The principles of facility in teaching and learning

    2.1. Nature begins with a careful selection of materials.

    2.2. Nature prepares its material so that it actually strives to attain the form.

    2.3. Nature develops everything from a beginning which, though insignificant in appearance, possesses great potential strength.

    2.4. Nature advances from what is easy to what is more difficult.

    2.5. Nature does not overburden herself but is content with a little.

    2.6. Nature does not hurry but advances slowly.

    2.7. Nature compels nothing to advance that is not driven forward by its own mature strength.

    2.8. Nature assists its operations in every possible manner.

    2.9. Nothing is produced by nature for which the practical application is not soon evident.

    2.10. Nature is uniform in all its operations.

3. The principles of thoroughness in teaching and in learning

    3.1. Nature produces nothing that is useless.

    3.2. When bodies are being formed, nature omits nothing that is necessary for their production.

    3.3. Nature does not operate on anything unless it possesses a foundation or roots.

    3.4. Nature strikes her roots deep.

    3.5. Nature develops everything from its roots and from no other roots.

    3.6. The more the uses to which nature applies anything, the more distinct subdivisions that thing will possess.

    3.7. Nature never remains at rest but advances continually; she never begins anything fresh at the expense of work already in hand, but proceeds with what she has already begun and brings it to completion.

3.8. Nature knits everything together in a continuous combination.

3.9. Nature preserves a due proportion between the roots and the branches, with respect to both quality and quantity.

3.10. Nature becomes fruitful and strong through constant movement.

Chronology of Comenius's Life and Works

- 1592—Born, most likely at Uherský Brod or Nivnice (Moravia).
- 1608—High school in Přerov.
- 1611—Studied at the University of Herborn. Started to compile the *Poklad jazyka českého* [Treasury of the Czech Language], a phraseological and stylistic dictionary, on which he continued to work until 1656, when it was lost in the fire at Lešno.
- 1612—Continued in his studies at the University of Heidelberg.
- 1614—Served as a teacher in Přerov. Influenced by his reading of Ratke's work and drawing on his own teaching experience, he wrote *Pravidla snazší mluvnice* [Principles of a Simpler Approach to Grammar]—the first of his school textbooks (1st edition, Prague, 1616).
- 1616—Became a minister in the Czech Unitas Fratrum Church. During the following years he continued to work on the encyclopedia *Theatrum universitatis rerum* [Theater of Everything]. In its introduction he enumerated the subjects lacking in Bohemian culture which he intended to develop. He planned to accompany the *Theatrum* with an *Amphitheatrum* as well as a *Theatrum scripturae*, which he completed and published later on. During the years the Bohemians were suffering severe reverses he wrote books on theological and moral subjects, many of which were autobiographical. Among them was *Labyrint*

světa a ráj srdce [The Labyrinth of the World and the Paradise of the Heart].

- 1618—Outbreak of the Thirty Years War. Served as a teacher and minister at Fulnek (until 1623).

- 1620—Defeat of the Bohemians at White Mountain.

- 1623—During the sacking of Fulnek by imperial troops he lost his family, his house, and his library, which was publicly burned.

- 1627—While living and hiding in the mountains of Bohemia, he read Bodin's *Didactica*, which gave further stimulus to his studies. An imperial edict forced the Protestants to go into exile. Comenius started work on *Didaktika česká* [Czech Didactic], the first version of the *Didactica magna* [Great Didactic], conceived as part of a collection of writings to be entitled *Ráj český Ráj Církve* [The Bohemian Paradise, Paradise of the Church]. His *Navrženi krátké o obnovení škol o království českém* [Brief Proposal for the Regeneration of Schools in the Kingdom of Bohemia] (1st ed., Prague, 1849) may have been a first attempt to carry out this project.

- 1628—In exile at Leszno, in Poland. Between 1628 and 1633, he wrote several books on education: *Informatorium školy mateřské* [Book of Nursery School Teachers] (1st ed., Leszno, 1633); *Opera didactica omnia,* his first coordinated series of books on education, published first in German and later in Latin; *Vernaculae scholae classis sex libelli* [Six Booklets for the National School Classes]: Violarium, Rosarium, Viridarium, Labyrinthus, Balsamentum, Paradisus. Next came the *Janua linguarum reserata* [The Gate of Languages Unlocked] (1st ed., Leszno, 1631), conceived as the 'seed-plot of all arts and sciences,' which superseded his first textbook on *The Simpler Approach to Grammar* and was immediately translated into several languages. Lastly, as an easy introduction to Janua, he wrote *Januae linguarum reseratae vestibulum* [Vestibule to the Gate of Languages Unlocked]. In the following years, Comenius remained active in the educational field, explaining the use of his manuals for teachers in the towns that adopted them and making plans to improve and expand them. The culmination of this continuous educational activity was the translation into Latin of the *Czech Didactic,* as the *Great Didactic,* which was to be the first work in the series subsequently published in the *Opera didactica omnia* [Complete Didactic Works]. During the same period, the original plan to write a *Janua linguarum* or to cooperate with other scholars in writing a *Templum sapientiae* [Temple of Wisdom] developed into the project of 'pansophic' research into universal knowledge, which resulted in the drafting of *Pansophiae prodromus* [Introduction to Pansophy] (1st ed., London, 1637). This was sent to English friends asking for their private opinions; it was published by them without his knowledge.

- 1638—Invited to Sweden to reform the school system. Although he declined the invitation, it encouraged him to translate the *Czech Didactic* into Latin with a view to having it distributed throughout Europe.

- 1639—In reply to the comments received on the Pansophiae prodro-nus, he wrote the *Conatuum pansophicorum dilucidatio* [Explanation of the Endeavours of the Pansophists] (1st ed., London, 1639). In the meantime, he published separately a number of scientific writings, which formed part of this pansophic research, including *Physica ad lumen divinum reformanda* [Toward a Reform of Physics in Accordance with Divine Light] (1st ed., Leipzig, 1639).

- 1641—Travelled on the 4th of February to England (at Parliament's invitation) to collaborate in founding a college of learned men. In a letter (possibly to Ludovic de Geer), he mentioned the idea of a work made up of a Pansophia and a Pampaedia, his first recorded use of that term..

- 1642—Comenius was invited to France by Richelieu to reform the school system, at Mersenne's suggestion. On Richelieu's death, the project was dropped. In July, a meeting with Descartes at Endegeest. In August Comenius travelled to Sweden to discuss school reform with Oxenstiern. He resolved to give up the pansophic plans and return to education. In England he wrote *Via lucis* [The Way of Light], in which he proposed a general reform of cultural and political life. He was prevented from publishing it by the crisis in England, but it was eventually published in Holland (1st ed., Amsterdam, 1668). His *Consultationis brevissima delineatio* [A Very Brief Description of the Consultation] dates from the same period. It was the first real outline of what was to be his great work, the *General Consultation*. The plan that Comenius already had in mind was very close to that which he finally adopted, with the Pampaedia as the center of a triad, opened and closed in turn by a twofold introduction and a twofold conclusion:

4. Pampaedia

3. Pansophia   5. Panglottia

2. Panaugia   6. Panorthosia

1. Panegersia   7. Pannuthesia

ELBLAG PERIOD

- 1642—At Elblag, in Poland today but ruled by Sweden in Comenius's time. Comenius started work on the *Methodus linguarum novissima* [Newest Method of Language Instruction] (1st ed., Leszno, 1648) which, like the *Didactica*, was to provide the theoretical basis for a new series of handbooks: *Vestibulum latinae linguae/Vorthür der lateinischen Sprache* [Vestibule to the Latin Language] (1st ed.,Leszno, 1649), a new bilingual, Latin-German version of the preceding *Janua linguarum reserata* [Grammar of the Gate] with *Annotationes super grammaticam novam janualem* [Notes on the New Grammar of the Gate], and others.

- 1644—On the 24th of August he took part in the Council of Orlag.

- 1645—The Colloquium Charitativum took place from August 24 to September 20 in Torun. Comenius wrote several memoranda for the delegates of the Unitas Fratrum.

- 1646—Briefly returned to Sweden to discuss pansophic plans.

- 1648—Start of his second stay in Leszno. On October 24 the Peace of Westphalia was signed; the Bohemian claims were ignored.

SÁROSPATAK PERIOD

- 1650—In May Comenius moved to Sárospatak, Hungary. He went at the invitation of Zsigmond Rákóczyi, in order to start work on his third series of books on education. After explaining his projects for a pansophic school in a few short texts, he wrote the *Scholae pansophicae classibus septem adornandae delineatio* [Plan of a Seven-Grade Pansophic School], and this was followed by other brief commentaries. Subsequently, in response to a request for a shorter period of schooling, he drew up a new proposal in the form of the *Schola latina tribus classibus divisa* [The Three-Grade Latin School], which introduced the third series of his 'school instruction' handbooks: *Eruditionis scholasticae; Pars prima: Vestibulum* [School Instruction; Part One: Vestibule], followed in this case, too, by the necessary practical tools: *Rudimenta grammaticae* [Rudiments of Grammar], *Reportorium vestibulare sive Lexici latini rudimentum* [Repertory of the Vestibule or Rudiments of Latin Vocabulary] and the *Commonefaction ad praeceptorem* [Instructions for Teachers]; *Pars secunda: Janua* [School Instruction; Part Two: The Gate], again followed by a *Lexicon, a Grammatica, a Historiola and Annotationes; Pars tertia: Atrium* [School instructions; Part Three: Atrium] accompanied by a *Praefation ad praeceptorem* [Preface for the Teacher], the *In latinitatis atrium ingression* [Entrance to the Atrium of Latin Civilization] and the Lexicon Latino-latinum, which was published in Amsterdam (lst ed.,1657). There followed the Continuatio of his Sarospatak writings, which included the *Praecepta morum* [Rules of Life], the *Leges scholae bene ordinate* [Rules for a Well-Regulated School] and, lastly, two educational works that were to prove successful for several generations: *Orbis sensualium pictus* [The Visible World in Pictures] (lst ed., Nuremberg, 1658), which is a Lucidarium, or illustrated aid, to accompany the Vestibule and the Porta, and *Schola ludus* [School as Play] (lst ed., Sarospatak, 1654), which is a dramatized version of the Porta. From this period also was dated the *Artificii legendi et scribendi tirocinium* [Elements of the Art of Reading and Writing], which may perhaps be regarded as a preliminary draft for the Pampaedia.

- 1654—Returned to Leszno for the third time, on June 30.

- 1655—Dispersal of the Sarospatak school because of the plague. Comenius lost track of those of his texts that were in the press at that time.

- 1656—In the fire of Leszno on April 29 Comenius lost, among other works, the manuscript of the *Thesaurus linguae Bohemicae* and a portion of the *Consultatio Catholica*.

AMSTERDAM PERIOD

- 1656—Moved to Amsterdam in August.
- 1657—Convening of the Imperial Parliament in Regensburg.

- 1668—On May 28 he was invited to give an account of his pansophic projects to the Royal society of London. During this period Comenius saw to the publication of the Complete Didactic Works: Part I, written between 1627 and 1642 (Leszno period); Part II, written between 1642 and 1650 (Elblag period); Part III, written between 1650 and 1654 (Sárospatak period).; Part IV, new writings produced in 1657 (in Amsterdam); with short prefaces, dedications, linking paragraphs, and conclusions which, together with the prefaces and autobiographical notes contained in previous writings republished on this occasion, provide material of the highest importance for understanding the development of Comenius's thought. The brief writings in Part IV are as follows: Vita gyrus [Life Is a Circle]; Parvulis parvulus [The Child for Children], designed to serve as an Auctarium, i.e., a supplement to the Vestibolo and the Porta; Apologia (A Defense of the Approach to Latin Adopted in the Porta); Ventilabrum sapientiae [The Winnowing of Wisdom]; Ex labyrinthis scholasticis exitus [The Way Out of the Educational Labyrinth]; Latium redivido [Latium Reborn]; Typographeum vivum [A Typography for Our Time]; Paradisus juventuti christianae reducendus [The Paradise to Be Regained for Christian Youth]; Traditio lampadis [Handing on the Lamp]; Paralipomena didactica [Supplementary Notes to Educational Writings] (lst ed., Amsterdam, 1657). Closely linked to the Complete Didactic Works is the Synopsis methodi linguarum novissimae [Synopsis of the Newest Method of Language Instruction] (lst ed., Amsterdam, 1657), an informatorium for school administrators and teachers in Amsterdam. Concurrently with the printing of the Complete Didactic Works, Comenius gave the final sections of the General ConsultationSp to be printed, intending to present a few advanced copies to scholars and people in power. The printing of a few copies of the following writings was completed in the course of 1656/57: Praefatio ad europaeos [Preface to the Europeans]; Panegersia [Universal Awakening] (lst ed., Halle, 1702; Czech translation, 1895); Panaugia [Universal Dawning]. The fate of the other parts was as follows: Pansophia [Universal Knowledge]: twelve pages were printed and the rest remained in manuscript; Pampaedia [Universal Education] (Czech translation, 1948; Latin-German: Heidelberg, 1960) remained in manuscript; Panorthosia [Universal Reform] (Czech translation, 1950): nine chapters and part of the tenth were printed; Panuthesia [Universal Admonition], which, written after

1664, was printed but subsequently lost, except for twelve chapters and part of the thirteenth; Panglottia [Universal Language Study], preceded by the Novae harmonicae linguae tentamen primum [First Attempt to Devise a New Harmonious Language], which was written in 1665 and 1666, remained in manuscript. To these must be added the Lexicon reale pansophicum [Universal Scientific Vocabulary]. A complete edition of the whole of the Consultatio has been published by the Czechoslovak Academy of Sciences (Prague, 1966). At the end of Komenský's life, the following books were printed or reprinted: Theatrum scripturae [The Theatre of the Sacred Scriptures], planned in his youth as a companion to Theatrum universitatis rerum (lst ed., 1661); Lux e tenebris [A Light Shining in the Darkness] (lst ed., 1663), accompanied by a History of Prophecies, including a reprint of the prophesies of Kotter, Drabik, and Poniatowska, which he had already had printed in 1657; Labyrint světa a ráj srdce [The Labyrinth of the World and the Paradise of the Heart] (lst ed., 1663); Clamores Eliae [The Exhortations of Elijah] (lst ed., 1665); Angelus pacis [The Angel of Peace], addressed to the negotiators of the peace between Holland and England (lst ed., 1667); Unum necessarium [The One Thing Necessary] (lst ed., 1669).

- 1670—Died in Amsterdam on October 15 or November 25.

APPENDIX 4

Glossary of Special Terms

Apologetics: The term comes from the Greek *apologia*, meaning a verbal and rational defense. In relation to Christianity, it is the academic discipline that deals with a rational defense of the Christian faith.

Chiliasm: A specific concept of some varieties of Christian eschatology. The term comes from the Greek *chiliasmos*, meaning "a thousand years." The essence of the teaching is as follows: before the end of the world Christ will once again return to earth, defeat the Antichrist, resurrect only the righteous, and establish a kingdom on earth in which the righteous, as a reward for their struggles and sufferings, will reign with Him for one thousand years. After this will be another resurrection, in which the rest of the people will be raised from the dead. Then the Universal Judgment will take place, in which God will reward the righteous and punish the sinners. The defenders of this teaching base their arguments mainly on the 20th chapter of the book of Revelations in the Bible.

Emendation: From the Latin *emendare*, meaning an alteration designed to correct or improve.

Empiricism: A type of theory of knowledge based on the primacy of human experience. The term comes from the Greek *empiria*, meaning "experience." The primary source of knowing in empiricism is observation and experiment.

Encyclopaedism: An effort to encompass all human knowledge. The undertaking stretches back to classical antiquity but was significantly developed with the arrival of the scientific boom of the Enlightenment era. In pedagogy the term refers to acquiring a large amount of data, often isolated and adopted without a proper understanding of their inter-relatedness or substantial meaning.

Epistemology: The philosophic discipline that deals with human knowledge, investigating its origin, nature, possibilities, processes, etc. The term is derived from the Greek *episteme* and *logos*, meaning the study of how we know. Sometimes the term "noetics" is used as a synonym.

Eschatology: From the Greek eschaton, meaning "last." It is the Christian doctrine which deals with the last things—either of an individual (death, judgment, etc.) or the world (endtimes, Apocalypse). The concept is also used in a secular sense.

Exegesis: Of Greek origin. It refers to the critical examination of a text (especially a religious one). The term itself means "pulled out." Exegetical work is objective, that is, the goal is the true meaning of the text.

Fabule: From the Latin *fabula*. A narrative, literary summary of events, or plot. A plot adds something to the reader, either during the reading or later, as the contrast between the story and plot is formed in the reader's consciousness. The story, or storyline, tells what happened, while the plot dictates how the reader gets to know the story.

Irenism: From the Greek *eiréné*, which means "peace." It is a concept which strives for reconciliation between religious denominations and churches. It is a tool of natural theology which attempts to establish religious unity using reason as an essential attribute.

Millenialism: The Latin equivalent of chiliasm, derived from the word *millenium*, meaning "thousand years."

Pansophy: From the Greek *pan-sophia*, meaning "universal wisdom." It is about philosophical orientation, method and skill all at once. The goal of pansophy is the harmonization of human knowledge in order to restore or repair the world.

Prophesy/prophetic: Prophesying, in the sense of speaking in the name of God, delivering a divine message.

Rosicrucian: The Rosicrucian order (Brothers of the Red Cross) was founded in the early seventeenth century. It was a secret international society which used philosophical-alchemistic methods to renew a degenerate society and humanity in general. Johann Valentin Andreae (1586–1654) was likely the author of the Rosicrucian Manifesto and legends.

Socianism: A (heretical) Christian movement, or religion, which, among other things, denied the orthodox doctrine of the Trinity. It was named after its founder, Faustus Socinus, whose teachings gained many followers in Poland during the sixteenth and seventeenth centuries.

Soteriology: Theological doctrine dealing with the salvation of human beings. The concept is derived from the Greek *soterion*, which is translated as "salvation."

Syncretism: From Greek *syn*, meaning "with," and *krinein*, meaning "to separate" or "to compare", referring to a method of comparison and contrast of parallel cases in the process of acquisition a unified knowledge.

Succession (Apostolic): From the Latin *successio*, it is a theological concept which refers to the uninterrupted spiritual continuity (for the most part) of Catholic bishops from the early Christian apostles.

Bibliography

Alston, William P. *Illocutionary Acts and Sentence Meaning.* Ithaca, NY: Cornell University Press, 2000.

Alt, Robert. *Pokrokový charakter Komenského pedagogiky* [Progressive Character of Comenius' Pedagogy]. Praha: Státní pedagogické nakladatelství, 1959.

Austin, John Langshaw. *Jak udělat něco slovy* [How To Do Things with Words]. Praha: Filosofia, 2000.

Balcar, Lubomír. "Theologické srovnání Komenského 'Labyrintu světa's Bunyanovou knihou 'Pilgrims Progress'" [Theological Comparison of Comenius' *Labyrinth of the World* and Bunyan's *Pilgrim's Progress*]. In *Archiv pro bádání o životě a spisech J. A. Komenského* 14 (1937) 113–25.

Baldermann, Ingo. *Úvod do biblické didaktiky* [Introduction to Biblical Didactics]. Translated by L. Beneš et al. Jihlava: Mlýn, 2004.

Bauman, Zigmunt. *Individualizovaná společnost* [The Individualized Society]. Praha: Mladá fronta, 2004.

Bayle, Pierre. *Dictionnairie Historique et Critique.* 1695. Reprint. Paris: Libraire, Rue Christine 1820.

Bečková, Marta. "Das Werk Komenský's in seinem Nachleben." In *Symposium Comenianum 1986*, edited by Marie Kyralová and Jana Přivratská, 215–26. Praha: Comenius Institute of Education of the Czechoslovak Academy of Sciences, 1989.

———. "On the Development of Comenius Research in Czechoslovakia since the War." In *Symposium Comenianum 1982*, edited by Marie Kyralová and Jana Přivratská, 143–50. Uherský Brod: Comenius museum, 1984.

Bílý, František. "Úvod" [Introduction]. In *Labyrint světa a ráj srdce*, 7–22. Praha: Česká grafická unie, 1939.

Bratrské vyznání [Brethren Confession]. In *Čtyři vyznání*, edited by Bartoš, František, Michálek, 113–76. Praha: Komenského Evangelická Bohoslovecká Fakulta, 1951.

Čapek, Jan Blahoslav. *Několik pohledů na Komenského* [Several Views on Comenius]. Praha: Karolinum, 2004.

Čapková, Dagmar. "Demokratizmus Komenského systému celoživotního vzdělávání" [Democratism of Comenius' System of Lifelong Learning]. In *Demokratizmus v diele Jana Amosa Komenského*. Bratislava: Slovenské pedagogické nakladateľstvo, 1974.

———. "John Amos Comenius, An Outline of his Life and Work." In *Digitalizace Komenián*, edited by Hýbl František. CD, no pages. Praha-Přerov: Pedagogické muzeum J. A. Komenského v Praze, 2002.

BIBLIOGRAPHY

———. "Kobrazu J. A. Komenského v české pedagogice 20. století" [A Picture of J. A. Comenius in Czech Pedagogy of the Twentieth Century]. In *Studia Comeniana et historica* 67–68 (2002) 203–40.

———. *Některé základní principy pedagogického myšlení J. A. Komenského* [Some Basic Principles of J. A. Comenius' Pedagogical Thought]. Praha: Academia, 1977.

———. "On the Impact of J. A. Comenius to the Theory and Practice of Education." In *Symposium Comenianum 1982*, edited by Marie Kyralová and Jana Přivratská, 11–28. Uherský Brod: Comenius Institute of Education of the Czechoslovak Academy of Sciences, 1984.

———. "Škola a utváření lidství v pojetí J. A. Komenského" [School and the Shaping of Humanity in the Concepts of J. A. Comenius]. *Pedagogica* 41 (1991) 5–6.

Červenka, Jaromír. "One Hundred Years of the Views on Comenius Pansophia." In *Consultationes de Consultatione*, 21–84. Praha: Czechoslovak Academy of Science, 1970.

———. "Pokračování vidění Drabíkových" [The Continuing Vision of Drabík]. In *Vybrané spisy Jana Amose Komenského* 6, edited by Jan Patočka, 403–30. Praha: Státní Pedagogické Nakladatelství, 1972.

———. "Úvod k Obecné poradě" [Introduction to the General Consultation]. In *Vybrané spisy Jana Amose Komenského* 4, edited by Otakar Chlup, 5–53. Praha: Státní Pedagogické Nakladatelství, 1966.

Chatman, Seymour. *Příběh a diskurs. Narativní struktura v literatuře a filmu* [Story and Discourse: Narrative Structure in Literature and Film]. Brno: Host, 2008.

Chlup, Otakar. "Zhodnocení Komenského myšlenky pansofické" [Evaluation of Comenius's Pansophic Concept]. In *Vybrané spisy Jana Amose Komenského* 4, edited by Otakar Chlup, 53–57. Praha: Státní Pedagogické Nakladatelství, 1966.

Cipro, Miroslav. *Prameny Výchovy, Galerie Světových Pedagogů I, II, III* [Sources of Education, a Gallery of World Educators]. Praha: Cipro, 2002.

Comenius, J. A. *Angelus pacis* [Angel of Peace], first printing. Unknown loc: unknown pub, 1667. Location

———. *Clamores Eliae* [The Exhortations of Elijah]. Written 1670. In *Dílo Jana Amose Komenského*, 23, edited by Jiřina Otáhalová-Popelová and Julie Nováková, 1–536. Praha: Academia, 1992.

———. *Didaktika analytická* [Analytic Didactic]. Written 1644–47. Praha: Samcovo knihkupectví, 1946.

———. *Didaktika česká* [Czech Didactic]. 4th ed. Praha: Národní knihtiskárna I. L. Kober, 1926.

———. *Didactica magna* [Great Didactic]. First printing 1657. In *Dílo Jana Amose Komenského* 15, 35–214. Praha: Academia, 1986.

———. *Didaktika velká* [Great Didactic]. First printing 1657. Praha: Grégr a syn, 1905.

———. "Geometria." In *Vybrané spisy Jana Amose Komenského* 5. Praha: Státní Pedagagické Nakladatelství, 1968.

———. *The Great Didactic (Didactica Magna)*. Translated by M. W. Keatinge. New York: Russell & Russell, 1967.

———. *Hlubina bezpečnosti* [The Depths of Safety]. First printing 1633. Praha: Spolek Komenského, 1927.

———. *Jedno potřebné* [The One Necessary Thing]. First printing 1668. Praha: Melantrich, 1920.

————. *Labyrint světa a ráj srdce*. First printing 1631. In *Veškeré spisy Jana Amose Komenského* 15, edited by Jan Kvačala, 181–328. Brno: Ústřední spolek jednot učitelských na Moravě, 1910.

————. *Obecná porada o nápravě věcí lidských* [A General Consultation on the Restoration of Human Affairs], 1, 2, 3. First printing 1664. Praha: Nakladatelství Svoboda, 1992.

————. *Opera didactica omnia*. 4 vols. First printing 1657. Praha: Státní pedagogické nakladatelství, 1955.

————. *Předchůdce vševědy* (Pansophiae praeludium). In *Vybrané spisy Jana Amose Komenského* 5. Praha: Státní pedagogické nakladatelství, 1966.

————. *Truchlivý I*. In *Veškeré spisy Jana Amose Komenského* 15, edited by Jan Kvačala, 94–139. First printing 1624. Brno: Ústřední spolek jednot učitelských na Moravě, 1910.

————. *Vševýchova* [Universal Education]. First printing 1664. Praha: Státní nakladatelství, 1948.

Čuma, Aleš. "Vztah ruskej školy k demokratickému odkazu J. A. Komenského v 2. polovici 19. Storočia" [The Relationship of the Russian School to the Democratic Legacy of J. A. Comenius]. In *Demokratizmus v diele Jana Amosa Komenského*, 5–12. Bratislava: Slovenské pedagogické nakladateľstvo, 1974.

Darling, John, and Sven Erik Nordembo. "Progressivism." In *The Blackwell Guide to Philosophy of Education*, edited by N. Blake et al., 288–309. Oxford: Blackwell, 2003.

Dobiáš, František Mrázek. *Víra a vyznání českých bratří* [Faith and Creed of the Czech Brethren]. Praha: Vydavatelské oddělení KSML pro Evangelické dílo, 1941.

Dolejšová (Noble), Ivana. *Accounts of Hope: A Problem of Method in Postmodern Apologia*. European University Studies, ser. 23; Theology 726. Bern: Lang, 2001.

Doležel, Lubomír. "Kompozice 'Labyrintu světa a ráje srdce' J. A. Komenského" [The Composition of Comenius's *The Labyrinth of the World and the Paradise of the Heart*]. In *Česká literatura* 17 (1969) 37–54.

————. *Narativní způsoby v české próze* [Narrative Methods in Czech Prose]. Praha: Československý spisovatel, 1993.

Eagleton, Terry. *The Illusions of Postmodernism*. Oxford: Blackwell, 1996.

Eco, Umberto. *Meze interpretace* [Limits of Interpretation]. Praha: Karolinum, 2004.

————. *Šest procházek literárními lesy* [Six Win the Fictional Woods]. Olomouc: Votobia, 1997.

Erickson, Millard J. *Truth or Consequences: The Promise and Perils of Postmodernism*. Downers Grove, IL: IVP, 2001.

Floss, Pavel. *Nástin života, díla a myšlení Jana Amose Komenského* [Outline of the Life, Work, and Thought of Jan Amos Comenius]. Přerov: Vlastivědný ústav, 1970.

————. *Od divadla věcí k dramatu člověka* [From the Theater of Things to the Drama of Man]. Ostrava: Profil, 1970.

————. *Poselství J. A. Komenského současné Evropě* [Messages of J. A. Comenius to Contemporary Europe]. Brno: Soliton, 2005.

Friedman, Jill, and Gene Combs. *Narativní psychoterapie* [Narrative Psychotherapy]. Praha: Portál, 2009.

Geissler, Heinrich. "Das Christus-Verständnis in der Pädagogik des Johann Amos Comenius" [The Understanding of Christ in the Pedagogy of Jan Amos Comenius]. In *Das Wort Gottes in Geschichte und Gegenwart*, edited by Wilhelm Andersen, 196–207. München: Kaiser, 1957.

Greer, Robert C. *Mapping Postmodernism*. Downers Grove, IL: IVP, 2003.

Greer, Thomas H., and Gavin Lewis. *A Brief History of the Western World*. 7th ed. Florida: Harcourt Brace, 1997.

Grenz, Stanley J. *A Primer on Postmodernism*. Grand Rapids: Eerdmans, 1996.

Hábl, Jan. *Lessons in Humanity From the Life and Works of Jan Amos Komenský*. Bonn: Verlag für Kultur und Wissenschaft, 2011.

———. *Teaching and Learning through Story: Comenius' Labyrinth and the Educational Potential of Narrative Allegory*. Bonn: Verlag für Kultur und Wissenschaft 2014.

Haman, Aleš. "Estetický rozměr světa v Komenského Labyrintu" [The Aesthetic Dimension of the World in Comenius' *Labyrinth*]. *Tvar* 16.21 (2005) 8–9.

Hanesová, Dana. "Aktivizujúce metódy v kresťanskom vzdelávaní" [Activating Methods in Christian Education]. In *Evanjelikálny teologický časopis* 2 (2002) 33–36.

Harbo, Tomáš. "Humanizace vzdělání a současné teorie kurikula" [The Humanization of Education and Current Theories in Curricula]. *Pedagogika* 41.3 (1991) 247–55.

Harvey, David. *The Condition of Postmodernity: An Enquiry into the Conditions of Cultural Change*. Oxford: Blackwell, 1989.

Helus, Zdeněk. "Culture of Education at the Beginning of the New Millenium, Current Educational Challenges." In *Jan Amos Komenský. Odkaz kultuře vzdělávání*, edited by Svatava Chocholová et al., 671–85. Praha: Academia, 2009.

———. "Humanizace školy—samozřejmost či rozporuplná výzva" [The Humanization of Education—a Given, or a Contradictory Challenge]. In *Pedagogická Revue* 55.5 (2003) 427–40.

Hendrich, Josef. *Jan Amos Komenský ve světle svých spisů* [Jan Amos Comenius in Light of His Writings]. Praha: Družstevní práce v Praze, 1941.

Heřmánek, Pavel. *Jan Amos Komenský a Kristýna Poniatowská*. MA diss., Prague: Charles University, 2005.

Hessen, Sergěj. *Filosofické základy pedagogiky* [Philosophical Basis of Pedagogy]. Praha: ČSGU, 1936.

Hošek, Pavel. *C. S. Lewis, mýtus, imaginace a pravda* [C. S. Lewis, Myth, Imagination, and Truth]. Praha: Návrat, 2003.

———. *Cesta ke kořenům: Odkaz šlechtického rodu Milnerů z Milhausenu a jeho nositelé* [Journey to the Roots. The Legacy of the Noble Family of Miller from Milhausen and Its Descendents]. Brno: Centrum Demokracie a Kultury, 2010.

———. "Proměňující moc příběhu" [The Transforming Power of Story]. In *Církevní dějiny* 3.5 (2010) 87–96.

Hrabák, Josef. "K stylistické výstavbě Komenského 'Labyrintu'" [The Stylistic Construction of Comenius's "Labyrinth"]. *Listy filologické* 93 (1970) 284–88.

Ingarden, Roman. *O poznání literárního díla* [Knowledge of Literary Works]. Praha: Československý spisovatel, 1967.

Kalhous, Zdeněk et al. *Školní didaktika* [Teaching Methodology]. Praha: Portál, 2002.

Kant, Imanuel. *O výchově* [On Education]. Translated by Josef Jančařík. Praha: Dědictví Komenského, 1931.

Karšai, František. "Democratizmus v pedagogickom odkaze J. A. Komenského" [Democracy in the Pedagogical Legacy of J. A. Comenius]. In *Demokratizmus v diele Jana Amosa Komenského*, 197–206. Bratislava: Slovenské pedagogické nakladateľstvo, 1974.

Kasper, Tomáš, and Dana Kasperová. *Vybrané kapitoly z dějin pedagogiky* [Selected Chapters from the History of Education]. Liberec: Technická univerzita v Liberci, 2006.

Kolár, Jiří, and Věra Petráčková. "Komentář." [Commentary or Afterword]. In *Truchlivý I, II, Labyrint světa a ráj srdce*, 365–97. Praha: Nakladatelství lidové noviny, 1998.

Kopecký, Milan. "J. V. Andreae a J. A. Komenský: literární analogie a diference." [J. A. Komenský: Literary Analogy and Differentness]. In *Studia Comeniana et historica* 18.35 (1988) 160–68.

————. *Komenský jako umělec slova*. Brno: Masarykova Univerzita, 1992.

Kostlán, Antonín. "K 'negaci světa' v raných dílech J. A. Komenského." [On "Refutation of the World" in Comenius's Early Works]. In *Studia Comeniana et historica* 15.29 (1985) 149–55.

Kožmín, Zdeněk, and Drahomíra Kožmínová. *Zvětšeniny z Komenského* [Magnifications in Comenius]. Brno: Host, 2007.

Králík, Stanislav, ed. *Otázky současné komeniologie*. Praha: Academia, 1981.

Krámský, David. "Komenského svět jako labyrint ve fenomenologické interpretaci." [Comenius' World as Labyrinth in Phenomological Interpretation]. *Studia Comeniana et historica* 35.73–74 (2005) 27–35.

Krasnovskij, Archip Aleksejevič. *Jan Amos Komenský*. Praha: Státní Pedagogické Nakladatelství, 1955.

Kratochvíl, Ladislav. "Pedagogický realismus Komenského." [Comenius' Pedagogical Realism]. In *Jan Amos Komenský*, edited by Jiří Václav Klíma, 123–31. Praha: L. J. Peroutka, Unie, 1947.

Kreeft, Peter. *Ethics: A History of Moral Thought*. Recorded books, LLC, 2003. Online: https://richardconlin.files.wordpress.com/2015/06/peter-kreeft-ethics-modern-scholar.pdf.

————. *Making Choices. Practical Wisdom for Everyday Moral Decisions*. Grand Rapids: Servant, 1990.

Krofta, Kamil. *Dějiny československé* [History of Czechoslovakia]. Praha: Sfinx, 1946.

Kubíček, Tomáš. *Vypravěč. Kategorie narativní analýzy* [Narrator: Category of Narrative Analysis]. Brno: Host, 2007.

————. *Vyprávět příběh. Naratologické kapitoly k románům Milana Kundery* [To Tell a Story: Narratological Chapters on the Works of Milan Kundera]. Brno: Host, 2001.

Kučera, Karel. "Lidová rčení v Labyrintu světa a ráji srdce J. A. Komenského" [Folk Sayings in Comenius's *Labyrinth of the World and the Paradise of the Heart*]. In *Studia Comeniana et historica* 2.3 (1972) 27–34.

Khun, Pavel. *Humanizácia výchovy a vzdelávania* [The Humanization of Education]. Bratislava: Státní Pedagogický Ústav, 1994

Kulič, Vaclav. "J. A. Comenius and Contemporary Psychodidactics." In *Symposium Comenianum 1982*, edited by Marie Kyralová and Jana Přivratská, 122–31. Uherský Brod: Comenius Institute of Education of the Czechoslovak Academy of Sciences, 1984.

Kumpera, Jan. "Comenius and England." In *Comenius in World Science and Culture*, C-III, edited by Jaroslav Pánek, 91–97. Prague: Historical Institute of Academy, 1991.

————. *Jan Amos Komenský*. Ostrava: Amosium Servis & Nakladatelství Svoboda, 1992.

Kvačala, Jan. *Jan Amos Komenký, jeho osobnost a soustava věd pedagogických* [Comenius, His Character and System of Pedagogical Science]. Praha: Muzeum Jana Amose Komenského, 1920.

Kyrášek, Jiří. *Synkritická metoda v díle J. A. Komenského* [Syncretic Methods in the Works of Comenius]. Praha: Československá Akademie Věd, 1964.

BIBLIOGRAPHY

Lášek, Jan Blahoslav. "Der Bekenner, Bischof und Wissenschaftler J. A. Comenius" [The Confessor, Bishop, and Scientist J. A. Comenius]. In *Internationales Comenius Koloquium*, edited by Kotowski et al., 13–19. Prague: Husitská Teologická Fakultá, 1992.

———. "Komenský kazatel" [Comenius the Preacher]. In *Teologická Revue Husitské Teologické Fakulty* 4 (1992) 56–61.

Lewis, C. S. "Bluspels and Flalansferers." In *Selected Literary Essays*, edited by Walter Hooper, 251–65. Cambridge: Cambridge University Press, 1969.

———. *Pilgrims Regress*. Grand Rapids: Eerdmans, 1996.

———. *Surprised by Joy: The Shape of My Early Life*. London: Harcourt, Brace, Jovanovich, 1955.

Lochman, Jan Milič. "Comenius as Theologian." *Acta Comeniana* 10.34 (1993) 35–47.

Lyotard, Jean-François. *O postmodernismu* [The Postmodern Condition]. Praha: Filosofie, 1993.

Machovec, Milan. *Filozofie tváří v tvář zániku* [Philosophy in the Face of Extinction]. Brno: Nakladatelství Zvláštní vydání, 1998.

MacIntyre, Alasdair. *After Virtue*. Notre Dame, IN: Notre Dame University Press, 1981.

Marklund, Sixten. "School Stages and Student Development: An Application of Comenian Thinking." In *Symposium Comenianum 1982*, edited by Marie Kyralová and Jana Přivratská, 55–63. Uherský Brod: n.p., 1984.

Masaryk, Tomáš Garrigue. *J. A. Comenius*. Lecture, delivered in 1892 in "Slavia." Online: http://www.czp.cuni.cz/filv/phprs/download.php?sekce=2 [accessed 14 July 2012].

Menck, Peter. "The Formation of Conscience: A Lost Topic of Didactic." *Journal of Curriculum Studies* 33.3 (2001) 261–75.

Michálek, Emanuel. "Tradiční rysy v slovní zásobě Komenského Labyrintu" [Traditional Features in the Vocabulary of Comenius's *Labyrinth*]. *Acta Comeniana* 26 (1970) 229–38.

Miller, Joseph Hillis. "Narativ." *Aluze* 12.1 (2008). Online: www.aluze.cz/2008_01/05_studie_miller.php, [accessed 14 July 2012].

Mirvaldová, Hana. "Alegoričnost v Labyrintu světa a ráji srdce J. A. Komenskeho" [Allegory in Comenious's *Labyrinth of the World and the Paradise of the Heart*]. In *Slovo a slovesnost* 31.4 (1970) 353–64.

Mitoseková, Zofia. *Teorie literatury. Historický přehled* [Theory of Literature. Historical Overview]. Brno: Host, 2010.

Mišíková, Katarína. *Mysl a příběh ve filmové fikci* [Mind and Story in Cinematic Fiction]. Praha: Nakladatelství Akademie múzických umění, 2009.

Molnár, Amedeo. *Bratr Lukáš, bohoslovec Jednoty* [Brother Luke, a Divinity Student in the Unity of Brethren]. Praha: Kalich, 1948.

———. *Českobratrská výchova před Komenským* [Brethren Education before Komenský]. Praha: Státní Pedagogické Nakladatelství, 1956.

———. "Eschatologická naděje české reformace" [Eschatological Hope of the Czech Reformation]. In *Od reformace k zítřku*, edited by Mrázek Dobiáš František, et al., 13–101. Praha: Kalich, 1956.

———. "Martin Luther a Jednota." In *Acta Reformationem Bohemicam Illustrantia* 3, edited by Noemi Rejchrtová, 109–35. Praha: Kalich, 1984.

———. "O Komenského jako teologa" [On Comenius as a Theologian]. In *Sedm statí o Komenském*, edited by Mrázek Dobiáš František et al., 3–15. Praha: Komenského evangelická bohoslovecká fakulta, 1971.

BIBLIOGRAPHY

————. *Valdenští* [Valdenses]. Praha: Kalich, 1991.

Molnár, Amedeo, and Noemi Rejchrtová. *J. A. Komenský o sobě* [J. A. Comenius on Himself]. Praha: Odeon, 1987.

Murphy, Daniel. *Comenius: A Critical Reassessment of His Life and Work.* Dublin: Irish Academic Press, 1995.

Murphy, Nancey. *Anglo-American Postmodernity: Philosophical Perspectives on Science, Religion, and Ethics.* Oxford: Westview, 1997.

————. *Beyond Liberalism and Fundamentalism: How Modern and Postmodern Philosophy Set the Theological Agenda.* Valley Forge, PA: Trinity, 1996.

————. *Theology in a Postmodern Age.* Prague: International Baptist Theological Seminary, 2003.

Murphy, Nancey, and James Wm. McClendon Jr. "Distinguishing Modern and Postmodern Theologies." *Modern Theology* 5.3 (1989) 191–214.

Nastoupilová, Alena. *Pojetí odpovědnosti v díle bratra Lukáše a J. A. Komenského* [The Notion of Responsibility in the Work of Brother Lukáš and J. A. Comenius.]. Hradec Králové: Gaudeamus, 2002.

Novitz, David. "Umění, narativ a lidská povaha." *Aluze* 13.3 (2009). Online: http://www.aluze.cz/2009_03/04_studie_novitz.php, [accessed 21 July 2012].

Nový, Lubomír. "Dialektika vnějšího a vnitřního v Labyrintu světa" [External and Internal Dialectic in the World of the Labyrinth]. *Studia Comeniana et historica* 13.26 (1983) 95–97.

Neval, Daniel. "An Approach to the Legacy of Comenius' Theology." In *Bohemian Reformation and Religious Practice III*, edited by Zdeněk V. David and David R. Holeton, 215–28. Praha: Academy of Sciences of the Czech Republic. Main Library, 2000.

————. *Die Macht Gottes zum Heil, Das Bibelverständnis von Johann Amos Comenius in einer Zeit der Krise und des Umbruches* [The Power of God to Salvation, the Biblical Understanding of Jan Amos Comenius in a Time of Crisis and Upheaval]. PhD diss., University of Zürich, 2004.

Novák, Jan Václav. "*Úvod k Centrum Securitatis*" [Introduction to the Centrum Securitatis]. In *Veškeré Spisy Jana Amose Komenského* 15, edited by Jan Kvačala, 381–84. Brno: Ústřední spolek jednot učitelských na Moravě, 1910.

————. "*Úvod k Listové do nebe*" [Introduction to Letters to Heaven]. In *Veškeré Spisy Jana Amose Komenského* 15, edited by Jan Kvačala, 3–5. Brno: Ústřední spolek jednot učitelských na Moravě, 1910.

————. *Labyrint světa a ráj srdce J. A. Komenského a jeho vzory* [Labyrinth of the World and the Paradise of the Heart of J. A. Comenius and Its Patterns]. Praha: Časopis Českého Muzea, 1895.

Palouš, Radim. *Čas výchovy* [Time for Education]. Praha: Státní Pedagogické Nakladatelství, 1991.

————. "J. A. Komenský—náboženský myslitel" [J. A. Comenius—Religious Thinker]. *Studia Comeniana et historica* 51.24 (1994) 7–12.

————. *Komenského Boží Svět* [The World of Comenius's God]. Praha: Státní Pedagogické Nakladatelství, 1992.

Pánek, Jaroslav. "The Heritage of the Czech Humanist J. A. Comenius." In *Comenius in World Science and Culture*, 9–20. Praha: Historical Institute of Academy, 1991.

———. "The Labyrinth of Czech Lands in the Period before the Battle of the White Mountain." In *Symposium Comenianum 1986*, edited by Marie Kyralová,and Jana Přivratská, 202–18. Praha: Academia, 1989.

Pascal, Blaise. *Pensées*. English translation by A. J. Krailsheimer, New York: Penguin, 1995.

Patočka, Jan. *Aristoteles, jeho předchůdci a dědicové* [Aristotle, His Predecessors and Heirs]. Praha: Nakladatelství Československé akademie věd, 1964.

———. *Komeniologické studie 1, 2, 3.* 3 vols. Praha: Oikoymenh, 1997, 1998, 2003.

———. "Mezihra na prahu moderní vědy: Cusanus a Komenský." [Interlude on the Threshold of Modern Science: Cusanus and Comenius]. In *Muž bolesti a naděje, Sborník k 400. výročí narození J. A. K.*, edited by Emil Havlíček, 30–44. Praha: Blahoslav, 1992.

———. "Nový obraz Komenského" [A New Picture of Comenius]. In *Archiv Jana Amose Komenského* 18 (1959) 385–92.

———. "*Úvod*" [Introduction]. In *Svazku vybraných spisů J. A. Komenského*, edited by Otakar Chulup et al., 5–57. Praha: Státní Pedagogické Nakladatelství, 1958.

Pařízek. Vlastimil. "Komenského pedagogická soustava" [Comenius's Pedagogical System]. In *Jan Amos Komenský a jeho odkaz dnešku*, edited by Josef Polišenský and Vlastimil Pařízek, 37–54. Praha: Státní Pedagogické Nakladatelství, 1987.

Pelcová, Naděžda. "Komeniův výchovný sen v reflexi moderní filosofické a pedagogické antropologie" [Comenius's Educational Dream in the Reflection of Modern Philosophical and Pedagogical Anthropology]. In *Jan Amos Komenský. Odkaz kultuře vzdělávání*, edited by Svatova Chocholová et al., 229–41. Praha: Academia, 2009.

———. "O krizi pojmu humanismus" [On the Crisis of the Concept of Humanism]. In *Mezigenerační porozumění a komunikace*, edited by Věra Jirásková et al., 139–60. Praha: Eurolex Bohemia, 2005.

———. *Vzorce lidství. Filosofie o člověku a výchově* [The Pattern for Humanity: A Philosophy of Man and Education]. Praha: ISV, 2001.

Petrů, Eduard. "Filozofie a filozofové v Labyrintu J. A. Komenského" [Philosophy and Philosophers in the *Labyrinth* of J. A. Comenius]. In *Studia Comeniana et historica* 15.29 (1985) 121–26.

———. "Parodie u Erasma Rotterdamského a Jana Amose Komenského" [Parody in Erasmus of Rotterdam and Jan Amos Comenius]. In *Studia Comeniana et historica* 18.35 (1988) 137–43.

Pešková, Jaroslava. "Aktuální aspekty filosofické argumentace v Komenského 'Konsultaci'" [Current Aspects of the Philosophical Arguments in Comenius' *Consultations*]. In *Filosofický časopis* 40.1 (1992a) 51–56.

———. "Jan Amos Komenský ve světle nového bádání" [Jan Amos Comenius in Light of New Research]. *Studia Comeniana et historica* 22.46–47 (1992b) 21–28.

Pešková, Jaroslava et al. *Homage to J. A. Comenius*. Praha: Karolinum, 1991.

Piaget, Jean. *Jan Amos Comenius, Prospects* (UNESCO, International Bureau of Education) 23.1/2 (1993) Online: http://www.ibe.unesco.org/sites/default/files/comeniuse.PDF.

Polkinghorn, Donald. "Narrative Therapy and Postmodernism." In *The Handbook of Narrative and Psychotherapy*, edited by John McLeod and Lynne E. Angus, 53–68. London: Sage, 2004.

Polišenský, Josef. *Jan Amos Komenský*. Praha: Svobodné slovo, 1963.

Popelová, Jiřina. *Komenského cesta k všenápravě* [Comenius's Way to the Restoration of All Things]. Praha: Státní Pedagogické Nakladatelství, 1958.

BIBLIOGRAPHY

Pospíšil, Jiří. *Filosofická východiska cílů výchovy a vzdělávání v období novověkého obratu* [Philosophical Basis of the Goals of Education in the Period of the Shift to Modernity]. Olomouc: Hanex 2009.

———. "Náboženská pedagogika a cíle výchovy v Obecné poradě o nápravě věcí lidských J. A. Komenského" [Religious Pedagogy and the Goal of Education in Comenius's General Consultation on Human Affairs]. *Paidagogos* 16.4 (2004) Online: http://old. paidagogos.net/16/1.html.

Prázný, Aleš. "Komenský—myslitel krize" [Comenius—Critical Thinker]. *Pedagogika* 3 (2008) 236–40.

Propp, Vladimír Jakovlevič. *Morfologie pohádky a jiné studie* [The Morphology of Fairy Tales and Other Studies]. Praha: Nakladatelství H&H, 1999.

Příhoda, Václav. *Racionalizace školství* [Rationalization of Education]. Praha: Orbis, 1930.

Ricoeur, Paul. *Reflection and Imagination*. Edited by Mario J. Valdés, London: Harvester Wheatsheaf, 1991.

Röd, Wolfgang. *Novověká filosofie* [New Age of Philosophy]. Praha: Oikoymenh, 2004.

Rousseau, Jean-Jacques. *Emil, čili o vychování* [Emil, or on Education]. Translated by Jan Novák and M. Svoboda, Praha: Dědictví Komenského, 1911.

Ryba, Bohumil, ed. *Sto listů Jana Amosa Komenského* [One Hundred Letters of Jan Amos Comenius]. Praha: Jan Laichter, 1945.

Rýdl, Karel. "Didaktické perspektivy inovujících procesů v rámci humanizace výchovy a vzdělávání" [Didactic Perspectives on Innovative Processes within the Framework of the Humanization of Education]. In *Historie a perspektivy didaktického myšlení,* edited by A. Vališová, 350–57. Praha: Karolinum, 2004.

———. "Jak vlastně rozumíme Komenského odkazu dnešku?" In *Idea harmonie v díle Jana Amose Komenského,* edited by Věra Šifferová, et al., 207–14. Pavel Mervart: Univerzita Pardubice, 2014.

Říčan, Rudolf. *Dějiny Jednoty bratrské* [History of the Unity of Brethren]. Praha: Kalich, 1957.

Říčan, Rudolf, et al. *Bratrský sborník* [Brethren Anthology]. Praha: Komenského Evangelická fakulta bohoslovecká, 1967.

———. *Od úsvitu reformace k dnešku* [From the Dawn of the Reformation to the Present]. Praha: YMCA, 1947.

Sadler, John Edward. *J. A. Comenius and the Concept of Universal Education*. London: Allen & Unwin, 1966.

Šalda, František X. "O literárním baroku cizím i domácím" [On Foreign and Domestic Baroque Literature]. In *Z období zápisníku* 1, edited by František Šalda, 282–307. Praha: Odeon, 1987.

Schaller, Klaus. *Die politische Pädagogik des J. A. Comenius* [The pedagogy of J. A. Comenius]. *Acta Comeniana* 3.27 (1972) 67–77.

———. *Die Pädagogik des Johann Amos Comenius und die Anfänge des pädagogischen Realismus im 17. Jahrhundert* [The Pedagogy of Jan Amos Comenius and the Beginnings of Educational Realism in the Seventeenth century]. 2nd ed. Heidelberg: Quelle & Meyer, 1967.

———. *Die Pampaedia des J. A. Comenius. Eine Einführung in sein Hauptwerk* [The Pampaedia of J. A. Comenius: An Introduction to His Main Work]. Heidelberg: Quelle & Meyer, 1958.

————. "Komenský a otevřená duše—Patočkův výklad Komenského" [Comenius and the Open Spirit—Patočka's Interpretation of Comenius]. *Filosofický časopis* 40.1 (1992) 35–47.

————. "Několik poznámek k problematice revelací u Komenského" [Some Remarks on the Problems Revealed in Comenius]. *Studia Comeniana et historica* 7.17 (1977) 172–76.

Searle, John R. *Speech Acts: An Essay in the Philosophy of Language.* Cambridge: Cambridge University Press, 1969.

Shapiro, Rami. *Chasidské povídky* [Hasidic Tales]. Praha: Volvox Globator, 2006.

Schank, Roger, and Gary Saul Morson. *Tell Me a Story: Narrative and Inteligence.* Evanston, IL: Northwestern University Press, 2000.

Schmid, Wolf. *Narativní transformace.* Brno: Ústav pro českou literaturu, 2004.

Skalková, Jarmila. *Humanizace vzdělávání a výchovy jako soudobý pedagogický problém* [The Humanization of Education and Training as a Current Pedagogical Problem]. Ústí nad Labem: Univerzita Jana Evangelisty Purkyně, 1993.

Skorunka, David. *Narativní přístup v psychoterapii: pohled psychoterapeuta a klienta* [The Narrative Approach in Psychotherapy: A Look at the Psychotherapist and Client]. Phd diss.,. Brno: Masarykova univerzita, Fakulta sociálních studií, 2008. Online: http://is.muni.cz/th/71263/fss_d/DISERTACE.pdf [accessed 8 February 2012].

Skutil, Jan. "Comenius's *Labyrinth of the World* as the Culmination of the Pedagogical, Didactic and Patriotic Ideas of Žerotín's Apologia." In *Symposium Comenianum 1982*, edited by Marie Kyralová and Jana Přivratská, 140–49. Uherský Brod: Comenius Museum, 1984.

Smolík, Josef. "Teologické a ekumenické motivy v Komenského všenápravném díle" [Theological and Ecumenical Motifs in Comenius's Pan-restoration Works]. *Křestanská Revue* 59.7 (1992) 153–56.

Sokol, Jan. *Filosofická antropologie. Člověk jako osoba* [Philosophical Anthropology. The Individual as a Person]. Praha: Portál, 2002.

Souček, Josef B. "Hlavní motivy bratrské theologie ve světle novějšího biblického bádání" [Principle Motifs in Brethren Theology in Light of More Recent Biblical Research]. In *Od reformace k zítřku*, edited by František Mrázek Dobiáš, 103–18. Praha: Kalich, 1956.

Souček, Stanislav. "Dva české pramínky v Labyrintu" [Two Czech Streams in the *Labyrinth*]. *Listy filologické* 59 (1924) 271–80.

————. "Komenského Labyrint u nás a v cizině" [Comenius's *Labyrinth* at Home and Abroad]. *Archiv pro bádání o životě a spisech J. A. Komenského* 7 (1924) 2–53.

Sousedík, Stanislav. "Comenius chiliastische Rechtfertigungslehre" [Comenius's Chiliastic Doctrine of Justification]. In *Comenius als Theologe*, edited by Vladimír J. Dvořák and Jan Blahoslav Lášek, 174–83. Praha: Nadace Comenius, 1988.

Spilková, Vladimíra. "Pedagogika na Pedagogické fakultě UK—současný stav a perspektivy" [Pedagogy at the School of Pedagogy, Charles University—Current State and Perspectives]. In *Česká pedagogika: Proměny a výzvy*, edited by Eliška Walterová, 21–29. Praha: Univerzita Karlova, 2004.

————. *Proměny primárního vzdělávání v ČR* [Changes in Primary Education in the Czech Republic]. Praha: Portál, 2005.

Spinka, Matthew. *John Amos Comenius, That Incomparable Moravian.* Chicago: University of Chicago Press, 1943.

BIBLIOGRAPHY

Srogoň, Tomáš. "Comenius's Basic Principles of Teaching and Present-Day Didactics." In *Symposium Comenianum 1982*, edited by Marie Kyralová and Jana Přivratská, 109–13. Uherský Brod: Comenius Museum, 1984.

Strupl, Milos. "Confessional Theology of the Unitas Fratrum." *Church History* 33.3 (1964) 279–93.

Šifferová, Věra et al. *Idea harmonie v díle Jana Amose Komenského*. Pavel Mervart: Univerzita Pardubice, 2014.

Škarka, Antonín. "Doslov" [Epilogue]. In *Labyrint světa a ráj srdce*, by Jan Amos Komenský, 209–13. Praha: Naše vojsko, 1958.

——. "Slovesné umění J.A.Komenského" [Verbal Art of J. A. Comenius]. In *Vybrané spisy Jana Amose Komenského 7*, edited by Antonín Škarka, 5–90. Praha: Státní Pedagogické Nakladatelství, 1974.

Švankmajer, Milan. "K zákazu Labyrintu světa r. 1825." [The Ban of the *Labyrinth of the World* in 1825]. In *Archiv pro bádání o životě a spisech J. A. Komenského* 18 (1958) 169–71.

Švec, Štefan. "Humanistická didaktika a školovanie" [Humanistic Didactics and Training]. In *Humanizácia výchovy a vzdělávania*, edited by Pavel Khun, 24–48. Bratislava: Státní Pedagogický Ústav, 1994.

Thiessen, Elmer John. *Teaching for Commitment, Liberal Education, Indoctrination and Christian Nurture*. Montreal: McGill-Queen's University Press, 1993.

Tichý, František Rut. "S J. A. Komenským do budování socialistické školy" [With J. A. Comenius in Building a Socialist School]. In *Jan Amos Komenský, Didaktické spisy*, edited by František Rut Tichý, 5–22. Praha: Státní Pedagogické Nakladatelství, 1951.

Tolkien, J. R. R. *Netvoři a kritikové* [The Monsters and the Critics and Other Essays]. Praha: Argo, 2006.

Trávníček, Jiří. *Vyprávěj mi něco. Jak si děti osvojují příběhy* [Tell Me Something: How Children Learn Stories]. Praha-Litomyšl: Paseka, 2007.

Toulmin, Stephen. *Cosmopolis: The Hidden Agenda of Modernity*. Chicago: University of Chicago Press, 1990.

Urbánek, Vladimír. "Konflikt ortodoxního luteranismu a mosaického pansofismu" [The Conflict of Orthodox Lutheranism and Mosaic Pansophism]. *Studia Comeniana et historica* 24.51 (1994) 149–57.

Uspenskij, Boris Andrejevič. *Poetika kompozice* [Poetics and Composition]. Brno: Host, 2009.

Válka, Josef. "Problém výkladu revelací v Komenského životě a díle" [The Problem of Interpreting the Revelations in the Life and Work of Comenius]. *Studia Comeniana et historica* 7 (1977) 114–19.

Vlček, Jaroslav. *Dějiny české literatury* [The History of Czech Literature]. Praha: Československý spisovatel, 1951.

Volf, Josef. "Horologium Hussianum—Orloj husitský" [Hussite's Clock]. *Časopis Českého Muzea* 86 (1912) 133–34.

Vomáčka, Jiří. *Proměny školního vzdělávání v našich dějinách* [Changes in School Education in Our History]. Ústí nad Labem: Univerzita Jana Evangelisty Purkyně, 1993.

Walterová, Eliška. "Humanizace vzdělávání jako prostředek kultivace člověka" [The Humanization of Education as a Means of Cultivating the Person]. *Pedagogická revue* 43 (1991) 327–33.

White, Michael, and David Epston. *Narrative Means to Therapeutic Ends*. New York: Norton, 1990.

Wilson, Douglas. *The Case for Classical Christian Education*. Wheaton, IL: Crossway, 2003.

Wright, Andrew. *Religion, Education and Postmodernity*. London: Routledge, 2004.

Zoubek, František Jan. "O proroctvích za války třicetileté, zvláště o Kristýně Poňatovské" [Prophecy during the Thirty Years War, Particularly about Christina Boňatovský]. In *Časopis Českého Muzea* 49 (1872) 3–16.

Zeman, Jarold K. "Restitution and Dissent in the Late Medieval Renewal Movements: The Waldensians, the Hussites and the Bohemian Brethren." *Journal of the American Academy of Religion* 44 (1976) 7–27.

Index of Names

INDEX OF NAMES

Index of Names

www.ingramcontent.com/pod-product-compliance
Lightning Source LLC
Chambersburg PA
CBHW061735270326
41928CB00011B/2249